INTEGRATED CRAFT AND DESIGN

INTEGRATED CRAFT AND DESIGN

Colin Caborn
and Ian Mould

Harrap Books

Acknowledgements

The authors and publishers wish to thank the following for permission to use questions from their papers:

East Anglian Examinations Board (EAEB)
Oxford and Cambridge Schools Examination Board (O&C)
Oxford Delegacy of Local Examinations (O)
University of London University Entrance and School
Examinations Council (L)
Welsh Joint Education Committee (WJEC)
Yorkshire Regional Examinations Board (YREB)

The Authors

Colin Caborn is Head of the Creative Design Faculty, John Howard Upper School, Biddenham Turn, Bedford. He has taught in grammar and comprehensive schools since 1966.

Ian Mould is Head of Technical Studies, Wootton Upper School, Wootton, Bedford. He has taught in comprehensive schools since 1974.

First published in Great Britain 1981
by HARRAP LIMITED
19-23 Ludgate Hill, London EC4M 7PD

Reprinted 1981; 1982 (*twice*); 1983 (*twice*)

ISBN 0 245-53633-7

Designed and typeset by DP Press Ltd, St Julians, Sevenoaks
Printed in Great Britain by J. W. Arrowsmith Ltd, Bristol

Contents

1 What is design?

The word 'designing' is used to describe a wide range of activities. These range from purely visual work which aims to make our environment more attractive, to entirely functional work which aims to make our lives easier and more comfortable. The specialists involved in these many different areas of design, such as visual design, product design, graphic design and engineering design, each have their own ideas of what design means to them. There are therefore many different answers to the question "What is design?", and it is very easy to become confused.

Design as a problem solving activity

All these different design activities do however share a number of common features; identifying a problem, thinking about it, arriving at a solution and realising (making) that solution.

A general definition which brings together all these important parts of the design process and which could be applied to the whole range of design activities might therefore be:

'a thinking process resulting in the realisation of a solution to a problem in ways involving changes in materials'.

This might be further summarised by saying simply that:

'design can be described as problem solving',

and this is the definition which we will use. While the relative importance of the visual and functional parts of the problem, and the best way to tackle it, will depend on the type of project being undertaken, this basic problem-solving process remains the same for them all.

The purpose of design

We must now think about what we are trying to achieve when we design and about the problems which designers face, so that we can learn to judge both our own and other people's solutions to design problems objectively.

Since there would be no point in changing something if this made it worse, it is obvious that *the purpose of design is to make things better.*

For example, if a designer was asked to produce a car which was safer, quicker, stronger, cheaper, lighter, faster and more economical than existing models, and he succeeded in doing all these things, we would all agree that he had made a better car.

In practice he would find that many of the design requirements in the example above conflicted with each other and that he had to choose between them. For example, speed might conflict with economy, and cheapness and lightness with strength and safety. Therefore *design is always a compromise* and he would have to put the requirements in order of importance before producing the design which fulfilled as many of them as possible.

In some cases, after following a design process, we will come up with a result which is very different from our preconceived ideas of what the solution should be. This is good and shows why it is important when designing to explore all the possible solutions and not to settle for the first idea which comes to us. On other occasions after thoroughly investigating the problem we will find that the best solution is similar to existing ones. *There are few completely new and innovatory designs and a design does not have to be entirely different to be good.* A recent example of a completely novel design would be the hovercraft. Earlier examples would be the wheel and the internal combustion engine.

Changes in design

Many of the objects which we use today have evolved from products first produced a long time ago, and the changes in design have been slow because of the strong influence of the existing designs and because people are reluctant to accept major steps forward. The motor car is a very good example of how a design has evolved over many years. While changes from year to year have usually been small the differences between current models and the carriage-like originals is very marked.

The rate of change is therefore controlled by two basic factors. Firstly, the introduction from time to time of new materials or processes which present opportunities for a major redesign of the product, and secondly changes in the needs of the people who will buy the product which create a demand for change. Examples of changes in the motor car resulting from new materials or processes include the invention of the pneumatic tyre, and the change from cars with a separate chassis to cars with a *monocoque* construction combining body and chassis. Changes resulting from public demand include the current switch to smaller and more economical cars because of rising petrol prices, and increased attention to safety and pollution control because of government action in many countries.

At other times cars judged to be too revolutionary have not been successful, even though they were excellent vehicles, simply because the public were not ready to accept them.

The effect of design on our lives

In deciding how to use the resources available to us, the designer must sometimes make decisions which could change all our lives. For example, we must choose between the peaceful versus the military uses of nuclear power, or the conservation of open spaces versus the need for more homes, factories and roads. Designers have the power to make or destroy our future, because the results of a mistake when tackling projects of this size could be catastrophic. The chances of a mistake increase when the project gets too big for any one person to oversee and when designers are working at the limits of their knowledge and experience.

For example, a decision was taken in the 1950's to rehouse thousands of people in high rise blocks of flats in order to save land, which could then be used to provide more open spaces, or to prevent towns getting ever larger. This has proved to be a disastrous mistake in many places. Not only were the buildings more difficult and more expensive to build than expected, but they often failed to provide the good low-cost housing which was needed and were unpopular with those forced to live in them. The living conditions they created have been blamed for a large increase in social problems such as vandalism, violence, loneliness, stress and mental illness. Now many people are no longer prepared to live in them. Also running repairs to high rise buildings have proved to be very expensive. As a result, it has at last been admitted that the policy was wrong, and in some cases buildings only a few years old are being demolished to make way for new types of housing.

Understanding the designer's work

It is generally agreed that the best way to avoid such mistakes in the future is to make design decisions more public, in such areas as architecture, planning and industrial design, which affect everyone's lives, so that everyone who is affected can have a say in deciding what should be done. This will only be possible when people understand enough about how designers work and about the problems facing them, and also keep themselves well-enough informed about important matters, to be able to discuss what should be done sensibly and constructively.

Our understanding of design and our experience of designing will help us to do this. In the same way it will prove valuable in helping us to make decisions about choosing things. Deciding what type of chair to buy for example can involve the same careful and objective study of the functional and aesthetic aspects of chair design as is involved in designing one to fit the same situation. Design training is therefore a valuable introduction to making decisions and solving problems in a wide range of situations in later life.

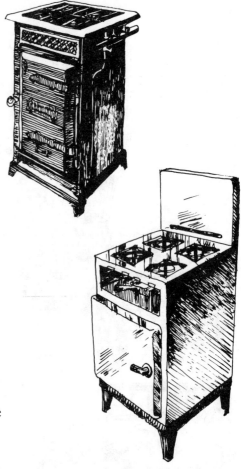

Evaluating design

Since the success of a design is measured by how well the final solution fulfills the need which the designer set out to meet, and since we are surrounded by examples of professional designers' solutions to what they, or the manufacturers who employ them, saw as the needs of the public, we can learn more about design and develop our own sense of good design by looking carefully and critically at everyday objects such as buildings, cars, bicycles, furniture and electrical equipment. We can make this activity even more valuable by keeping a scrap book of our own notes, sketches and cuttings from magazines and catalogues to illustrate what we consider to be good designs or parts of designs, and by writing down what we consider to be the good and bad points of a design, together with the reasons for our decisions.

It is also helpful to study the development of things to see how they have improved (or worsened). For example, while all the cookers shown, satisfy the basic need for a means of cooking food, each has advantages over the one it replaced. You might like to write down what you think these advantages are and compare your list with other people's.

Communicating ideas

It is wrong to think that we can study or practise design in isolation because before we can begin to design we must learn how to communicate our ideas clearly and fluently; before we can see a design project through to a successful conclusion we must have a good working knowledge of the materials available to make our solution, together with the tools and processes used to shape, join and finish them; and before we can use our knowledge of design usefully and responsibly, for the benefit of everyone, we must have a sound general knowledge of the needs of our society and of the role of the designer in it.

2 Sources of design ideas

We have already said that the decisions which we must make when designing can be divided into functional judgements and aesthetic judgements.

Function

The most important consideration when designing an article is that it should perform its intended job correctly, and a careful analysis of what the article has to do will provide many starting points for design.

The *key questions* which we must ask ourselves are those which seek to investigate the *functional requirements* of the design, such as its weight, size, strength, materials, durability, safety, construction and cost.

Visual judgements

The second most important consideration is the appearance of the article, and the *key questions* here should seek to investigate the *aesthetic requirements* of the design, such as its appearance, finish and the environment in which it will be used.

In some cases the primary function of the article will be to look visually attractive and this will then become the most important consideration when designing. These two sources of design ideas will be studied in more detail later, but we must first make sure that we are all using the same words and meanings when we discuss design.

A design vocabulary

In the same way that we have to learn to recognise and understand words, in order to be able to read, we must learn to recognise and understand the words used when talking about aesthetic principles, in order to be able to discuss the visual judgements which we must make when designing. Some of these words have different meanings in general conversation and we must therefore be careful to use them accurately.

As well as making design understandable and definable by isolating and considering some of the basic units of design, this vocabulary provides many sources of design ideas, and we have shown examples of projects and everyday objects based on them.

Line

Lines can be used in many ways.

Direction. Lines can be used to indicate directions. For example, they can be vertical, horizontal, inclined (sloping), converging, diverging, radiating or curving.

The way in which lines are applied to shapes or forms can create significantly different visual effects. For example, the dimensions of a room can appear to be altered by the use of wallpapers which have strong lines of direction:

1. Vertical pattern lines will tend to make a room appear higher, but smaller in other directions.

2. Horizontal lines will tend to make the walls look longer, but the ceiling lower, etc.

Movement. Lines can be used to indicate movement in a particular direction.

Rhythm. Lines can also be used in ways which will create a visual rhythm (flow). Functional objects, which may be rather dull, can be transformed by the application of more interesting linear detailing. For example, the appearance of cars is often completely changed by the addition of patterns of lines.

Texture. Various combinations of lines can give the impression of textured surfaces and create interesting effects.

Shape. This is simply a two-dimensional area defined by lines, and lines can be used to do this in two ways:

1. By using a series of measured lines which will cover a specific area and suggest an outline.

2. By joining lines together to enclose a space.

Free form design. This can be used when objects are to be created for their appearance, but when you have no particular shape in mind. A limitless number of ideas and shapes can stem from using this method. Here are some ways of producing a variety of shapes:

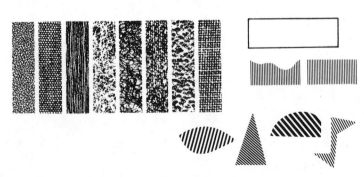

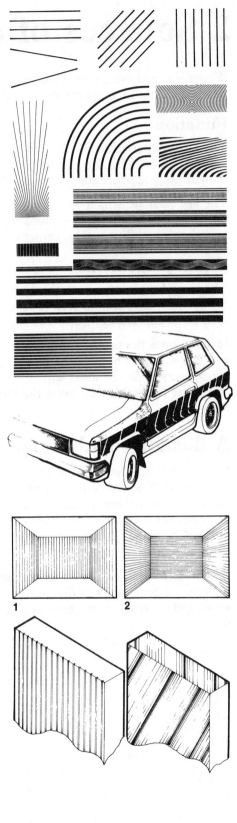

1. Shapes can be created by drawing random curved lines which cross each other. Suitable shapes can be outlined boldly and the best ones can be developed as required.

2. Straight lines can be used in the same way. Here they create suitable outlines for a door number plate.

3. Curved and straight lines can also be used together. Here for example, they are used to design decorative panels on a container top.

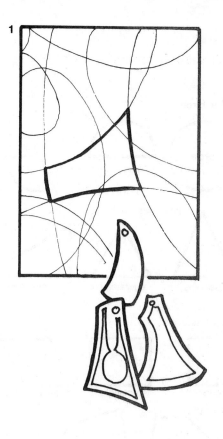

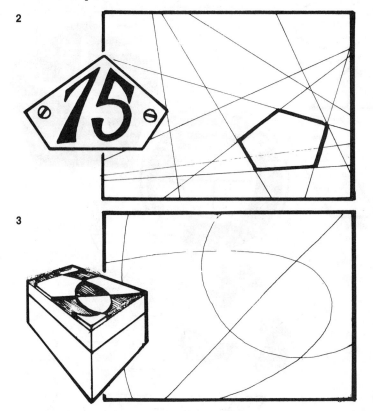

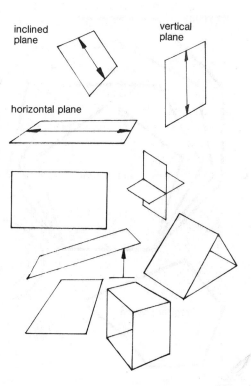

Planes

The word 'plane' usually refers to a flat, smooth surface. A table top is considered to be a horizontal plane, a door front is a vertical plane and many roofs are inclined planes.

One can use a plane as a base in which to work and we can add further planes by overlapping, penetrating, joining and so on. In this way, many interesting compositions can be created, and two-dimensional shapes can be built-up into three-dimensional constructions.

Plane geometric shapes. Look very carefully around you and you will see that most of our man-made environment and some of our natural environment are based on geometric shapes, (e.g. honeycombs are hexagonal).

Many of these geometric shapes can be developed into grids for use in basic pattern design work. (*See* next section.)

11

The circle

circle

semi-circle

$1/3$ circle

quadrant

ellipse

Triangles

isoceles

equilateral

right-angled

scalene

Quadrilaterals

square

rectangle

rhombus

parallelogram

trapezium

trapezoid

Polygons

octagon (8)

heptagon (7)

hexagon (6)

pentagon (5)

irregular polygon

12

Units and grids

By using grids developed from tessellating (interlocking) geometric shapes such as rectangles, equilateral triangles, hexagons etc., we can develop new pattern designs which may be difficult to produce in any other way.

The first drawing shows how a square grid is built up. From this simple grid quite complex designs can be produced by:

1. Drawing any shape into the sub-unit.

2. Copying this shape into all four sub-units within the larger unit. (Here the sub-units have each been rotated through a quarter turn.)

3. Repeating the unit design onto the large grid or super-unit.

Notice how this shape is repeated throughout the grid so that both positive and negative shapes are identical, i.e. the shape itself also tessellates as well as the units.

Here are some patterns developed from one sub-unit design. To create the full effect, the shapes have to be drawn out carefully before they can be inked or coloured in.

With the use of drawing instruments a straightforward pattern can be drawn accurately and quickly. However, difficulty arises when the sub-unit becomes complex, or is a random shape, or has to be rotated frequently. Therefore, you may find the stencil, template or tracing methods easier to use.

Below are examples of designs produced from the same unit using a template. These are just some methods of varying the original shape but there are many more.

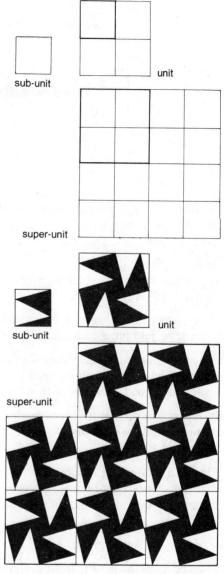

sub-unit

unit

super-unit

sub-unit

unit

super-unit

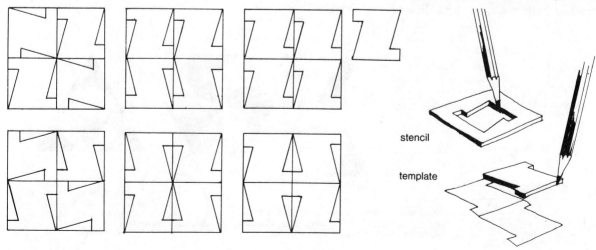

stencil

template

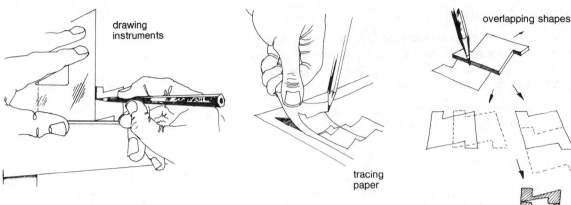

drawing instruments

tracing paper

overlapping shapes

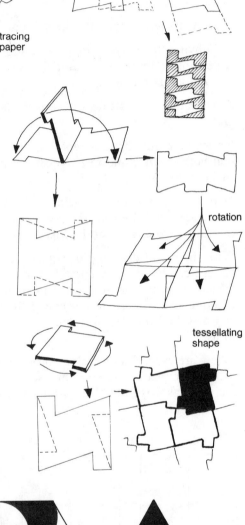

rotation

tessellating shape

Symmetry. Symmetrical shapes are those which can be halved equally, resulting in two identical parts, with one part reversed.

Hence by flipping over the stencil shown, symmetrical shapes can be produced either by extending the design over the grid or by repeating it within the same sub-unit.

With a good use of *negative* and *positive* the sub-units can be made to join onto each other to form new shapes.

Some sub-units can be developed to form many different shapes which in turn can be used as units. The equilateral triangle is a good example of this.

By separating the negative and positive shapes, and colouring both in the same way, we can rearrange them to create new shapes.

Hints on designing a sub-unit.
1. If the shapes are to tessellate well the design on the sub-units must touch the edges of each sub-unit grid.

2. It is advisable to limit yourself to two colours when designing units and grids.

The above methods of pattern designing can often form the basis of both two- and three-dimensional work.

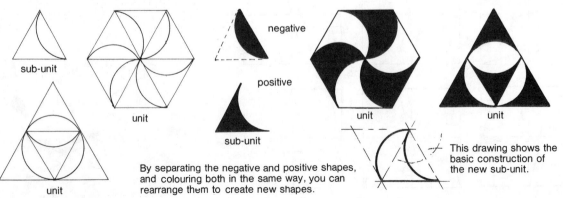

sub-unit

unit

unit

negative

positive

sub-unit

unit

unit

By separating the negative and positive shapes, and colouring both in the same way, you can rearrange them to create new shapes.

This drawing shows the basic construction of the new sub-unit.

Form

When we give flat two-dimensional planes or shapes a third dimension we refer to the three-dimensional solids which we have made as forms. Many objects around us are developed from geometric forms.

To fully describe a form we must give details of all its characteristics: shape, size, proportion, weight, opacity, colour and texture. The design language which we have learnt in this chapter will help us to do this.

Size. This is a relative concept in which we rely upon comparisons to help describe the magnitude of an object. For example, we only consider someone to be particularly small (or tall) because they are below (or above) the height of most people of the same age and sex.

Shape. As shown earlier, two-dimensional shapes define specific areas. When shape is used in connection with a three-dimensional form it defines the overall outline of the object.

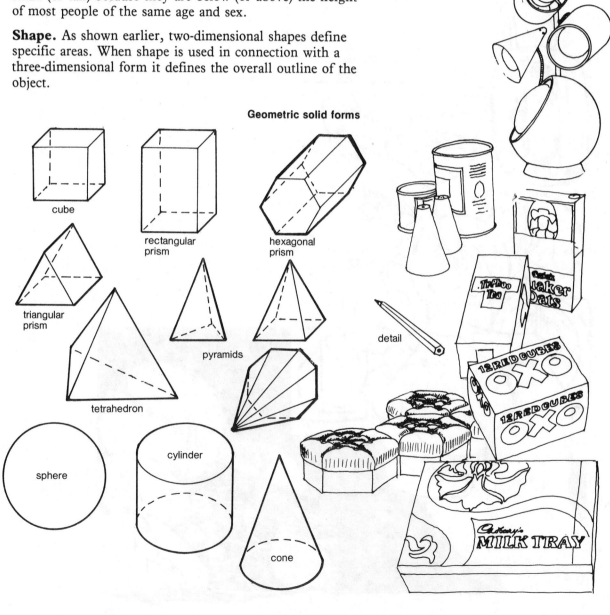

Geometric solid forms

cube

rectangular prism

hexagonal prism

triangular prism

pyramids

tetrahedron

detail

sphere

cylinder

cone

Natural forms

The study of natural forms such as leaves, flowers, insects, fishes, fruit, pieces of wood and stones provides an endless source of shapes for design.

The usual approach is to make analytical drawings of these forms, often using some form of magnification to obtain detailed knowledge of the internal and external structure of them, and then to develop the shapes which have been suggested into designs for jewellery, decorative panels, ceramics, etc. Alternatively, the objects can be used as models for sculpture, work in clay, etc., as patterns for the casting of exact replicas, or as subjects for embedding.

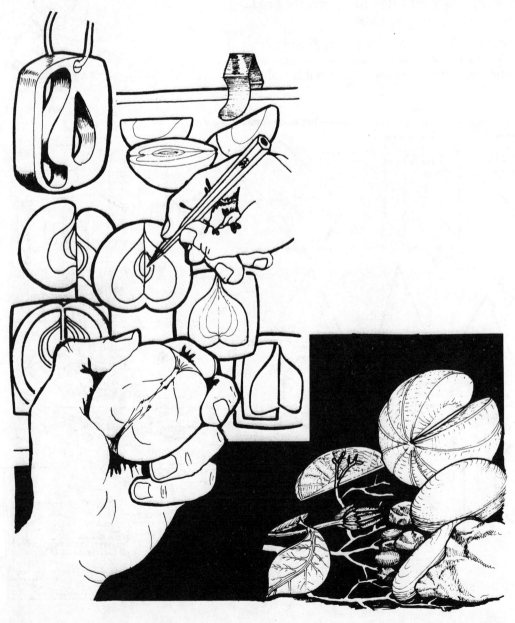

Visual properties of materials

When we think about the materials available to us as designers we must look at their properties. In addition to those such as strength, hardness and weight discussed in the sections on materials we must consider:

1. Opacity. If we can see through the material, it is transparent. If we cannot see through it, but light shines through, it is translucent. If we cannot see light through the material at all, it is *opaque*.

2. Texture and finish.
This is the physical surface condition of a material, which may range from rough to smooth in an infinite number of ways, and any finish which we might apply to it.

3. Colour. This is made up of three basic elements:

(a) Hue, which is the actual colour or complexion, i.e. whether it is red, yellow, orange etc.

(b) Chroma, which is the brilliance of colour (intensity).

(c) Tone, which is the amount of black or white in a colour. The maximum contrast one can gain is by the use of black and white alongside each other.

Primary colours are the basic pigments from which other colours (secondary colours etc.) can be mixed.

Complementary colours are those colours which are opposite each other on the colour wheel (spectrum). They give maximum contrast.

Harmony comes from using colours which are close to each other around the colour wheel. Harmony can also be gained when using complementary colours, by toning down both colours with equal amounts of black or white.

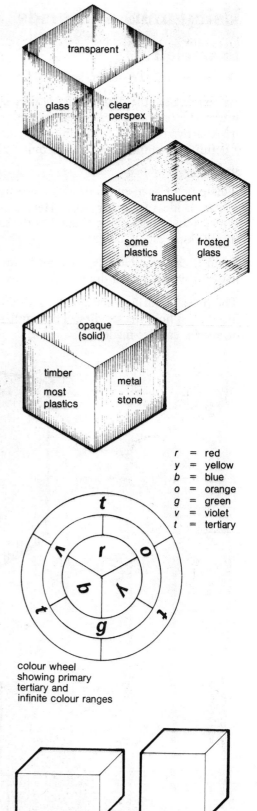

r = red
y = yellow
b = blue
o = orange
g = green
v = violet
t = tertiary

colour wheel showing primary tertiary and infinite colour ranges

Proportion

This refers to the relationship of one part of a form to another and gives an object its particular composition. A good composition is one in which all the characteristics of an object are visually correct. This gives agreeable proportions. Too much or too little of any characteristic gives bad proportions.

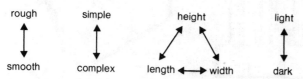

rough ↕ smooth

simple ↕ complex

height / length ↔ width

light ↕ dark

Using units and grids

Example 1

Design brief. 'To design an interlocking shape.'

As you can see the design brief is very short leaving much interpretation to the individual. Not all design problems necessarily result in the making of a particular product with a definite function. Some can be quite open ended.

Solution.

This type of open-ended design problem can be a good source of ideas for other work. Here the original two-dimensional interlocking shape has developed into interlocking candle holders.

Resin is cast into moulds, vacuum formed from wooden patterns which have a draw angle for easy release.

The holes are drilled and polished aluminium sleeves inserted to hold the candles. The candles could be bought or special candles made.

Investigation.

To design an interlocking shape

INTERLOCKING SHAPES | TIM WATTS | 4S

19

This type of basic work is often used to create schemes for wall coverings, upholstery, textiles, tiles, paving, etc.

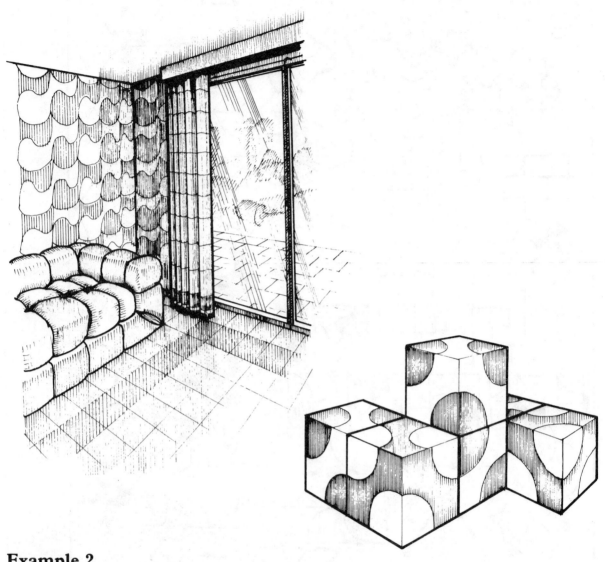

Example 2

Design brief. To design a pattern for a tile that is to be used on a coffee table top. There must be no more than two different patterns. (*See* Units and grids.)

One pattern should be selected for further development after preliminary investigation of several alternatives (as shown in example 1).

Solution.

This simple example shows the build up towards a final solution. The solution satisfies the requirements stated in the design brief and need go no further.

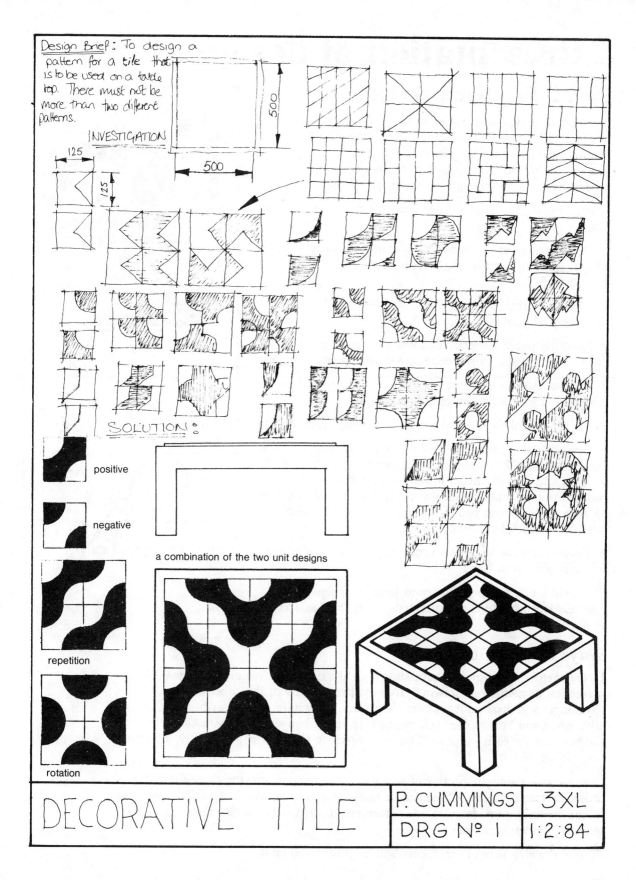

Design Brief: To design a pattern for a tile that is to be used on a table top. There must not be more than two different patterns.

500

500

125

125

INVESTIGATION

SOLUTION:

positive

negative

a combination of the two unit designs

repetition

rotation

DECORATIVE TILE

P. CUMMINGS

3XL

DRG No 1

1:2:84

21

3 Presentation of design

Part 1 Freehand sketching

If we are to design well, we must have efficient ways of recording our ideas and communicating them to other people. Freehand sketching is the quickest way of doing this. However, sketching must not be mistaken for a rough type of drawing, but should be presented carefully.

If you follow a few simple rules, learning to sketch can be quite easy:

1. Decide which of the numerous techniques you wish to use. (If in doubt read through the following pages before going any further.)

2. Choose a suitable pencil (HB) and make sure it has a *sharp* conical point.

3. Hold the pencil correctly as shown in the diagram. This position will enable faint lines to be drawn in any direction.

4. *Crating.* Always start by making a faint framework or box into which details can be drawn simply.

Never try to make a finished looking drawing straight away.

5. *Lining in.* Once you are satisfied that your faint sketch is correct increase the pressure on the pencil to produce bold outlines and medium detail lines. As some degree of confidence is required when lining in, it is an advantage to be able to move your papers around to the most suitable position for each line to be drawn.

6. *Curves.* Use the wrist as a compass point around which you can pivot your hand.

Sketch in a tidy manner and try to keep the proportions (the relationship of one measurement to another) as accurate as possible.

Ways of sketching

In the sketches opposite we have shown a cube drawn in five different ways. Each projection or method of drawing gives a different view of the cube, and each has advantages and disadvantages over the others. Therefore, you must become familiar with when and how to use each method, so that when sketching you can choose the best one for each purpose. This is in order to show on paper exactly what you want to put over.

One and two point perspective offer a good way to start drawing three-dimensional objects, either completely freehand or using ruler and pencil. Simple flat views can be drawn easily provided that you remember to keep the different views lined up with each other as shown.

Formal drawing using instruments will be introduced later.

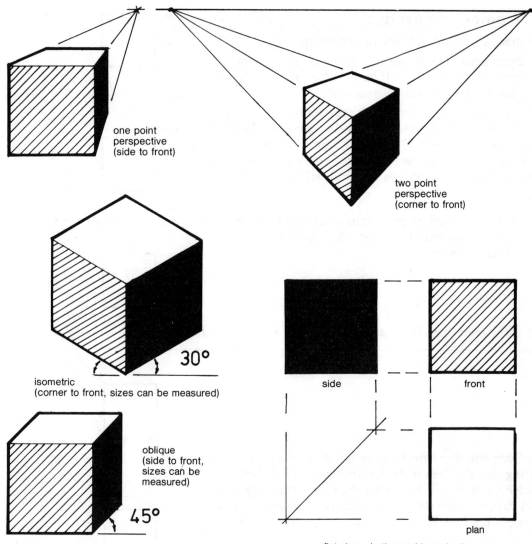

one point perspective (side to front)

two point perspective (corner to front)

isometric (corner to front, sizes can be measured) 30°

oblique (side to front, sizes can be measured) 45°

side | front | plan

flat views (orthographic projection show each side separately)

Perspective drawing

This allows us to draw shapes quickly and easily in a way which closely resembles their actual appearance. We can, therefore, use it to see what our finished design would look like.

When we look at objects drawn in perspective we see that:

(a) Parallel lines appear to converge (get closer together) as they recede (go away) from us.

(b) Equal lengths at different distances from us no longer look equal, but appear to get smaller as they recede.

(c) Objects of similar size appear to get smaller in size as they recede from us.

Perspective makes objects look solid and gives a sense of depth to the picture.

One point perspective

To draw a simple box-shape in one point:

(a) Draw a flat view of one side of the object in faint construction lines. This will be the true shape of the side and can be drawn to scale if required.

(b) Draw the horizon line which represents your eye level as you look at the object. This can be above the flat view if you want to see the top, below it if you want to see the bottom, and through the flat view if you want to make the drawing look as though you are level with it.

(c) Mark the vanishing point somewhere along the horizon line. Its position will determine which side of the completed shape will be seen.

(d) Draw faint lines from each corner of the flat view to the vanishing point.

(e) Complete the shape by drawing the back of the shape, noting that the lines from the flat view towards the vanishing point will be shorter than their true length. You will have to judge the correct lengths for yourself. In this example the back lines are parallel to the front shape.

This example shows how we can alter our view point by raising or lowering the eye level, and vary the amount of each side seen by changing the position of the vanishing point along the eye level. Notice how some views have only two sides showing.

Once you can draw these shapes practice drawing other three-dimensional geometric forms until you feel confident, and then use them to construct recognisable objects.

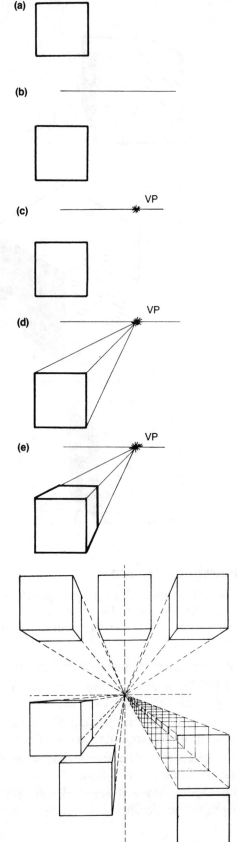

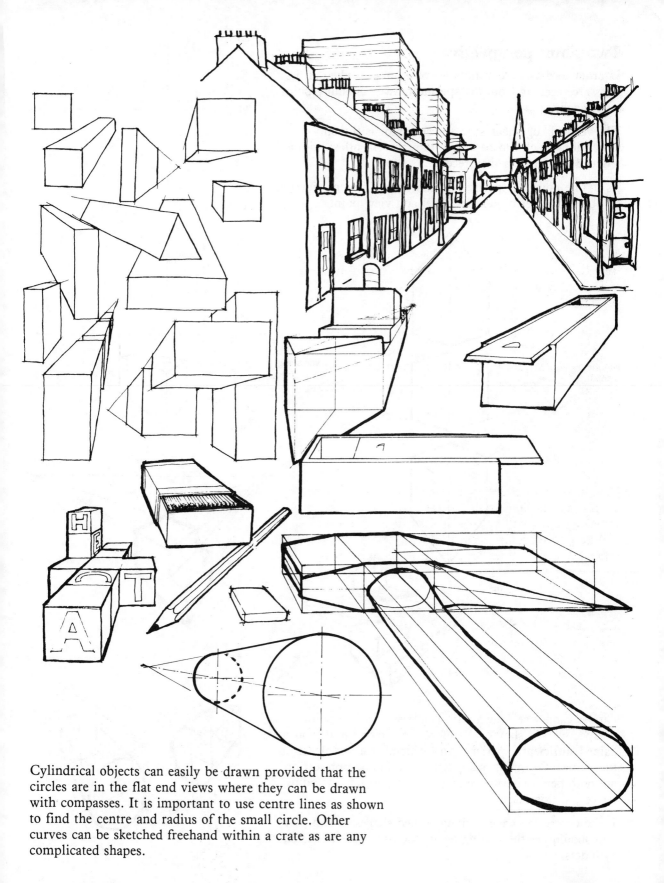

Cylindrical objects can easily be drawn provided that the circles are in the flat end views where they can be drawn with compasses. It is important to use centre lines as shown to find the centre and radius of the small circle. Other curves can be sketched freehand within a crate as are any complicated shapes.

Two point perspective

In order to draw a realistic view of an object when all its sides are receding from the spectator, two vanishing points are needed.

The vertical edge nearest to the spectator is the only dimension which can be drawn to scale. All other lines are reduced in length as they recede.

As in one point perspective we can draw different views of an object by altering our eye level and view point.

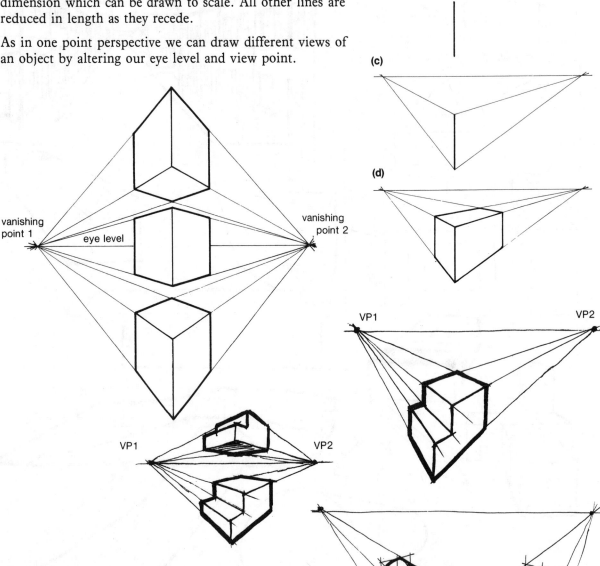

Circles cannot be drawn with compasses in two point perspective and should, therefore, be avoided until you have gained sufficient experience in freehand work to sketch in the curves. One point perspective and oblique projection are both better alternatives for drawing objects including curves, at this stage.

If, however, you have to draw curved shapes in two point you should use the crating technique used here to sketch cylinders.

Oblique views

These are similar to one point perspective views in that the true shape of one side is drawn first, see (a). However, the oblique lines in the drawing (those which are angled between horizontal and vertical) do not recede as they do in perspective drawing. Instead they are drawn parallel to each other at an angle of 45°, see (b). This angle will produce a well-shaped realistic drawing. To give the impression of foreshortening the 45° lines are drawn half their true length, see (c). Unless you do this your drawing will look too long from front to back. The shape is then completed.

The main *advantage* of oblique over one point perspective is that lines can be measured accurately on the front shape and along the 45° lines. The main *disadvantage* is that it does not look quite as realistic as perspective because the lines at the back of the drawing remain the same size as those at the front, when they should be smaller.

Oblique projection, like one point perspective, is very good for drawing curves as the drawing can usually be arranged so that the curves can be drawn on the flat front face with a compass. Curves on the sloping sides (right) have to be drawn freehand as in isometric and two point perspective. All the other curves in this section can be drawn with compasses.

Crating. Oblique and one point perspective views become a little more difficult to draw when there is no true shape at the front to work from. However, this can be overcome by using the crating technique already introduced (see the example on the right).

Complex detailing is possible when using oblique drawing (see right). In this, oblique is easier than one point perspective which would involve reducing the size of the detailing as it receded towards the vanishing point.

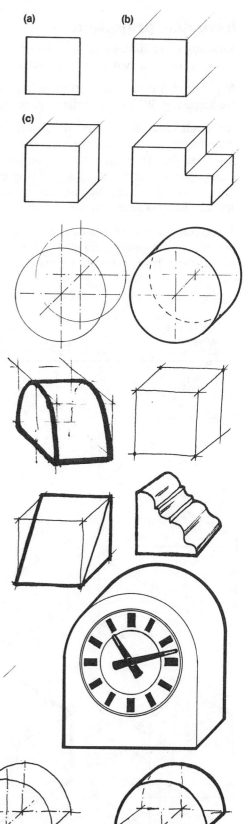

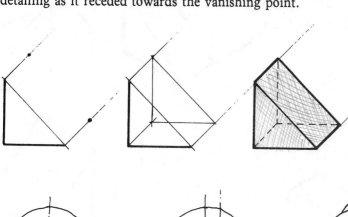

Isometric projection

This allows us to draw views with one corner of an object at the front as in two point perspective.

All vertical lines remain vertical while all horizontal lines are angled at 30° to the horizontal, see (a).

Although none of the sides in an isometric view appear as true shapes, all the sides are measured out to their actual sizes, see (b). The shape is then completed using more 30° lines, see (c). One disadvantage of isometric is that these lines at the top of the drawing often look as though they are too long because they are drawn full size.

More complicated shapes can easily be drawn using crating, but curves can prove difficult to draw as they usually have to be drawn freehand within a crate.

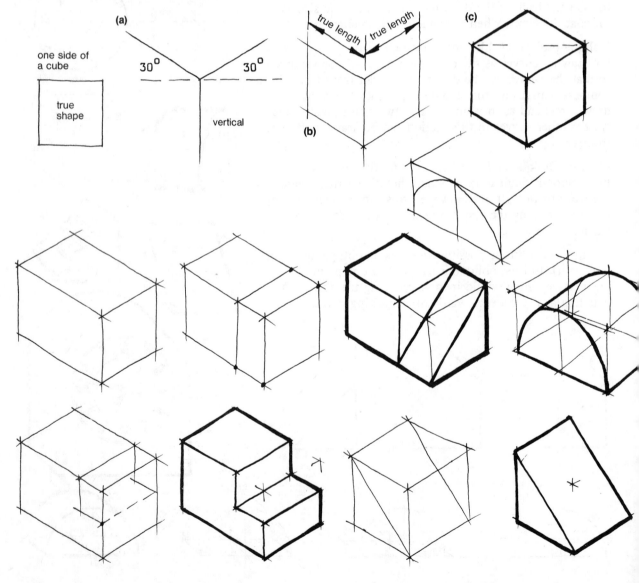

(a)

one side of a cube

true shape

30°   30°

vertical

true length   true length

(b)

(c)

Flat views (orthographic projection)

1. Flat work involving an element of design (for example, designing the pattern for a tiled table top) can easily be communicated on paper as it only has two dimensions, length and width, see (a). However, any shape which is to be developed in three dimensions is more difficult to visualise.

2. When we wish to show length, width *and* thickness we have to resort to drawing a second view in order to avoid changing from a flat to a pictorial drawing, see (b).

3. As the form of the object becomes more complicated, we have to add more views to show all parts of it, see (c). However, the number of views can often be reduced by using dotted lines to show hidden details, see (d), and three views; front, plan (top) and one side, are usually sufficient.

We must be careful to keep these views in their correct position in relation to each other, and to project lines across and down from one to the other so that we can see how they fit together to give a complete picture of the design.

Flat views are a simple way of showing an object accurately with all the sides drawn to their correct size. You can add dimensions and notes to give all the information needed to make the object. Therefore, flat views are especially useful for drawing the final solution, see (e).

As it is often difficult to visualise the appearance of the proposed solution from flat views alone, they are often accompanied by a pictorial view and/or a model, see (f).

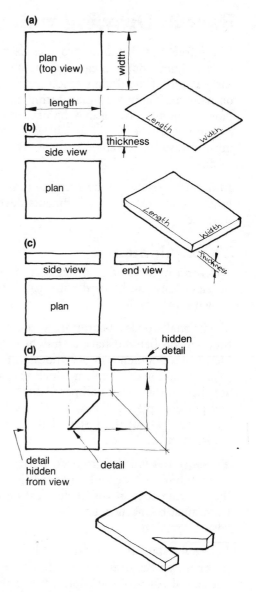

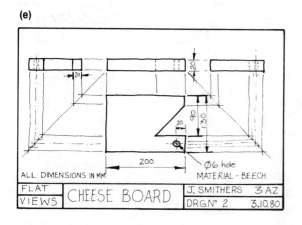

(e)

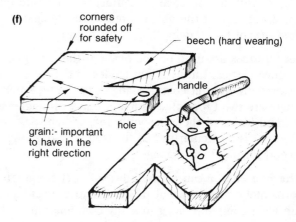

(f)

Part 2 Drawing with instruments

While freehand sketching provides us with a very good way to record and communicate our ideas quickly during the early stages of the design process, it is not always sufficient on its own. There are times during an investigation when more accurate drawing may be needed to work out sizes and to prove whether ideas will work, and the final solution must always be presented sufficiently accurately for it to be made.

In order to produce such accurate drawings quickly we must use the specialist instruments developed for the purpose.

The equipment

Drawing boards vary in size according to the largest size of paper they can be used with, e.g. A1, A2, A3, A4 as shown on the right.

Traditional wooden boards are specially constructed so that they remain flat and have a straight edge at each end. Newer developments in board design include the fitting of a parallel motion mechanism which keeps the tee-square attached to the board and parallel to the top of the board, and portable plastic boards which are light, simple to use and have many of the instruments normally used with a board built in.

Tee-squares are used to draw horizontal lines. To work accurately the blade and butt must join rigidly at 90° and the drawing edge of the blade must be absolutely straight. Care must be taken not to weaken the joint or chip the edge by misuse.

Before we start drawing we use the tee-square to line the paper up on the drawing board. This ensures that the horizontal edges of the paper are parallel to the tee-square blade and that all subsequent lines drawn on the paper are parallel with its top edge. When using a separate tee-square it is essential that the butt is pressed firmly against the *left-hand edge* of the drawing board during use.

Set squares are used on the blade of the tee-square to produce vertical lines at right angles to the tee-square and for drawing lines at common angles to the tee-square. There are two types of set square, one with angles of 30°, 60° and 90°, and the other with 45°, 45° and 90° angles. The first is particularly used for isometric drawing and the second for oblique drawing.

The protractor can be used to construct any angle to the horizontal or vertical, but it is easier to use set squares to construct common angles and any combination of these.

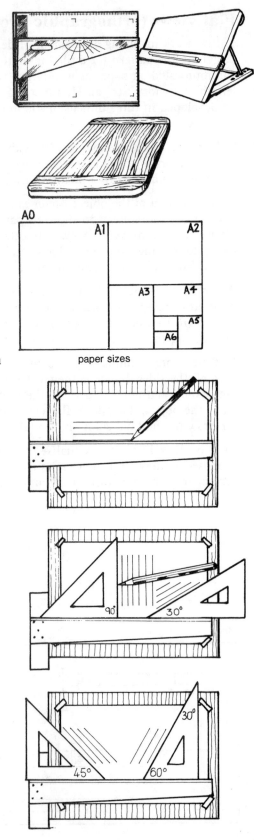

paper sizes

Pencils are probably the most important items of equipment you will use. If inaccurate drawings are to be avoided it is essential that the correct pencil is chosen for each job and that the correct *sharp point* is maintained throughout its use:

(a) *Conical points* should be used on HB and H pencils for sketching and lettering.

(b) *Chisel points* should be used on harder pencils. These are first sharpened with a knife and then finished on fine emery cloth. These pencils are used for all line work and are essential if a good standard of draughtsmanship is to be maintained.

Compasses are of many types, but all must be used with sharp leads sharpened to match the pencils used for straight lines.

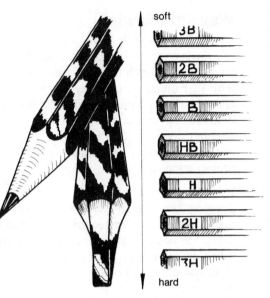

Types of line

Types of line are standardised by British Standard B.S. 308 along with most of the rules governing engineering drawing. Correct line strengths are a very important part of the language of drawing and each type of line has its own exact meaning. Study carefully the example below, practice using correct line strengths and remember them.

1. Projection lines.
2. Hatching/Section lines.
3. Cutting planes.
4. Centre lines.
5. Dimension lines.
6. Hidden detail lines.
7. Outlines.
8. Lettering.

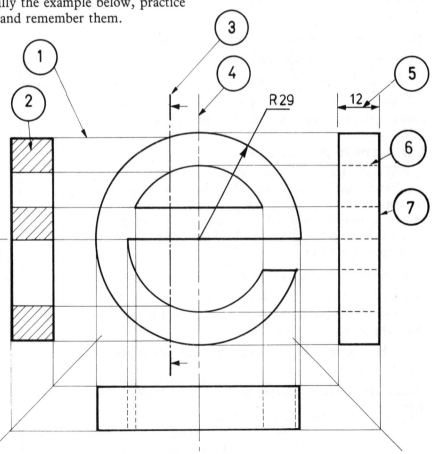

Ways of drawing

When drawing with instruments we use the same five ways of drawing (or projections) already introduced in the section on freehand sketching. You can, therefore, practice drawing with instruments simply by working through the examples given in the previous section and then finding everyday items to measure and draw. It is also valuable to go back to simple design projects for which you prepared only freehand sketches, and draw accurate flat views and pictorial presentation drawings.

It is not possible to provide a complete course in formal drawing here and so we have tried firstly, to introduce as many useful drawing techniques as possible in just enough detail for you to start using them and secondly, to give fuller details of those not so easily found in readily available technical drawing books.

Orthographic projection

Drawings which will be used in the workshop must contain all the information needed to make the design. The simplest way to convey this amount of detail is by using flat views or to give them their correct name *orthographic projection*.

There are two types of orthographic projection:

(a) First angle projection (English).

(b) Third angle projection (American).

It is important that you understand the basic differences between the two systems which are shown below.

First angle projection

Imagine that the letter is suspended in a box and that we are drawing on the box sides. The final views shown in A4 are constructed by looking at the letter in the directions shown by the arrows in A1 and projecting the images *through* the object onto the inside of the box (A2). This is then opened out (A3).

The important points to note are:

(i) Start with view F, the front elevation.

(ii) The view from E, the end elevation, will be drawn to the right of the front elevation.

(iii) When looking down from P, the plan will appear below the front elevation.

Summary. Project *through* the object away from the viewing position.

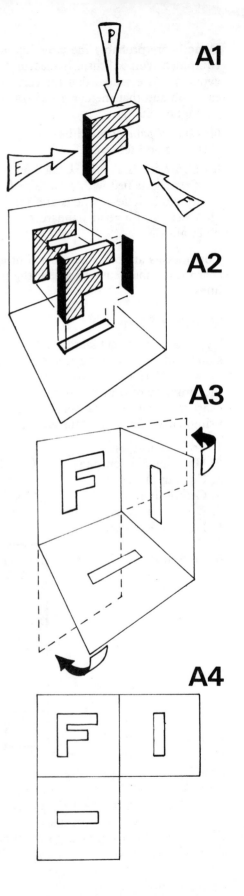

A1

A2

A3

A4

Third angle projection

In third angle we construct the final views shown in B4 by looking at the letter from exactly the same angles as before (B1). However, this time the images are projected *back* towards the onlooker through the box onto the outside of it (B2). The box is then opened out (B3). The important points to note are:

  (i) Start with F, the front elevation.

  (ii) The view from E, the end elevation, will be drawn to the left of the front elevation.

(iii) When looking down from P, the plan will appear above the front elevation.

Summary. Project *back* to the viewing position.

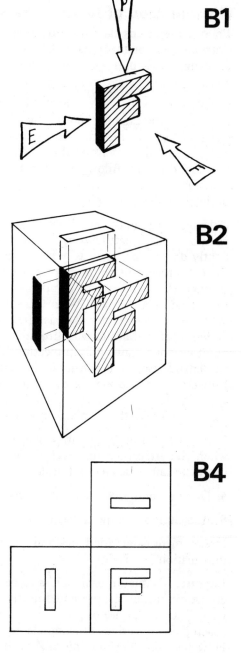

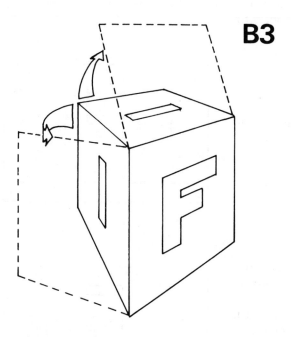

Drawing to scale

This allows us to see views of an object in true proportion. Drawings need not be full size, but can be enlarged or reduced provided that the scale is printed on the drawing. Full size is shown as 1:1; half size as 1:2; twice full size as 2:1; etc. However, any dimensions on the drawing are always printed *full size* giving the actual sizes to which the object will be made.

Presentation of formal drawings

Follow these steps carefully when presenting formal drawings. Although we have shown an orthographic drawing, these rules apply to all drawings.

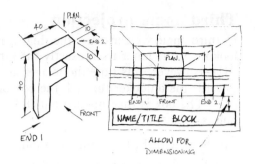

1. Work out the overall sizes and the best way to space the views in rough first. If orthographic projection is being used, as in the example shown, decide now how many elevations will be needed. Also decide if sections or hidden detail are needed to ensure that mistakes are not made on the final drawing. Allow room for dimensioning and other necessary information such as a name/title block, scale and projection used (see right).

2. Using very faint pencil lines (3H or harder) draw in the position of each part (*crating*). Check this arrangement as faintly drawn lines can easily be corrected at this stage. If correct, proceed to *project* further details from one view to another. (Use 45° lines or compasses to project through 90° from plan to end views.) When drawing symmetrical shapes or shapes involving curves, it is often best to start by drawing centre lines to work from. It is essential that you build up your drawing by projecting lines from one view to another and do not construct each view separately. Projection is much more accurate and ensures that each view lines-up correctly with the others. Every time you measure there is the chance of making a mistake.

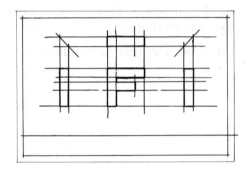

3. Begin to fill in detail with a sharp medium line only when you are certain that everything is correct. Once lined-in, lines cannot be changed neatly.

4. Draw around each view with a sharp bold outline.

5. Add limit and dimension lines.

6. Complete name/title block and any additional information (see right).

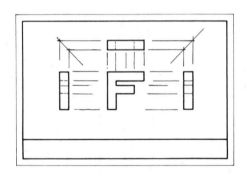

Layout. If visual information is to be communicated efficiently it must be presented neatly and in an organised way. The careful use of projection lines will ensure correct spacing of the various drawing elements involved. However, when written information has also to be included, such as name, date, title, scale, materials, etc., a system of name/title blocks is usually adopted. There are many ways in which these blocks of information can be arranged but in each case the emphasis must be on clarity.

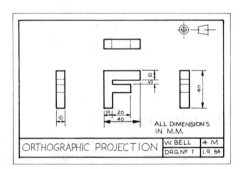

Lettering. The success of a name/title block will depend almost entirely on the standard of lettering used. For this reason it is important that a simple straightforward letter type is used. Decorative lettering should be avoided. Use guide lines when printing.

ABCDEFGHIJKLMNOPQRSTUVWXYZ

Hidden detail. You may have noticed that very little of the detail on the 'F' block shown on the previous page has been included on the end elevations or plans. This is because these details are hidden when looking from the chosen view points. Hidden detail lines enable us to show this hidden information and may reduce the number of elevations needed.

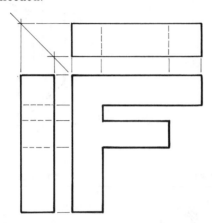

Dimensioning. Usually the main purpose of an orthographic projection is to give information as to the size and proportions of an object. Therefore, measurements must be given to indicate the size of the individual parts, and overall length, width and height. As the drawing may be required for continuous reference in the workshops, it is important that dimensions can be easily and quickly read.

Study the following rules carefully when dimensioning drawings:

1. You must be able to read all lettering and dimensions from the bottom or right hand side of the sheet, so that you do not have to rotate the paper.

2. To avoid confusion, space the dimensions well away from the drawing.

3. All letters and figures should be clear and of the same height (use guide lines which sit above not on the dimension lines).

4. Use neat, bold but sharp arrow heads.

5. Leave 1 mm space between the part being dimensioned and the limit lines.

6. Try not to show the same dimension more than once. For further details consult B.S. 308. It is not necessary to show dimensions which can be easily worked out by adding or subtracting others.

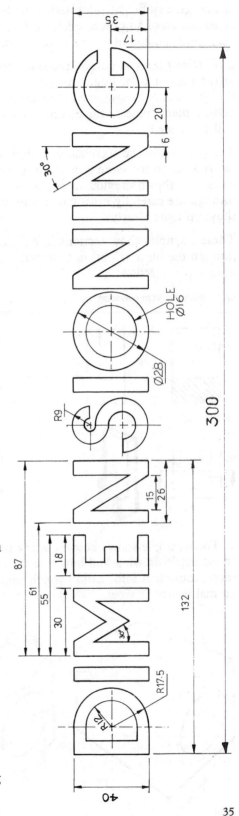

35

Sectional views

1. Sometimes additional views and even hidden detail cannot give sufficient information to clearly illustrate the construction of an object. Sectioning provides us with a very good method of seeing inside an object.

2. *Cutting planes.* A cutting plane on one of the elevations or the plan of an orthographic projection indicates where the object is to be sectioned. The arrows attached to the cutting plane indicate the direction from which the section will be viewed.

The position of the sectional elevation on the paper is worked out in the same way as for any of the other elevations shown previously. Surfaces which have been cut through are carefully cross-hatched to make the section show up more clearly.

These examples show sections in different directions through the block (right) in both orthographic and isometric projections.

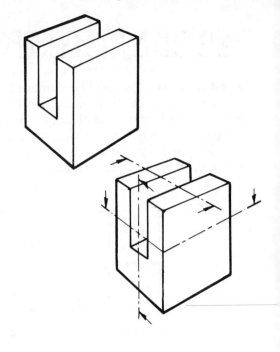

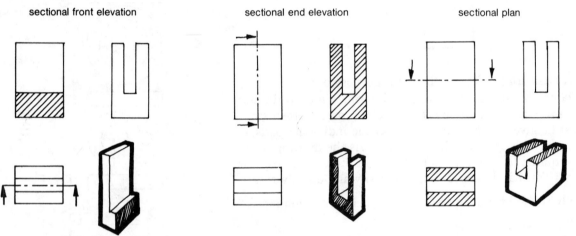

| sectional front elevation | sectional end elevation | sectional plan |

3. This example shows how a cutting plane is marked on an isometric drawing and how a section can be used to reveal important information which cannot be seen on the normal isometric view.

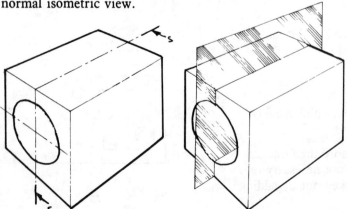

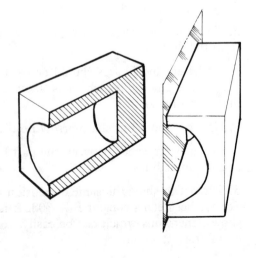

36

The drawing below illustrates how inadequate a pictorial
view alone is compared to an orthographic projection
including hidden detail, and the use of orthographic and/or
isometric sectional elevations.

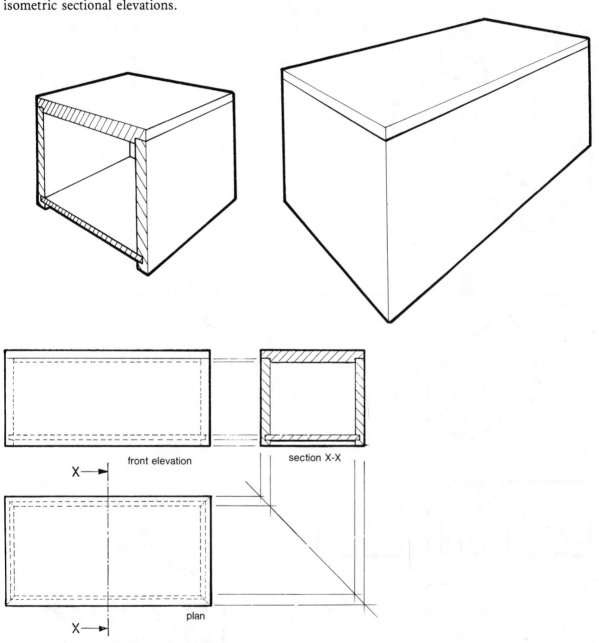

front elevation

section X-X

plan

Note Only the view indicated by the cutting plane X-X
appears as a sectional view. The other views must be drawn
as complete views unless further cutting planes are added.

Ways of drawing; a summary

The exploded view (left) shows a simple toy garage made from several wooden blocks. Compare the different techniques used on this page to show the garage and choose the one most suited to the drawing you want to do.

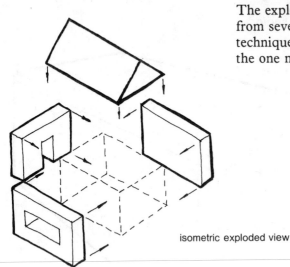

isometric exploded view

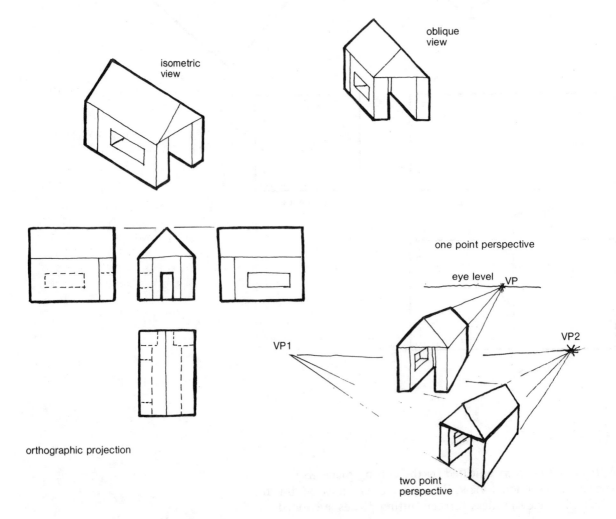

isometric view

oblique view

orthographic projection

one point perspective

eye level VP

VP1

VP2

two point perspective

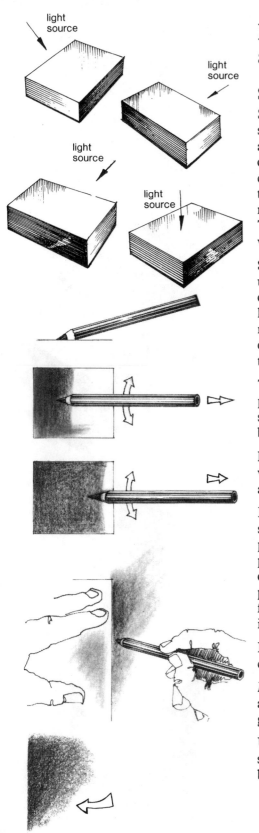

Part 3 Use of shading, colour and line rendering

Shading

Simple flat views given in orthographic projection are sufficient to explain the basic proportions of each side of an artefact. Pictorial views are used to give an overall picture of an object. However, as these views are still merely two-dimensional line drawings of three-dimensional objects, they often lack the appearance of being solid. Hence, the need for a method of successfully representing an object. There are many ways of achieving this aim using a wide variety of media.

Simple colouring and shading. We see objects around us because they reflect light. Therefore, the position of the object, and our viewing position in relation to the source of light are primary factors regarding the view we see. A rectangular form for example will reflect varying amounts of light from each of its sides as each side is at right angles to the others.

To make possible a simple demonstration of shading, the position of light in each example has been assumed and shadows that would usually be cast from an object have been left out.

Pencil and pencil crayons can be used to create some very 'professional' results. However, this can only be achieved by extremely careful use of the media.

Hold the pencil about halfway down its length and at the same time lower the pencil so that the side of the conical point, and not the point itself, comes into contact with the paper. Begin shading/colouring by moving the pencil from one side to the other, merely allowing the weight of the pencil to provide the light pressure needed to build up a faint layer of colour. Repeat this process as many times as is required to sufficiently cover the area being shaded.

In this way it is possible to build up a very flat layer of colour.

Masking. It takes quite a lot of skill to colour up to a line and so the use of a sheet of paper may prove beneficial in giving a good crisp edge.

Using scraps of paper in this way (they must have good straight edges) is a simple method of keeping the background to a drawing clean.

However, if the background has also become shaded and hence the edges of the drawing will appear woolly, this masking technique can be used to correct the situation. Put a piece of paper over your drawing but line one straight edge of the paper up to the edge of the drawing and proceed to erase any unwanted pencil marks. Repeat this process on all edges to give a good clean finish to the drawing. (Of course this technique is more difficult if curves are involved.)

Before you begin to render objects make sure you can control the media first. Practice creating the flat areas of tone described above. Make each one slightly lighter or darker than the next. Now try shading from the faintest tone you can possibly make to the darkest, which should be almost black.

The cube. Follow the instructions below very carefully:

1. Apply a very faint tone over all three surfaces as practiced above.

2. Ignoring face A, apply a second tonal layer over faces B and C. Already the cube will have a more solid appearance.

3. Now complete the process by adding a third layer to face C, which should then appear to be in shadow.

For a more three-dimensional effect graduate the density of tone (using the practice exercise above) so that it looks similar to the given illustration (4).

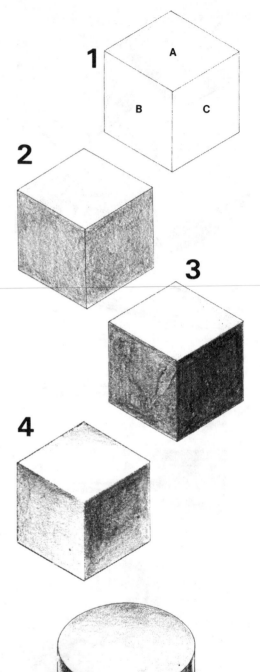

The cylinder.

1. Apply a faint layer of tone covering the whole of the drawing.

2. Ignoring the uppermost surface, graduate the tone on the rounded surface so that a light-to-dark effect is gained as illustrated.

Water based paints/ink

Many people are frightened off the idea of using paints because of one or two early disastrous attempts. Indeed, there are more problems involved with paints but the effects of these can be reduced considerably if tackled in an organised way.

There are many types of paint available which are suitable for graphic work but here are the main ones which you are likely to use.

Water colours. (Students and Artists Quality should be used if possible.) These can be bought in small tubes as a paste or as a small tablet. A very small amount of pigment is needed to produce a good colour wash. (A large amount of water is used to dilute the pigment into a colour tint.)

This colour wash is applied to faint drawings in the same way as the faint layers of pencil were applied when rendering the cubes. However, each colour wash must be allowed to dry in between coats which have to be added quickly. Thick cartridge, water colour paper, or card should be used as a base.

Poster colour. There are many types and qualities. Unlike water colours, poster colours have to be mixed with a small amount of water. The water merely allows a thick coat of pigment to be applied smoothly over the paper. A good paint, applied correctly will leave a flat even colour which does not allow the white of the paper to show through.

Although only one coat should be necessary, poster colour has the disadvantage of having to be mixed to the right colour for each detail on the drawing. A greater degree of accuracy has to be shown and it can very easily look messy if mistakes are made.

Designer's gouache is used in the same way as poster colour but it can give a very professional finish. It does not make the base paper wrinkle as quickly as the other paints.

Ink. Some inks can be used in the same way as water colour, but they do not usually give such a good finish. If waterproof inks are used, be very careful as brush strokes tend to show up. To avoid this work quickly.

Of course ink does not have to be used to form layers of colour as with paints, therefore line techniques can be used.

Nowadays the best way to achieve good line drawings is with the use of one of many makes of *technical pen*. These can be bought with nib widths ranging from less than 0.1 mm to over 2 mm. (They usually go up in 0.05 mm stages.) However these are very expensive.

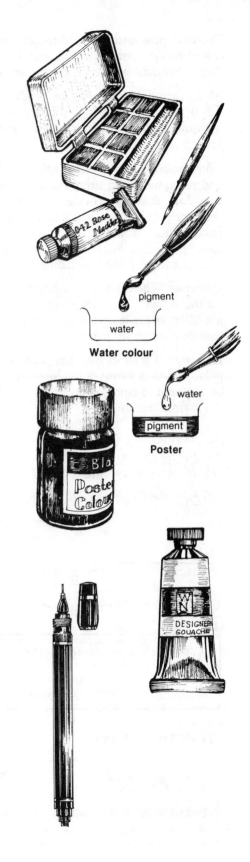

Water colour

Poster

Drawing pens with the traditional type of nib are also very useful but are also expensive and difficult to use when doing technical work. They are good for sketching.

Many manufacturers are now producing a wide range of felt tipped, fibre tipped and ball point pens, some of which are quite suitable for fine drawing work and are relatively inexpensive.

Line rendering can be done with pencils, coloured pencils and pens, but avoid using medium and thick felt and fibre tips. Line drawing provides us with a simple method of rendering which can, if handled properly, produce very good results. However, success does rely on accurate spacing of lines. Study the illustrations carefully. Gradation of tone can be gained by fading out lines.

Lettering. When drawing orthographic projections and other technical work, hand lettering or letters drawn in with the aid of letter guides are quite efficient methods of communicating information.

However, if a lot of time has been spent rendering a final presentation drawing of a design, good, tidy lettering will be required to complement the work. Below are illustrated the main alternatives:

~Hand Lettering

ABCDEFG abcdefghi

Abcdefghi ~ italic

Abcdefg
— cap line
— waist line
— base line
— drop line

ABCDEFG — Upper case

abcdefgh — Lower case

transfer letters :

sans serif
Extra Bold **Bold** Medium
Light OUTLINE *Italic* EXTENDED

Serif
Extra Bold Bold Medium
OUTLINE *Italic*

DECORATIVE
Old English ⋆ Bottleneck
Palace Script Flash
Fancy DAVIDA

Part 4 Presentation of design

The first part of this chapter has introduced the basic techniques needed before meaningful design can be explored. This section is devoted to how and when these techniques should be used within the design process. Four main areas of presentation can be identified as follows:

1. Preliminary sketches.
2. Development sketches.
3. Working drawings.
4. Presentation drawings.

These stages will enable the whole design process from the first thoughts and ideas about a problem to the final 'rendered' solution, to be illustrated clearly.

1. Preliminary sketches. This first step in the presentation of design includes a simple investigation of the problem, research notes and sketches, and a series of annotated sketches (sketches and notes) outlining first thoughts and ideas.

Annotated sketches are used because this is the most efficient way of getting information and ideas down on paper. Sketches are used to convey information related to shape, form and overall appearance. Notes are added as the quickest way of indicating possible details such as fixing methods, manufacture, materials etc., in addition to general points which may be of use later. As many ideas as possible should be collected before one or two are chosen for further development.

2. Development sketches are used to transform the rather vague ideas brought forward from the preliminary sketches, into workable solutions ready for drawing up to scale.

To achieve this aim, each individual detail has to be developed (there may be many possible solutions to each) to fit within the whole scheme or design. Study the example given carefully.

3. Working drawings can include quite a varied selection of sketches or drawings, depending on the type of problem and the level of design required. A scale drawing will in itself help to finalise the dimensions and proportions brought forward from the development sketch stage.

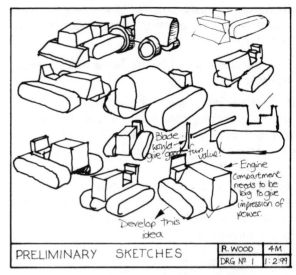

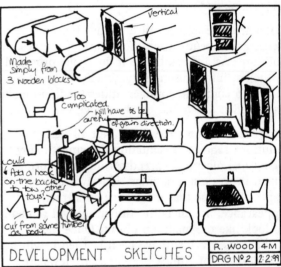

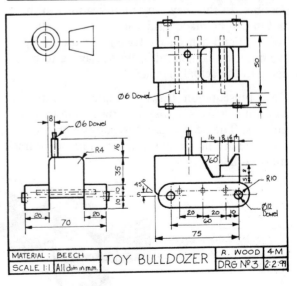

However, the main purpose of working drawings is to provide all the information needed to make the artefact.

This information can be displayed in a number of ways:

(a) *Orthographic projections* give specific information about dimensions and materials to be used and usually take the form of either:
(i)   Assembly drawings, or
(ii) Parts drawing.

(b) *Pictorial views* are more commonly used to give instructions for assembly, but can be used as an alternative to (a). They may include:
(i)   Dimensions.
(ii) Sections.
(iii) Detail views.
(iv) Exploded views.

Of course the number of drawings that may be necessary depends upon the nature of the design solution. As a check to see if you have provided sufficient information ask yourself the question, 'Could a complete stranger understand and make the artefact illustrated on the drawings?'.

4. Presentation drawings. Not all design solutions require presentation drawings, many being manufactured directly from the information given in working drawings. However others, especially those that must have an attractive appearance, are far better drawn up and rendered to look like the made up object. Once the techniques involved have been learned it will not take long before quick presentation views are possible. In this way, any modifications to the design can be made easily on the presentation drawing, and hence save time and expense by avoiding the same modifications having to be made to the actual artefact.

Good presentation drawings show your intentions and can suggest suitable materials, colours and finishes. They can even illustrate the object in use. You are in a way selling the idea to yourself and to others.

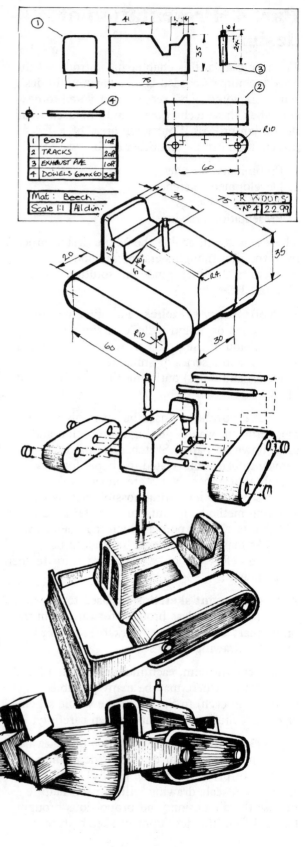

Presentation techniques; a summary

Simple geometric solids have been used to explain the presentation techniques used in this chapter, but with practice you should develop a rendering technique which you can use to tackle almost any type of drawing. In order to improve your skill try to render the shapes on this page using different techniques. You will soon find out for yourself the 'do's' and 'don'ts' of rendering.

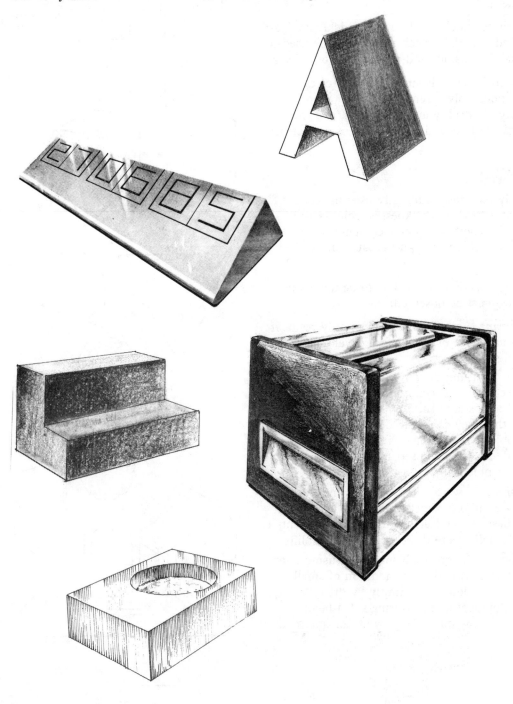

Part 5 Soft model making

We have seen how working drawings and presentation drawings can be used to give a realistic impression of an intended product. While these may give a good representation of materials, colour and perhaps finishes, some designs require more realistic methods of representing three-dimensional proportions. For this purpose we use models and mock-ups.

Soft models are those which can be made quickly and easily from easily worked materials. Such models can be used to work out the final dimensions and proportions of a design.

A number of suitable materials such as paper, card, polystyrene, expanded polystyrene, wire, balsa wood, plasticine and clay are readily available to us, and the choice of materials will depend on the type of project being tackled.

Paper and card

These are possibly the most commonly used materials because of the range of sheet thicknesses, colours and finishes available, in addition to their comparative cheapness, their ease of working and because most glues will stick them.

However, if a good standard of work is to be maintained certain procedures must be observed:

  (i) *Technical drawing*. Accurate models can only result if precise drawings are made of the surface development of a three-dimensional solid object.

  (ii) *Developments*. By using drawing instruments and adhering to correct drawing techniques it is possible to draw the sides of almost any solid object on a sheet of paper or card so that they can be folded to make the form of the required object. Developments should be drawn so that they are made up of as few separate pieces as possible and in one piece if practical.

(iii) *Geometric forms*. As we observed earlier, most artefacts around us are made up of geometric forms. Therefore, it follows that the best way to learn to make developments is to practise on gradually more difficult geometric solids.

  (iv) *Detailing*. One of the great advantages of using paper and card to make models is that the addition of small intricate details can be done very simply by drawing them onto the flat development and colouring them before it is even cut out. In this way quite simple but realistic models can be made.

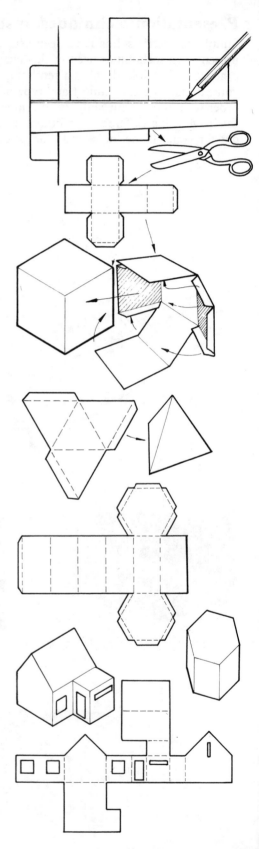

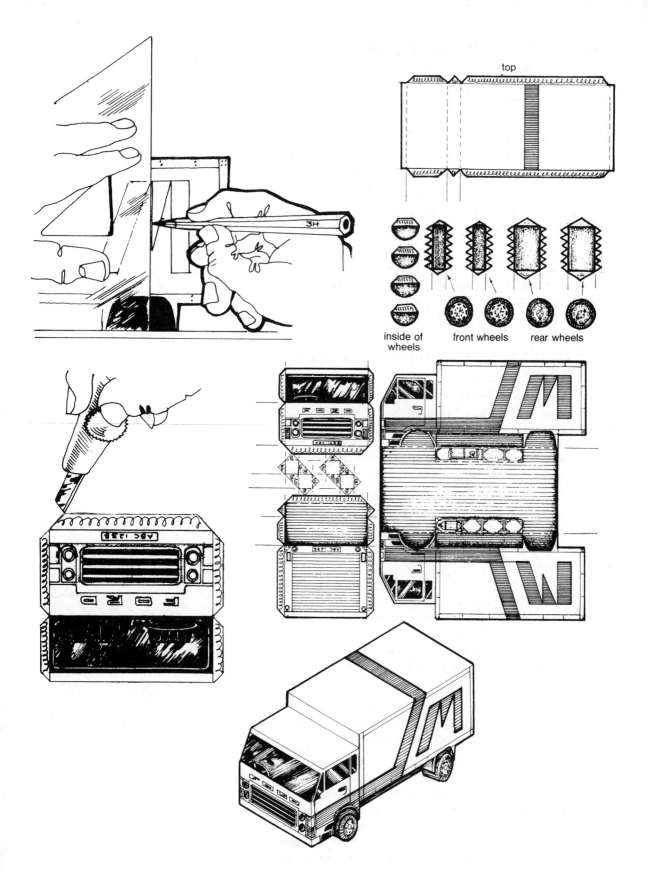

top

inside of
wheels.

front wheels

rear wheels

Cutting and scoring paper and card

Although, for many simple tasks scissors can be used to cut paper and some card accurately, for more detailed work a modelling knife should be used.

However, remember that if knife blades are to cut efficiently they must be very sharp and so are *very dangerous*!!! Also remember that the edge of paper can cut quite deeply into a careless finger.

To make straight line cuts use a steel straight edge if possible. Make sure that bevel edges are not used and that hands are always kept well behind the cutting edge of the blade.

Carefully and lightly score down the line you have previously made in pencil. This score line will act as a guide for your next cut which should go right through the card. Repeat this process several times if thicker materials are being used.

Always cut on scrap materials or special boards to protect furniture etc.

To make curved cuts. Where possible use a graphic type compass and a cylindrical modelling knife. With this method, accurate arcs and circles can be cut. If irregular curves are to be cut follow the pencil lines freehand very slowly, making a light score line at first and then a heavier cut as described above. Scissors should be used where possible!

To make bends in card. Paper will of course bend quite easily to any required curve, but because thicker card is more rigid other methods have to be found.

To make a bend along a straight line merely score along the previously drawn pencil line and bend downwards. This method will give you a very strong, sharp, accurate bend which will be better than any attempts to join two separate pieces of card to achieve the same bend. However, when using this method be careful not to cut too deeply as this may result in the bend coming apart as you try to bend it to the required angle.

To make a radiused bend, divide the section to be bent into a series of lines going across the bend. Score along these lines as above. Manipulate the bend to the required curve.

To make a cylinder from card which is too thick to bend on its own, draw out the flat development on the card. Then mask and score equally spaced, parallel lines along the length of the cylinder and simply bend into the cylindrical form required. Finally, fix the ends together. If calculated correctly, good accurate cylinders can be formed, although to be precise these forms are really multi-sided polygons.

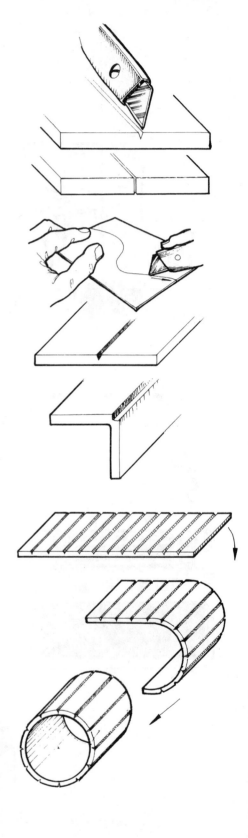

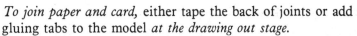

To join paper and card, either tape the back of joints or add gluing tabs to the model *at the drawing out stage.*

Paper and card mock-ups

Paper and card can be used, instead of the more expensive and harder to work materials which will eventually be used to make the product, when we are uncertain about what the shapes should be. When the shape has been finalised these mock-up parts can often be used as templates to mark out the real pieces.

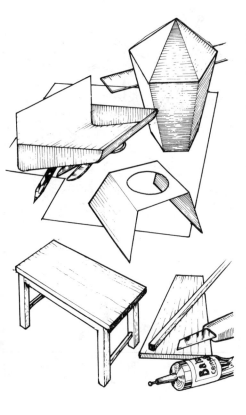

Balsa wood is a convenient material to use to develop simple frameworks for furniture etc. It can also be used to develop slab constructions. However, many jobs which could be done with balsa can be done more cheaply and efficiently with card.

Polystyrene sheet can be used in the same way as card and will often give a much better finish. Bends can be made simply by local heating and bending round a former.

Many scale models are made from polystyrene. Therefore, the many paint finishes available for use on models can also be used on home-made polystyrene models.

Sheet polystyrene is an excellent material for vacuum forming. Those schools which are fortunate enough to have a vacuum forming machine can produce quite complex product forms using this process. For example, the body shells for custom-made, motorised model cars are made in this way. Various rod and strip sections of polystyrene can be bought from model shops and these too can prove very useful. Polystyrene is fixed together using polystyrene cement.

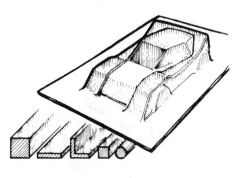

Expanded polystyrene is available in sheets, slabs and blocks, but can also be salvaged from the packaging material widely used to protect toys, household and electrical goods. However, it is difficult to cut using conventional tools which usually leave a rough finish. Glass paper can be used to smooth down the material as much as possible, but due to the air pockets which give expanded polystyrene its special characteristics, a really good finish is not possible without the addition of fillers. 'Polyfilla' can be used for this purpose.

The hot wire cutter is the best tool for cutting this material. Using this method of cutting, expanded polystyrene can be a very convenient material for exploring the three-dimensional form of an object. For example, it is sometimes used in industry to make full-size mock-ups of cars.

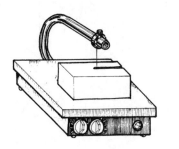

Warning. Do not use polystyrene cement to join expanded polystyrene. Use P.V.A., natural latex, or spots of contact adhesive.

49

Wire and thin rod. Used carefully metal wire and rods can prove to be a very useful method of representing full-size, metal-framed furniture, thereby providing a relatively inexpensive method of investigating ideas.

Gas welding rod has proved to be an excellent material for this purpose, as it is easy to bend, is available in a range of gauges, has a protective copper coating and is simple to solder together.

Thicker mild steel rod is available in a range of cross-sections, but is harder to shape and join, and may have to be painted to prevent rusting.

Any available material or combination of materials can be used for modelling, especially if the model is to be the end product of the design project. A model can, of course, be made in exactly the same materials as the full-size object it represents or a very realistic impression can be given, either by simulating the materials which would be used, or by applying exactly the same paint finish as would be used on the full-size product.

This chapter has shown you how to design using visual techniques. Once fully conversant with these you are ready to attempt more difficult design problems using a more detailed method of solving them. The aim of the next chapter, therefore, is to guide you in developing a more advanced design method.

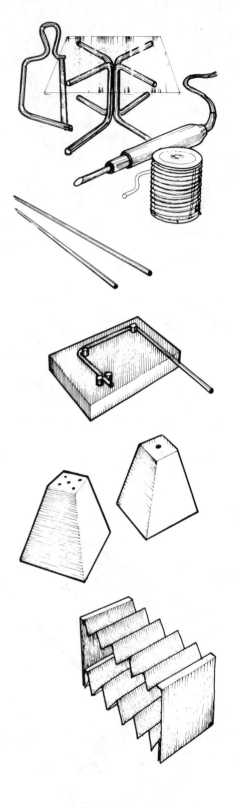

4 Design method

It is not possible to produce solutions to design problems like rabbits from a magician's hat and if asked without warning to solve a design problem most people would not know where to start. The purpose of this chapter therefore, is to overcome the obstacles which most people think they are faced with when asked to solve design problems.

In chapter one we saw that the word 'design' can have many different meanings but that for our purpose it should be defined as problem solving. In chapters two and three we saw examples of how we can find solutions to simple design problems by developing ideas suggested by the many sources available to us.

When tackling these simple problems we can successfully record and develop our ideas entirely by sketching and this is how we start to design. However, when we are faced with more complicated problems a lot more thought and preparation are needed before we can even begin to get ideas to provide starting points for our designing.

We therefore, need a design method which we can follow stage by stage to ensure that no part of a problem is overlooked and no opportunities missed.

This chapter provides details of such a design method and then shows how it can be developed further to deal with advanced projects.

A simple design method

The cartoons on the preceeding page show the stages which we subconsciously follow when we seek to satisfy a *need*, and in doing so we are following a simple design process.

By consciously approaching every problem with which we are faced in the same step by step way, we can develop our ability to solve gradually more difficult and wide ranging problems.

Stage 1 Situations for design

The problems you are required to solve will usually arise from normal everyday situations. Some of them will be set by your teacher, but many others will occur to you as a result of your own and other people's interests and experiences.

For example:

(a) Visitors to your home have difficulty in finding the correct house as there is no identification on the outside.

(b) Having made hot drinks in your kitchen you find you have to make several trips before your family are served in the lounge. This routine often results in messy spillages.

(c) You have difficulty doing work on your desk in the evening because your back is to the light which is in the centre of the room. As a result, an irritating shadow is cast over the work surface.

(d) You have nowhere to keep your pens and pencils which always seem to be lost or broken when you need them.

Stage 2 The design brief

This is a short statement of the *need* you have identified from the situations as described above.

For example:
If you decide that the lack of proper storage for your pens and pencils in example (d) is a suitable design problem you should begin to tackle it by trying to state clearly what you need to do to solve the problem.
This could be:
To design and make a unit to hold pens and pencils.
This statement then is the *design brief* for the given problem. This must be worded in such a way that preconceived ideas of what the solution might be are avoided.

Such a short statement, clearly does not give sufficient information for design solutions to be found. Therefore, a full *investigation* into the problem is necessary.

Stage 3 Investigation

The nature of the investigation will vary considerably, depending on the type of design problem being tackled. Basically it consists of asking yourself a series of questions about the problem and finding the answers to them. Let us continue with the example specified by the design brief.

Below are examples of the type of questions which you might ask yourself:

Key questions
How many pens and pencils have to be held?
Should other items such as rubbers, sharpeners, etc. be included?
What are the sizes of the items to be held?
Where is the unit to be used?
Will the unit have to be carried at any time?
Could the pens, pencils, or other items be dangerous in any way?
What materials are available?
Which of these are suitable?
How much will the unit cost?
How much time have you got to make the unit? etc.

All of these questions are important. The answers to them will dictate the starting points from which design ideas can be found. When you first begin to tackle design problems you may be given these *key questions* to ensure that you isolate and research all the important factors, but experience will enable you to prepare your own.

Stage 4 Solution

From the information gathered by this investigation you can begin to make *ideas sketches* which investigate visually the possible answers to the problem. The best idea(s) are then chosen from these ideas sketches and *developed* further in sketch form to give one or more *partial solutions*.

One or more of these partial solutions are then chosen and put together to give the *final solution*. It is worked out in detail, and presented in a way which gives all the information needed to realize (make) it. (*See* Working drawings.)

These working drawings should include:

(a) dimensions,
(b) materials
(c) processes, (e.g. joints),
(d) fittings,
(e) finishes.

1. SITUATION FOR DESIGN.

2. DESIGN BRIEF
TO DESIGN AND MAKE A UNIT
TO HOLD PENS AND PENCILS

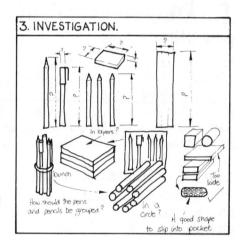

3. INVESTIGATION.

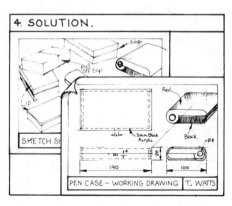

4. SOLUTION.

STRODE'S COLLEGE

53

The best way to present this information is in the form of annotated flat views, plus a pictorial presentation view showing what the finished product should look like and a cutting list if needed.

Stage 5   Realisation

This is the actual making of the solution from the working drawings described above.

Stage 6   Testing

The finished artefact must be tested to find out whether it satisfies the original design brief. This can only be done by using it and if necessary making modifications to it.

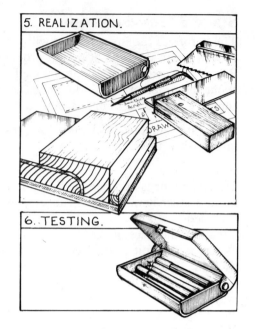

Tackling more advanced problems

While the design method which we have just described is adequate for fairly straightforward problems, we need to add additional detail to these basic stages in order to make a thorough examination of more advanced problems. These additional detailed stages can best be explained by going through the design process stage by stage again.

Stage 1   Situations for design

This should be expanded to ensure that all possible sources of information and all parts of the problem have been identified.

Stage 2   Design brief

With more advanced projects the design brief needs to be as concise as possible, yet fully specify the requirements of the prospective artefact without leading to preconceived ideas.
For example:

The design brief, 'To design a chair', could be criticised both for being too vague and for suggesting a preconceived solution, but by rewording the brief to say, 'To design a means of supporting a person in a comfortable position for working at a desk', we could overcome these criticisms and provide a good starting point for investigation.

Stage 3   Investigation

This can be broken down into two main areas:

(a) Research, the accumulation of useful data.

(b) Analysis, the consideration of all the factors which may have an influence on the final design.

We will now look more closely at each of these areas.

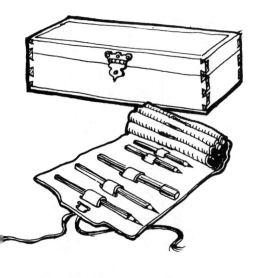

(a) Research. We have already seen that even the simplest design problems usually involve some research, such as the measurement of objects to be stored for example, and one of the main distinguishing features of more advanced projects is that they involve much more research. This information is often needed before designing can even begin.

Most of the information needed to design comes under the following headings:

(i)   Measurement of artefacts to be 'housed'.
(ii)   Measurements of the person(s) for whom an artefact is intended (anthropometrics).
(iii)   Study of the environment for which the artefact is intended (ergonomics).
(iv)   Finding out about the range of existing products, evaluating them, assessing their popularity and examining how they are made.
(v)   Market research.
(vi)   Collecting technological information.

(b) Factor analysis. Once you have become used to asking yourself the type of key questions shown earlier, you will soon become aware that many of them are the same for most design problems. It is important that we understand how these common *design factors* can interact with each other. *Factor analysis* is the study of the relationship between all the factors involved in solving a problem so that a *compromise* can be found.

Here are some common design factors:

(i) *Function.* This is the job which the artefact will have to do (specified by the design brief). The main job an artefact has to do is called its *primary function* and any others, the *secondary functions.*

For example, the primary function of a chair is to support people safely in a sitting position, but depending on exactly where it is to be used it may also have to look attractive, be easy to clean, match other furniture in the room, support people at the correct height for sitting at a table etc.

(ii) *Safety.* There are many safety considerations which may affect the solution of a design problem. These might include for example:

    Toxicity. Avoid using toxic materials where they are likely to cause danger, (e.g. do not use lead based paints on toys).
    Sharp corners and edges. Design smooth rounded shapes whenever possible so that, for example, you cannot hurt yourself when brushing past furniture and so that small items will not scratch furniture which they might be stood on.

Stability. Make sure that things cannot easily be knocked over. For example, a chair should not tip over even if someone rocks it back on two legs, and the base of a desk lamp must be large enough and heavy enough to prevent it from being knocked over.

Fire hazards. You must not use materials which are likely to catch fire easily, give off dangerous fumes, or melt during normal use.

(iii) *Materials.* These must be suitable for the job they have to do and should also be appropriate to the environment in which they are used.

Each of the materials available to us has its own properties and limitations which you should study carefully to make sure that you choose appropriate ones. This can prove difficult at times when you consider for example how many different alloys there are. (*See* Definitions of properties of materials and materials for craftwork.)

(iv) *Cost.* This includes not only how much *money* should be spent on materials, but also how much *time* will be needed to design and make the artefact. The choice of materials, processes and finishes will have a great effect on costs.

(v) *Manufacture.* The processes employed will depend on the materials, facilities and time available, as well as on the technical skills of the person using them. Make sure that it is possible to make your design with the resources available.

(vi) *Size and weight.* These are important factors when designing many jobs and their effect on the following should be considered:

   (a) Portability.
   (b) Storage.
   (c) Environment.
   (d) Materials used.

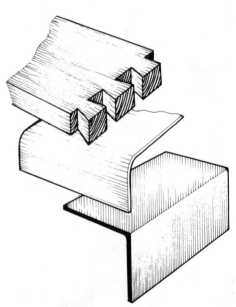

(vii) *Maintenance.* It is not enough merely to make an artefact which works for a short time. We must make sure that it will work for the maximum length of time without any problems, and that when maintenance or repairs are needed they can be carried out easily and economically.

(viii) *Appearance.* This is usually a very important factor because there are few situations in which we do not consider the appearance of a design and its effect on its environment. Appearance is also the first characteristic of an artefact which most people notice. We should therefore remember that:

   (a) The appearance should suit the nature of the job an artefact has to do.

(b) The appearance should suit the environment in which the artefact will be used.

(c) The overall appearance will depend on the materials which are used and the finishes which have been applied to them.

(d) Safety considerations may affect appearance, for example when rounding off edges as mentioned earlier.

(e) Colour and texture can play a very important role in the overall effect of an artefact.

(f) An aesthetically pleasing overall effect will enhance the quality of an artefact.

(ix) *Ergonomic and anthropometric data.*

(a) *Ergonomics.* This is the study of man in relation to his work and his environment.

(b) *Anthropometrics.* This is the study of the development of man.

Since the purpose of design is to make life better in some way for human beings, it is reasonable to expect that many design investigations will involve the study and measurement of man and his movements.

For example, when designing a chair we need to know where the users back, arms and legs should be supported to provide comfort in different sitting positions, and the range of measurements of the different people likely to use the chair (*see* Chair design example).

Once a compromise has been reached between the conflicting requirements of the many design factors, and the possibilities have been narrowed down to specific ranges of materials, approximate sizes and proportions, and the general character aimed at for the product, a visual investigation can begin. In other words, the purpose of the investigation stage in an advanced project is to provide the designer with everything he needs to know before he starts to make his preliminary design sketches, to resolve conflicts between the design factors and reduce the problem to manageable proportions.

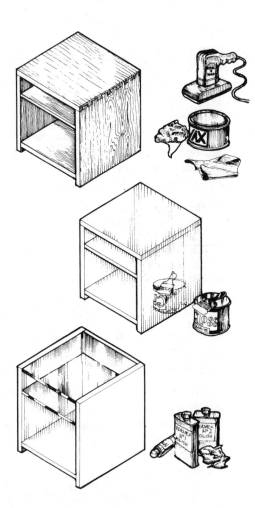

Stage 4 Solution

From the information provided by the investigation above a visual investigation is begun leading to the *synthesis* of a solution to the problem.

(The word 'synthesis' means the building up of a solution from the many, separate parts of a problem.)

The synthesis can be divided into five stages:

(i) *Preliminary ideas* recorded in notes and sketches.

(ii) *Development sketches* presented as annotated sketches, models and mock-ups.

(iii) *Working drawings* giving all the information needed to make the design.

(iv) *Presentation drawings* and models showing what the completed artefact would look like.

(v) *The final design compared with the original design brief* to make sure that it fulfills the original need.

Some aspects of this synthesis need to be explained further.

(i) *Preliminary ideas.* You should try to produce the largest possible number and range of ideas. All ideas, however unconventional they may seem, should be recorded by sketches (these sometimes turn out to be very good original solutions). Use sketching to think aloud. Your first sketches will probably be rather simple geometric forms. However, these will at least have given you a starting point on which to build new ideas. Be spontaneous!

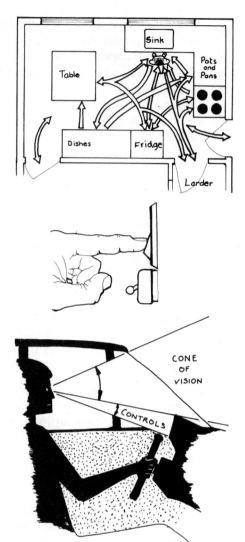

(ii) *Development sketches.* From your preliminary sketches you should take the best idea or ideas and begin to produce *partial solutions* from which a final solution can evolve. Partly developed ideas can usually only be finalised when they are drawn or modelled to scale so that the composition can be checked for proportions, etc. Mock-ups can be used at this stage so that accurate measurements can be worked out. From these sketches and models working drawings can be made.

(iii) *Working Drawings.* Remember that working drawings can be in many different forms but their purpose is always to ensure that all the information needed to make the artefact is given, (*see* previous chapter).

At this point a cutting list should be made of all the materials needed, (*see* Making a cutting list).

(iv) *Presentation drawings or models.* These are used to communicate a realistic impression of what the final artefact will look like well before it is actually made. In this way aesthetic and functional judgements can be made and any mistakes corrected before the prototype is started.

In industry several *visuals* may be presented to a client so that he may choose the most appropriate one for production.

(v) *Realisation.* This is the making of the artefact. Again in industry the *prototype* is made individually by craftsman technicians. Modifications are made as required and if it is given a good evaluation the go-ahead is given for production.

Other products may be designed on a one off basis. It is important that the final prototype is correct in every way and this can only be ensured by rigorous testing.

(vi) *Testing.* The artefact should be tested under the conditions under which the product will eventually be used. With 'one off' artefacts this will probably simply mean using it in its intended position. The artefact should be observed carefully under normal use for an initial period. If modifications are needed they should become apparent fairly early in its use.

In large scale production situations, prototypes are sometimes tested to destruction to identify trouble areas needing particular attention or modifications, or to indicate the potential spares back-up required.

Making a cutting list

Having designed a piece of work and made working drawings of it, a list of all the parts should be made showing the length, width and thickness of each. These will be the finished sizes of each piece.

Making a cutting list is very important because it allows you to check that you have all the materials needed to complete the job and that you have worked out the sizes correctly, making use of readily available standard sizes wherever possible, thus avoiding mistakes, waste and extra work.

Where the surfaces have a rough 'as sawn' finish we must allow extra material on all sides for planing, filing or machining the surfaces smooth and square, but where the width and thickness are already finished exactly to size and have a smooth surface we need only allow extra on the length where we have sawn it from a larger piece.

The allowances made depend on the materials being used.

For solid wood. The allowances on a board are: 3 mm extra on the thickness, 6 mm extra on the width, 12 mm extra on the length.

The allowances on square wood are 3 mm extra on the sides and 12 mm extra on the length.

Where a mortise is to be chopped out near the end of a piece of wood, the allowance on the length is increased to 25 mm so that enough wood can be left at the end to prevent the end-grain from splitting.

For man-made boards, metals and plastics the cutting list is simpler. It is necessary only to allow 3 mm for finishing any sides which have been left as sawn and have to be smoothed.

On metal and plastics rods, squares, flats, etc. allowances are usually needed only on the length.

On sheet materials of all kinds, allowances are required for smoothing the edges.

The following examples show a convenient way of making out a cutting list.

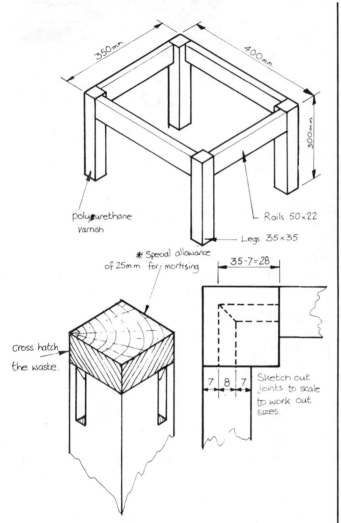

polyurethane
varnish

Rails 50×22

Legs 35×35

✳ Special allowance of 25m.m. for mortising

35 - 7 = 28

Cross hatch
the waste.

7 | 8 | 7

Sketch out
joints to scale
to work out
sizes.

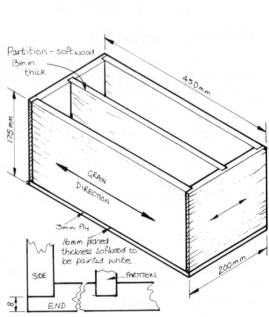

Partition - softwood
13 m.m. thick

450mm

175 mm

GRAIN
DIRECTION

3mm. Ply.

16 m.m. planed
thickness softwood to
be painted white.

SIDE

PARTITION.

END

200mm

PART	No. Req'd	MATERIAL	FINISHED SIZES			SAWN SIZES		
			L.	W.	Th.	L.	W.	Th.
LEGS	4	IROKO	300	35	35	325	38	38
LONG RAILS	2	IROKO	386	50	22	398	56	25
SHORT RAILS	2	IROKO	336	50	22	348	56	25

PART	No. Req'd	MATERIAL	FINISHED SIZES			SAWN SIZES		
			L	W	Th.	L.	W.	Th.
ENDS	2	P.B.S. SOFT WOOD	200	175	16	212	181	
SIDES	2	"	434	175	16	446	181	
PARTITION	1	"	434	175	13	446	181	
BOTTOM	1	"	450	200	3	453	203	

A simple design method

Example 1

Situation. You have a number of paperback books which are used frequently and are difficult to keep tidy, as they have no set place where they are to be stored.

Design brief. To design a holder to store paperback books neatly in a convenient position near your desk.

Investigation – How many paperback books are to be stored?
How big are they?
What is the best way of grouping the books?
Which materials are most suitable? (Look at the room where it will be used.)
Is the unit to be free standing or wall mounted?
If wall mounted, how will it be fixed?

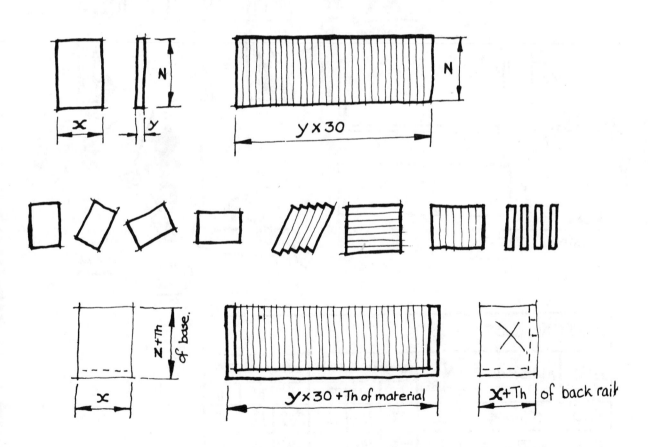

From the investigation a partial solution has been found which now needs to be developed so that the details can be finalised:

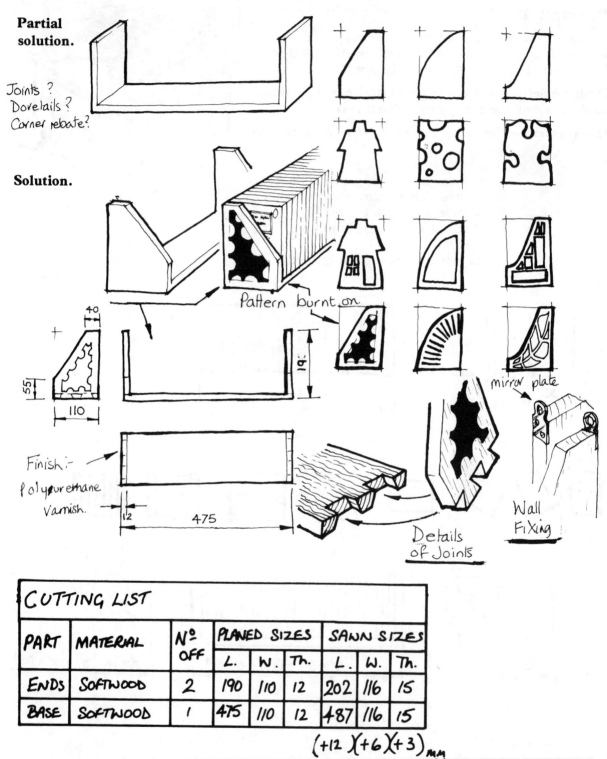

Partial solution.

Joints ?
Dovetails ?
Corner rebate?

Solution.

Pattern burnt on.

40

55

110

19

Finish :-
Polyurethane
Varnish.

12

475

Details
of Joints

mirror plate

Wall
Fixing

CUTTING LIST									
PART	MATERIAL	Nº OFF	PLANED SIZES			SAWN SIZES		
			L.	W.	Th.	L.	W.	Th.
ENDS	SOFTWOOD	2	190	110	12	202	116	15
BASE	SOFTWOOD	1	475	110	12	487	116	15

$$(+12)(+6)(+3)_{MM}$$

See Commonly available forms of hardwood and softwood and making a cutting list.

Example 2   Noughts and crosses game

Situation for design — Most of the games I own are quite large and cumbersome. and have parts that are easily lost or damaged. This makes them difficult to carry around and impossible to play when travelling.

Identification of problem :- A small compact game that can be easily carried.

Design Brief — To design a simple pocket game which can be used when travelling.

Investigation —
① Which game(s) do I prefer ?   ✓
② Which game do my brother + sister prefer?   ✓
③ How big are the pockets I am likely to   ✓
carry the game inside?   ✓
④ What material would be suitable/available?   ✓
⑤ Are there any safety factors I should be aware of? ✓
⑥ Where is the game likely to be played ?   ✓
⑦ How many people should be able to play the game ✓
at one time ?
⑧ How many parts does the chosen game include?

Monopoly X too complicated
Ludo ✓ possible — a bit complex for a small game.
Draughts X too many parts.
Chess X Sister + brother cannot play.
Noughts + crosses. ✓ — All prefer.

Nine pieces

Two players. rear passenger seats of car. room for two people. — sometimes at home.

About 100 m.m
square game would leave plenty of room for fingers.
— 4 Noughts.
— 5 crosses.
Will have to be careful of sharp corners.

180

Game has to be kept small and Compact — but can be brightly coloured — must not wear off inside pocket or by constant touch by hand — Acrylic would be suitable — there are plenty of small pieces in school!

| POCKET   GAME | J Topp | 11:12:82 |

Preliminary sketches

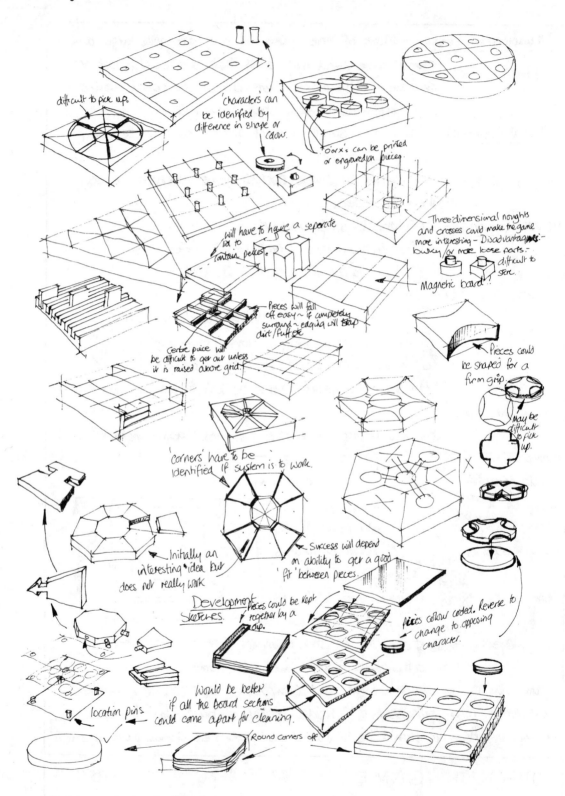

difficult to pick up.

'characters' can be identified by difference in shape or colour.

o'x's can be printed or engraved on pieces.

Three dimensional noughts and crosses could make the game more interesting - Disadvantages:- bulky / or more loose parts:- difficult to store.

Magnetic board?

Will have to have a separate lid to contain pieces.

Pieces will fall off easy - if completely surround - edging will trap dirt / fluff etc.

Centre piece will be difficult to get out unless it is raised above grid.

Pieces could be shaped for a firm grip.

May be difficult to pick up.

'corners' have to be identified if system is to work.

Initially an interesting idea but does not really work.

Success will depend on ability to get a good 'fit' between pieces.

Development sketches.

Pieces could be kept together by a grip.

Pieces colour coded. Reverse to change to opposing character.

Would be better if all the board sections could come apart for cleaning.

location pins

Round corners off.

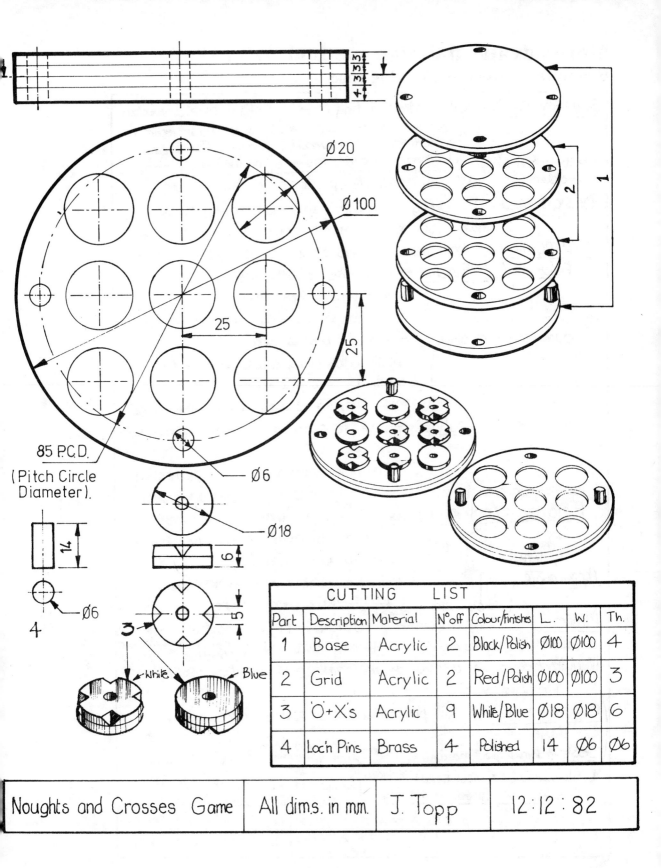

Ø20

Ø100

25

25

85 P.C.D.
(Pitch Circle
Diameter).

Ø6

Ø18

14

6

5

Ø6

4

3

White

Blue

CUTTING LIST							
Part	Description	Material	N°off	Colour/finishes	L.	W.	Th.
1	Base	Acrylic	2	Black/Polish	Ø100	Ø100	4
2	Grid	Acrylic	2	Red/Polish	Ø100	Ø100	3
3	O+X's	Acrylic	9	White/Blue	Ø18	Ø18	6
4	Loch Pins	Brass	4	Polished	14	Ø6	Ø6

Noughts and Crosses Game	All dims. in mm.	J. Topp	12:12:82

More advanced design method
Example 1   Record carrying case

SITUATION FOR DESIGN — When visiting friends I often take a selection of my records with me. However, these records sometimes get damaged in transit from being dropped, knocked, rained on or warped by heat.

Identification of problem :— Lack of adequate protection for the records.

DESIGN BRIEF:— To design a unit which will safely house a small number of records, during short journeys.

INVESTIGATION :— How many records should be carried — 20 ✓

Factors — Function —To house records safely
- must protect from bumps.
- must be secure — no danger to records damaging each other.
- must be weather proof —
- must allow easy access to records.
- must be easily carried
- must display records nicely when used

at home. — Safety — safe to carry — strong — no sharp edges.
- secure .
- Easy to clean without damaging records or case/unit.

(Handle) To pick out records
Ergonomics/Anthropometrics — Size of fingers/hand? length from my shoulder to carrying height of unit? Size of records (singles).

Appearance — must be attractive — impress friends
- Look like a record case.
strong durable.

Material - Light weight if possible — rigid — weather proof — attractive appearance — what's available? plastic/wood/metal. Textiles ?

Manufacture - will depend on materials and facilities — school workshop ✓. —

ENVIRONMENT — will probably sit on carpet beneath record player

Cost - about £5 maximum school prices Not rigid enough Brightly coloured
Aluminium X steel sheet X textile X Be good if it could match up with my stereo unit ǂ
Acrylic ✓ timber ✓ possibly

INVESTIGATION: ANALYSIS	M. MORRIS.	5 TL
	DRG Nº 1	27.8.85

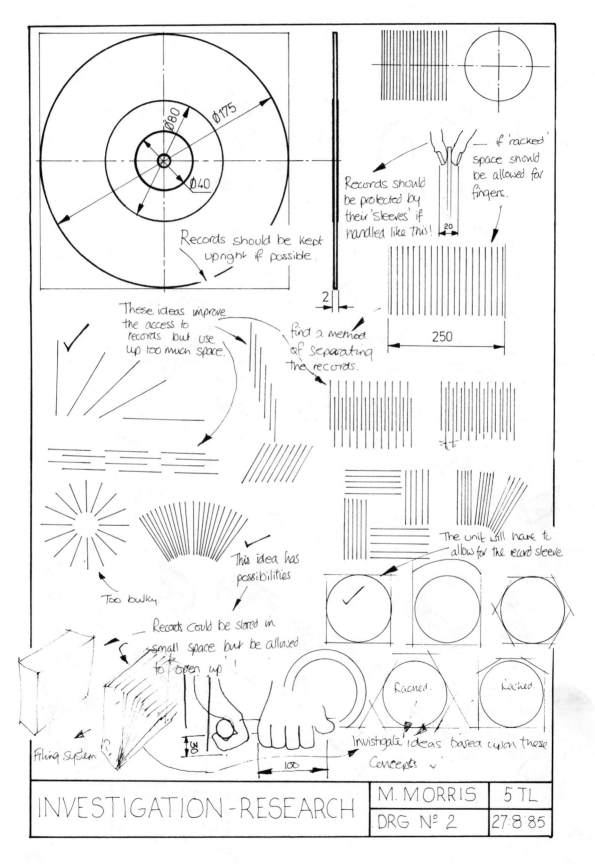

Ø175
Ø80
Ø40

Records should be kept upright if possible.

Records should be protected by their 'sleeves' if handled like this!

if 'racked' space should be allowed for fingers.

20

2

250

These ideas improve the access to records but use up too much space.

find a method of separating the records.

This idea has possibilities

Too bulky.

The unit will have to allow for the record sleeve

Records could be stored in small space but be allowed to 'open up'!

Filing System ?

100

Racked.

Racked.

Invistigate ideas based upon these Concepts ✓

INVESTIGATION - RESEARCH	M. MORRIS	5 TL
	DRG Nº 2	27·8·85

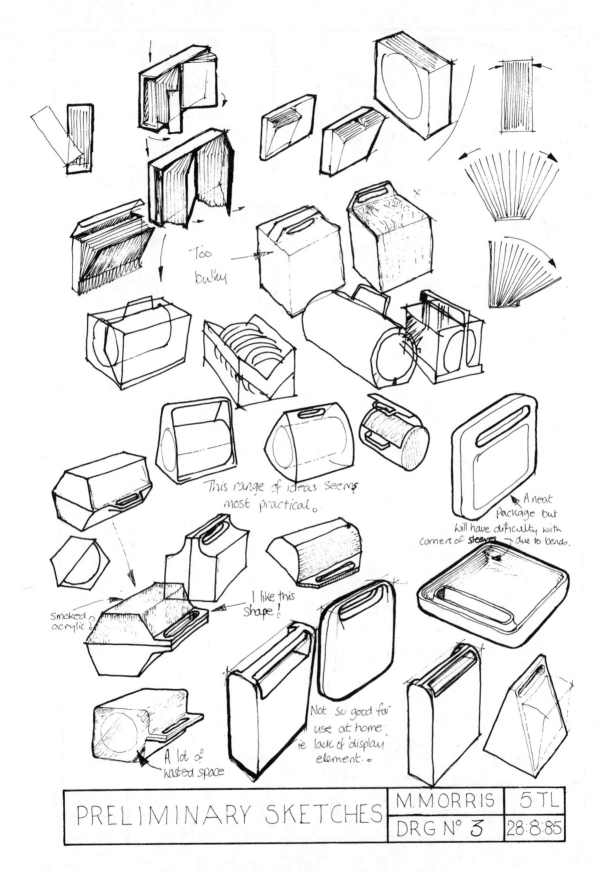

Too bulky

This range of ideas seems most practical.

A neat Package but will have difficulty with corners of sleeves due to bends.

smoked acrylic?

I like this shape!

A lot of wasted space

Not so good for use at home ie lack of 'display element.

PRELIMINARY SKETCHES	M.MORRIS	5 TL
	DRG N° 3	28·8·85

68

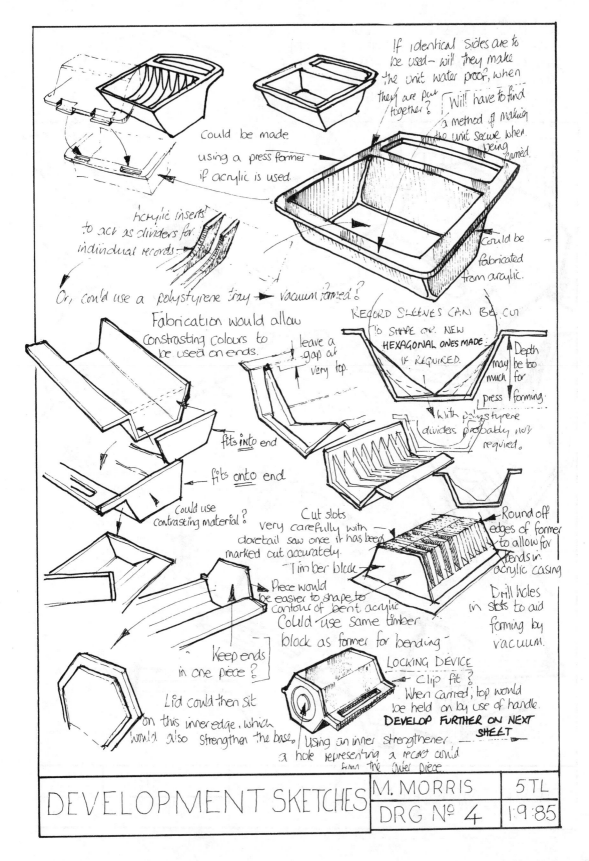

If identical sides are to be used — will they make the unit water proof, when they are put together?

Will have to find a method of making the unit secure when being carried.

Could be made using a press former if acrylic is used.

'Acrylic inserts' to act as dividers for individual records.

Or, could use a polystyrene tray → vacuum formed?

Could be fabricated from acrylic.

Fabrication would allow contrasting colours to be used on ends.

leave a gap at very top.

RECORD SLEEVES CAN BE CUT TO SHAPE OR NEW HEXAGONAL ONES MADE IF REQUIRED.

Depth may be too much for press forming.

With polystyrene dividers probably not required.

fits into end

fits onto end

Could use contrasting material?

Cut slots very carefully with dovetail saw once it has been marked out accurately.

Timber block

Piece would be easier to shape to contour of bent acrylic

Could use same timber block as former for bending.

Round off edges of former to allow for bends in acrylic casing

Drill holes in slots to aid forming by vacuum.

Keep ends in one piece?

LOCKING DEVICE
clip fit?
When carried, top would be held on by use of handle.
DEVELOP FURTHER ON NEXT SHEET

Lid could then sit on this inner edge which would also strengthen the base.

Using an inner strengthener a hole representing a record could from the outer piece.

DEVELOPMENT SKETCHES	M. MORRIS	5TL
	DRG Nº 4	1.9.85

69

AT THIS STAGE OF DEVELOPMENT A SIMPLE
CARD MODEL CAN HELP US TO DECIDE
FINAL PROPORTIONS IE:- IS THE HOLE
IN THE HANDLE BIG ENOUGH FOR
OUR FINGERS TO FIT IN?

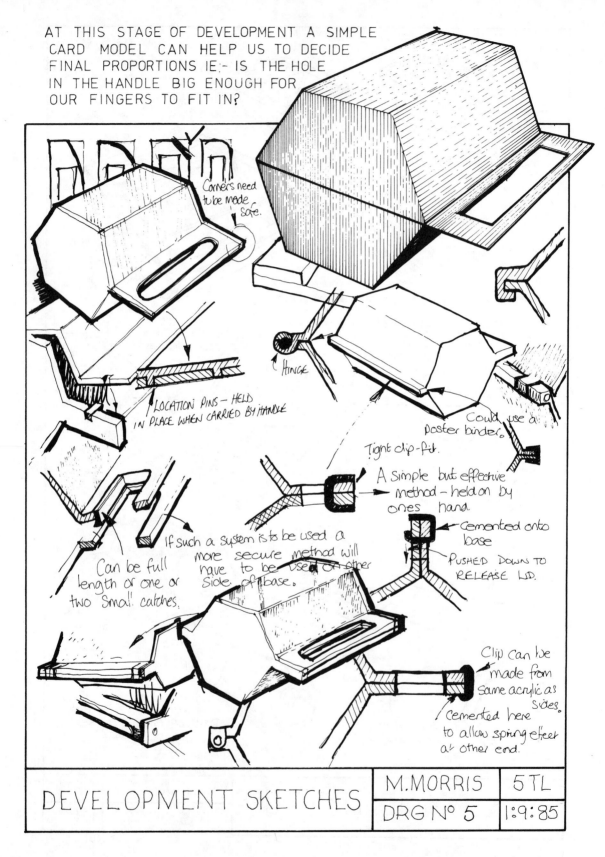

Corners need to be made safe.

LOCATION PINS — HELD
IN PLACE WHEN CARRIED BY HANDLE

HINGE

Could use a poster binder.

Tight clip-fit.

A simple but effective method - held on by ones hand.

Cemented onto base

PUSHED DOWN TO RELEASE LID.

If such a system is to be used a more secure method will have to be used on other side of base.

Can be full length or one or two small catches.

Clip can be made from same acrylic as sides.

cemented here to allow spring effect at other end.

DEVELOPMENT SKETCHES	M. MORRIS	5 TL
	DRG Nº 5	1:9:85

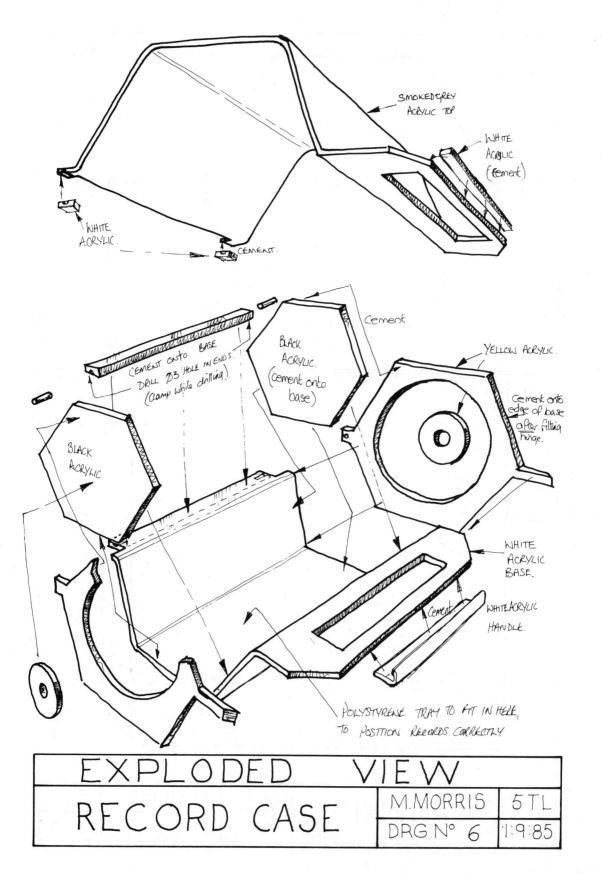

SMOKED GREY
ACRYLIC TOP

WHITE
ACRYLIC
(Cement)

WHITE
ACRYLIC.

CEMENT.

Cement

BLACK
ACRYLIC.
(cement onto
base)

CEMENT onto BASE
DRILL 23 HOLE IN ENDS.
(Clamp while drilling.)

YELLOW ACRYLIC.

Cement onto
edge of base
after fitting
hinge.

BLACK
ACRYLIC

WHITE
ACRYLIC
BASE.

WHITE ACRYLIC
HANDLE.

Cement.

POLYSTYRENE TRAY TO FIT IN HERE,
TO POSITION RECORDS CORRECTLY.

EXPLODED VIEW		
RECORD CASE	M. MORRIS	5 TL
	DRG N° 6	1·9·85

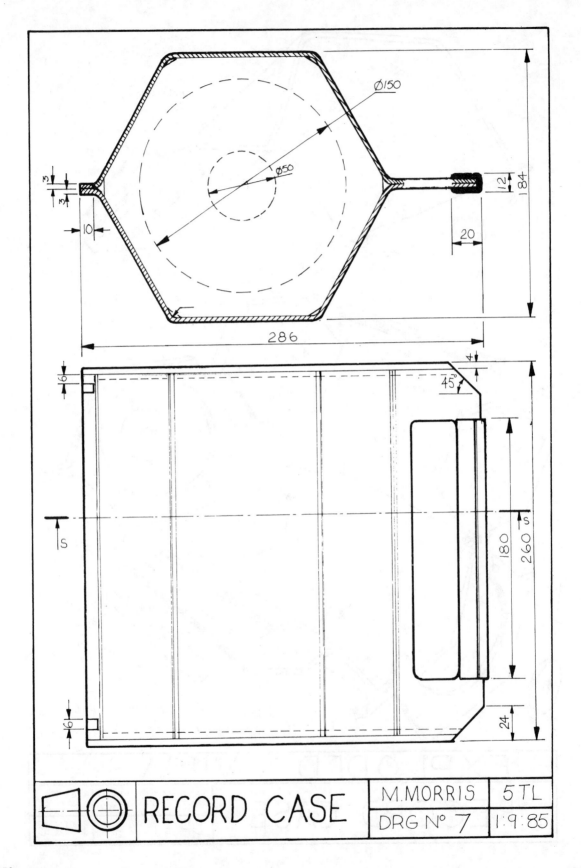

Ø150

Ø50

3

3

10

184

12

20

286

4

45°

6

6

180

260

24

S

S

RECORD CASE

M.MORRIS   5TL

DRG Nº 7   1:9:85

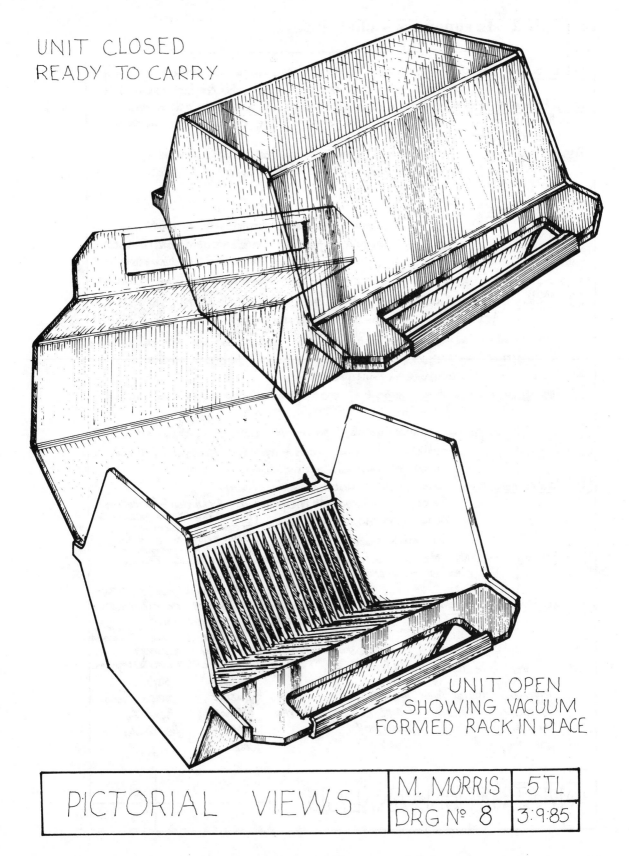

UNIT CLOSED
READY TO CARRY

UNIT OPEN
SHOWING VACUUM
FORMED RACK IN PLACE

PICTORIAL VIEWS	M. MORRIS	5TL
	DRG No 8	3·9·85

Example 2　Ergonomics – chair design

Situation for Design :- Existing seating in my lounge at home is becoming
　　　　　　　　talky and does not really give the comfort I would like

Identification of problem :- Need for a unit which will give comfortable support
　to those using it , and which will enhance the environment in which it
　will be used

Design Brief :- To design an attractive, low cost, unit which will give
　　　　comfortable support to the human body.

Design factors - ① Function -
　　　　　　　　　　　　　　　　　　　　　　　To give
　　　　　　　　　Primary function - comfortable support
　　　　　　　　　Secondary function - complete relaxation - allow comfortable
　　　　　　　　　　　　　　　　　　watching of TV - listening to music.
　　　　　　　　　　　　　　　　　　eating from a tray — reading

② Materials — Specifications — Strong, lightweight - (if unit is to be moved regularly)
　　　　　Availability ! cheap - safe, comfortable to touch, durable, steel, Plastics
　　　　　　　　　　　　　　will depend on environment　Aluminium　Timber, Textiles
　　— should allow simple construction yet give good appearance - suit other furniture

③ Manufacture — quick, simple, cheap methods, but strong construction
④ Cost — Inexpensive in money and time.
⑤ Appearance — suit environment , be attractive in colour and finishes - should
　　　　　look inviting.　　　　↗room
⑥ Strength/Weight — Must support 1 person efficiently but fairly lightweight.
⑦ Durability — Must last many years - materials /construction - should
　　　　　need the minimum of maintenance.
⑧ Environment — Where will the unit be used? - LOUNGE
　　　　　Where or relative to other furniture - BY WINDOW - for reading
　　　　　　　　　　　　　　　　　　　　　and near stereo music centre.
　　　　　What colour schemes have been used - CHROME - BROWNS.
　　　　　How much space is available. - Not enough space for
　　　　　　　　　　　　　　　　　　　a low, lying posture.
⑨ Safety — Non toxic materials , no sharp edges, - strong, stable, easily
　　　　　cleaned - non corrosive. - Fire proof as possible.

⑩ Ergonomics /Anthropometrics — Who will use the unit ? ↗whole family + visitors -
　　　　　　　　　　　　　　　　　　　　　　So base sizes on averages
　　　　　What will it be used for ? - see functions?
　　　　　What is the best position for these functions ? - semi upright
　　　　　Where should the human body be supported?
Other factors to be aware of : (Brainstorm)　　　↗Draw out to scale - ergonome

	Size	Balance	Style	
Efficiency	Appropriateness	Texture	Structure	trends - Taste
Suspension	Posture	Frame /Carcase Construction	Washable	Flexibility
Compatability		Water proof	Appeal	Reliability
Stain Proof		Quality	Wear	
				etc.

INVESTIGATION - ANALYSIS	MOULD	5M
	DRG N° 1	1 · 6 · 84

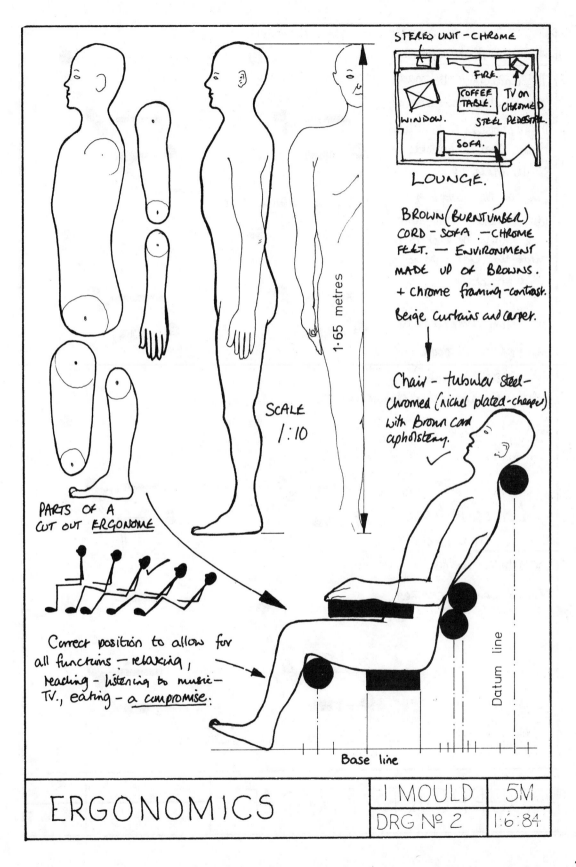

STEREO UNIT - CHROME

FIRE.

COFFEE TABLE.

TV on CHROMED STEEL PEDESTAL.

WINDOW.

SOFA.

LOUNGE.

BROWN (BURNTUMBER) CORD - SOFA - CHROME FEET. — ENVIRONMENT MADE UP OF BROWNS. + chrome framing - contrast. Beige curtains and carpet.

Chair - tubular steel - Chromed (nichel plated - cheaper) with Brown cord upholstery.

1·65 metres

SCALE 1:10

PARTS OF A CUT OUT ERGONOME

Correct position to allow for all functions - relaxing, reaching - listening to music - TV, eating - a compromise.

Datum line

Base line

ERGONOMICS

| | MOULD | 5M |
| DRG Nº 2 | 1·6·84 |

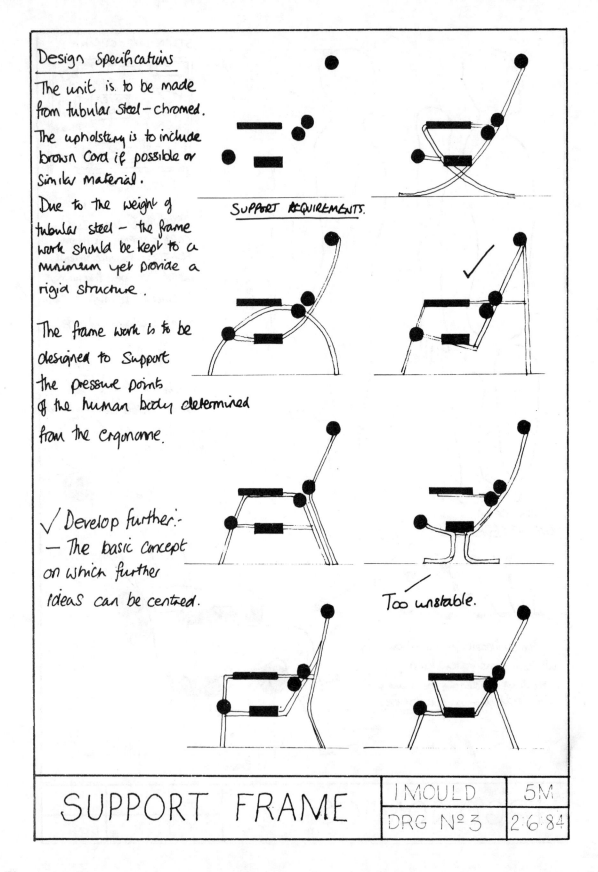

Design Specificatuins

The unit is to be made from tubular steel – chromed.

The upholstery is to include brown Cord if possible or similar material.

Due to the weight of tubular steel – the frame work should be kept to a minimum yet provide a rigid structure.

The frame work is to be designed to Support the pressure points of the human body determined from the ergonome.

√ Develop further:-
— The basic Concept on which further ideas can be centred.

SUPPORT REQUIREMENTS.

Too unstable.

SUPPORT FRAME

I MOULD	5M
DRG Nº 3	2·6·84

76

Tube/bar sections

Some of the ideas are becoming a little too complicated!

must be careful not to make the unit too heavy

Although an interesting idea tubing may get in the way of elbows

I like the way in which the seat is slung from the frame.

Could panel side piece!

PRELIMINARY SKETCHES	SEATING UNIT	I. MOULD	5M
		DRG Nº 4	3·6·84

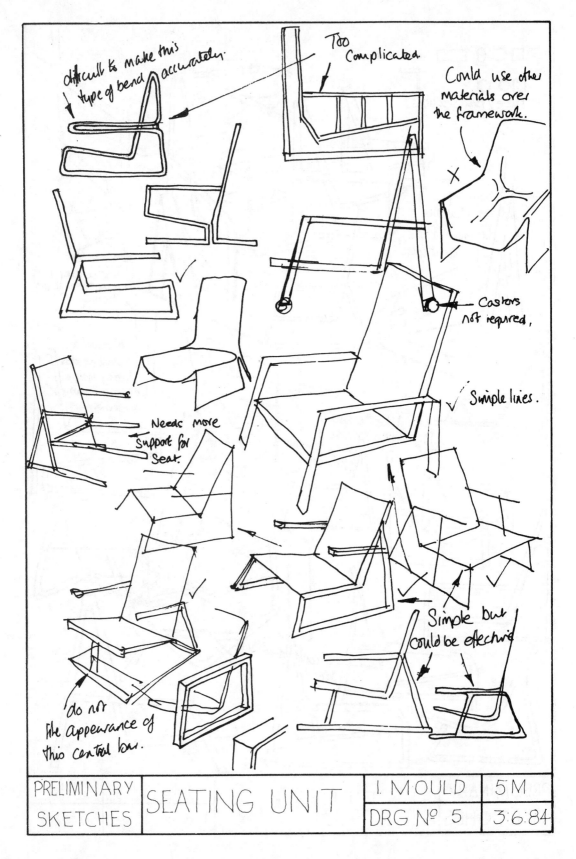

difficult to make this type of bend accurately.

Too complicated.

Could use other materials over the framework.

×

Castors not required.

Simple lines.

Needs more support for seat.

Simple but could be effective.

do not like the appearance of this central bar.

PRELIMINARY SKETCHES	SEATING UNIT	I. MOULD	5M
		DRG Nº 5	3.6.84

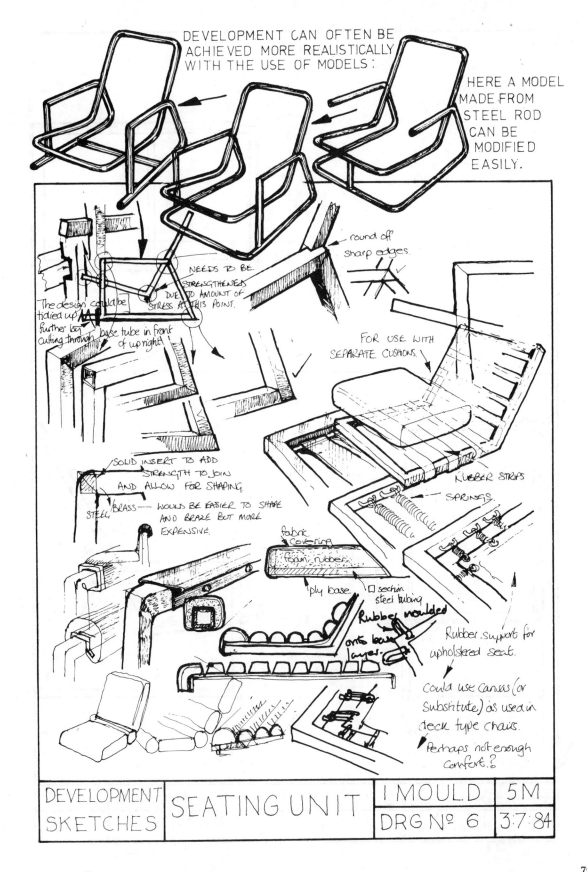

DEVELOPMENT CAN OFTEN BE ACHIEVED MORE REALISTICALLY WITH THE USE OF MODELS:

HERE A MODEL MADE FROM STEEL ROD CAN BE MODIFIED EASILY.

round off sharp edges.

NEEDS TO BE STRENGTHENED DUE TO AMOUNT OF STRESS AT THIS POINT.

The design could be tidied up further by cutting through

base tube in front of upright

FOR USE WITH SEPARATE CUSHIONS.

SOLID INSERT TO ADD STRENGTH TO JOIN AND ALLOW FOR SHAPING.

STEEL/BRASS — WOULD BE EASIER TO SHAPE AND BRAZE BUT MORE EXPENSIVE.

RUBBER STRIPS

SPRINGS.

fabric covering

foam rubber

ply base

☐ section steel tubing

Rubber moulded onto base layer.

Rubber support for upholstered seat.

Could use canvas (or substitute) as used in deck type chairs.

Perhaps not enough comfort.?

DEVELOPMENT SKETCHES	SEATING UNIT	1 MOULD	5M
		DRG Nº 6	3·7·84

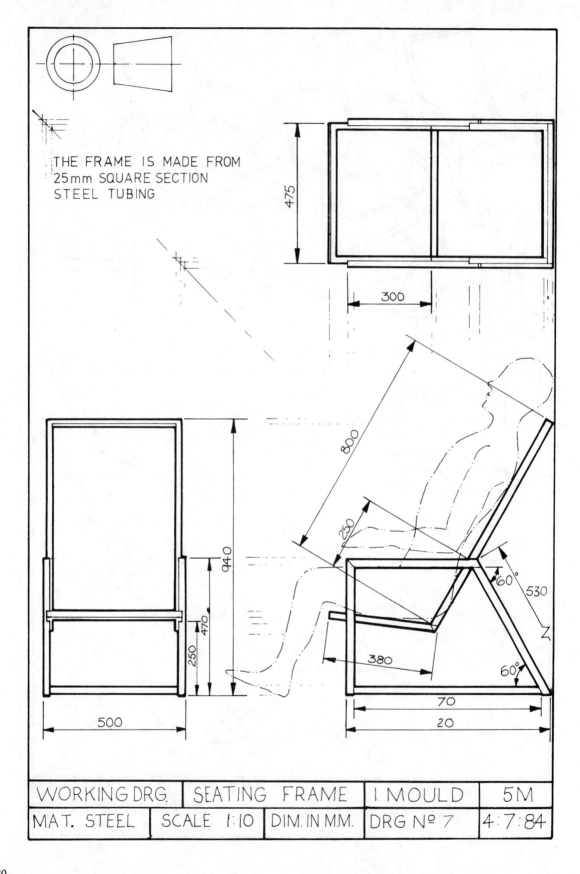

THE FRAME IS MADE FROM
25mm SQUARE SECTION
STEEL TUBING

475

300

800

250

530

940

470

250

500

380

60°

60°

70

20

WORKING DRG.	SEATING FRAME		I. MOULD		5M
MAT. STEEL	SCALE 1:10	DIM. IN M.M.	DRG Nº 7		4:7:84

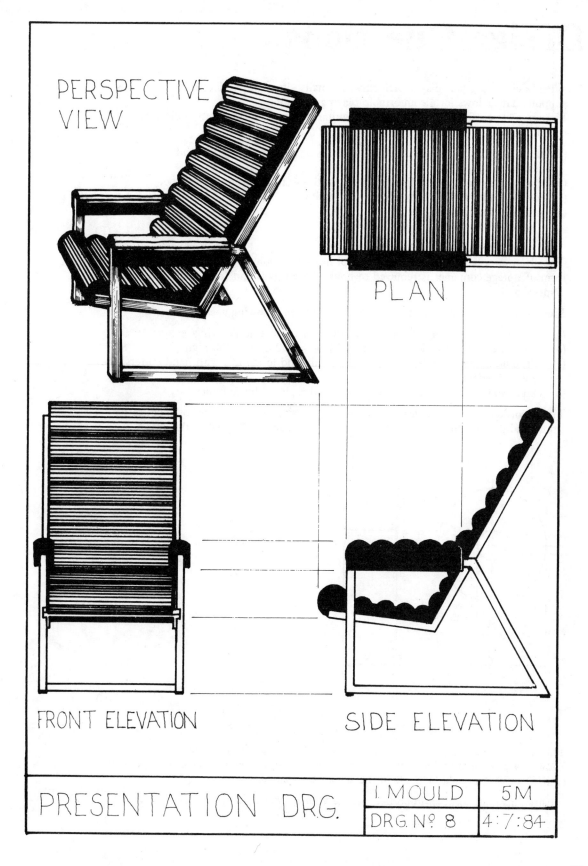

PERSPECTIVE
VIEW

PLAN

FRONT ELEVATION

SIDE ELEVATION

PRESENTATION DRG.

I. MOULD	5M
DRG. Nº 8	4:7:84

Design Questions

1. When a classical guitar player performs he usually sits with one foot raised on a special support. This allows for a comfortable playing position.

Prepare a design for a foot support for a guitarist that conforms to the following specifications:

  (a) the support is to have two height positions of approximately 140 and 170 respectively,
  (b) it should slope upwards from the back to the front i.e. from heel to toe,
  (c) it should fold flat for convenience of carrying,
  (d) it should be stable in use.

(L)

2. The electronics laboratory of a large school has a selection of wire on spools. Some form of storage container is required to house these spools and from which the wire is dispensed.

Prepare a design for a container that conforms to the following specifications:

  (a) it is to be stored in a cupboard and lifted out on to a desk during lessons,
  (b) it is to be compact and not exceed 500 long × 300 deep × 400 high,
  (c) it should be easy to select the particular wire and to cut off, with hand cutters, the required length,
  (d) empty spools should be easily extracted and replaced by full ones.

The spools are of similar construction but vary in size. The four sizes of spool to be stored and the maximum number of each size are as shown (below) in fig. 1.

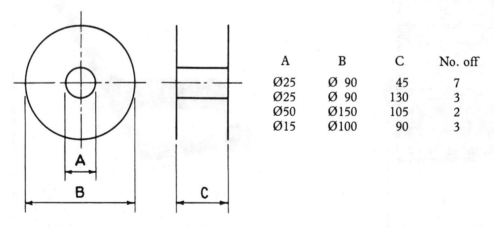

A	B	C	No. off
Ø25	Ø 90	45	7
Ø25	Ø 90	130	3
Ø50	Ø150	105	2
Ø15	Ø100	90	3

Fig. 1

(L)

3. The scientist frequently relies on the ingenuity of the engineer to develop his ideas. Show how any important scientific fact or principle can be demonstrated on a piece of equipment which could be made in the school workshops.

Illustrations must form an important part of your answer.

(L)

4. The bench vice is commonly used to hold material when carving irregular shapes in wood. Problems arise since chisel manipulation is often hampered by the position of the material in the vice and constant adjustment becomes necessary. To ease these problems you are to prepare a design for a portable vice made mainly in wood and which can be held securely to the bench during use.

The drawing, fig. 2, gives the beginnings of an idea for a woodcarver's vice which you are to develop and complete.

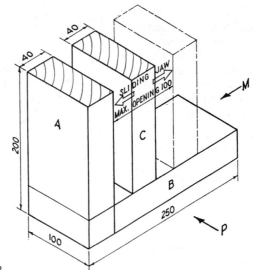

Fig. 2

Your design for the vice must conform to the following brief:

It must have–

(a) a fixed jaw 'A' soundly jointed to the base 'B',
(b) a moveable jaw 'C' with sufficient movement to accommodate 100 wide material,
(c) some means of activating the moveable jaw,
(d) some means of guiding the moveable jaw to prevent it from twisting and to keep it parallel to the fixed jaw. Your drawing should indicate how tapered, irregular or square material will be held.
(e) some means of temporarily holding the vice to the bench.

A base longer than the 250 shown can be incorporated should your solutions require it. Additional wood or other materials will need to be incorporated in your design,

(i) With the long edge of the paper placed horizontally, rule a line 200 from the left-hand side. To the left of this line list briefly the design problems stated above. Add to this list other design problems that occur to you, lettering them (*f*), (*g*), (*h*) etc.,

(ii) On the right-hand side of the line make preliminary sketch solutions for each of the problems stated, lettering them to conform with the brief given above. Use clear diagrams with explanatory notes indicating materials, constructions, critical dimensions, and finishes.

Answer (iii) *and* (iv) *on a separate sheet of drawing paper.*

(iii) Draw, approximately half full size, a pictorial view of the final design.
(iv) In orthographic projection prepare a side elevation viewed in the direction of arrow 'P' and a projected end elevation as seen from arrow 'M'.

Your drawings may be done either with instruments to a scale of 1 : 2, or freehand approximately half full size.

Fully dimension the moveable jaw only.

(L)

5. Many people have difficulty in carrying large, heavy cases when they travel by public transport. This difficulty may be eased by distributing the load and supporting the case on wheels and then pulling or pushing the case along.

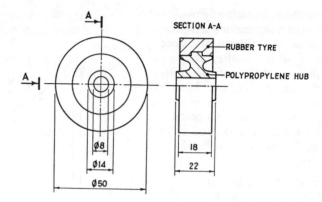

Fig. 3

Prepare a design for a suit case trolley, using the plastic wheels illustrated in fig. 3, to conform to the following brief:

The trolley must:

(a) be capable of use with a case of maximum size 650 × 450 × 200,
(b) be lightweight,
(c) be compact when stowed on a public transport vehicle, and also when stored. A folding platform, on which the case rests, must be included and it is suggested that a folding/collapsible handle may be considered,
(d) have adequate provision for securely attaching the case and any straps used must be specified,
(e) have wheels mounted so that the trolley may be pulled or pushed and remain stable,
(f) have a handle or handles ergonomically suited to their function.

(i) With the long edge of the paper placed horizontally, rule a line 200 from the left-hand edge. To the left of this line, list briefly the design problems stated above. Add to this list other design problems that occur to you, lettering them (g), (h), (i), etc.

(ii) To the right of the vertical line set down your solutions to the design problems, using clear diagrams with explanatory notes indicating materials, constructions, critical dimensions and finishes. Clearly letter your solutions to conform to the brief given above and label your final choice.

Answer (iii) *and* (iv) *on a separate sheet of drawing paper.*

(iii) Draw, approx. one-fifth full-size, a pictorial view of the complete trolley, incorporating your separately evolved solutions.

(iv) Make a detailed production drawing, in orthographic projection, of your solution to the problem of holding the wheels on their axles and of folding the platform flat. Appropriate additional views may be added to determine more completely the method of construction. Your drawings may be done *either* with instruments to a scale of 1 : 1, *or* freehand approx. full-size. Dimension the folding platform.

(L)

6. Design and make a machine for conveying a person on land for *either* sporting *or* transport purposes employing *either* the power of the wind *or* a hovercraft principle.

Your research and investigations should include accurate models to assist styling and a comprehensive appraisal of such equipment already in existence. Evidence of testing the machine would be desirable.

Should you experience difficulty in obtaining or costing of suitable materials, an *exact quarter scale model* would be acceptable as a solution.

(WJEC)

7. Design a compact, portable cotton reel holder as required for use by a student on her/his work table in the embroidery room of a school. It is to accommodate 20 reels and be made of either metal or plastics materials.

Present sketched ideas for such a holder, indicating material, construction, significant dimensions and finish. A standard cotton reel is ø32.5 × 32.5 and bored co-axially ø8.

(L)

8. You have been asked to complete the design of a mahogany box and lid to hold knitting needles. The overall sizes of the box are shown in fig. 4.

(a) Draw and describe the corner joints that you would use.

(b) Explain, stage by stage, how you would mark out and cut these joints.

(c) Draw and describe the type of lid that you would use, together with its method of fastening. Give *two* reasons for your choice of lid.

(d) Name the type of finish that you would apply to the box and give *one* reason for your choice of finish.

(e) Describe the finishing processes you would apply to the box.

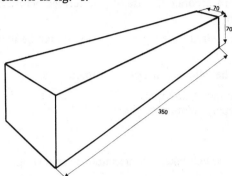

Fig. 4

(YREB)

9. Design and make a seat for a specified environment.

Your design study should include the following:

(i) Photographs of the proposed environment.
(ii) A full ergonomic and anthropometric investigation.
(iii) A mock-up *or* test rig to assess comfort, angles, shape etc.
(iv) Full size working drawings.
(v) An *accurate* scale model.

(WJEC)

10. Design a coffee service to be made in non-ferrous metal. Your design should follow a theme which relates the items visually.

You are required to make *only* the coffee pot and sugar bowl.

A set of presentation drawings should be included in your folio of graphic work.

(WJEC)

11. Design and make a piece of equipment for heating domestic hot water using the power of the wind.

Your studies should investigate the following:

(i) Average wind speeds and site locations.
(ii) Horizontal *or* vertical axis machines.
(iii) Feathering systems.
(iv) Heat transfer and storage systems.
(v) Economic viability analysis involving comparative studies of other heating methods.
(vi) Domestic hot water requirements of an average household.

(WJEC)

12. Design a tool which extends a person's reach to enable him to lift objects from shelves, one metre above eye level, *or* from the bottom of deep-freeze cabinets, 150 mm above floor level.

The objects to be moved could be *either* polythene packets *or* food cans. The instrument may be operated by one *or* two hands and should be easy to use.

(WJEC)

13. Design a container *or* rack for magazines and newspapers for a modern living room.

Your design must incorporate the use of post-formed acrylic sheet for at least one part of the construction.

Any jigs that are required for bending the acrylic may be manufactured prior to the 02 examination.

You may assume the following maximum dimensions:

(i)   magazine, 340 mm × 260 mm;
(ii) folded newspaper, 360 mm × 260 mm.

(WJEC)

14. Design a bird-table which takes into account the following:

(i)   provision for food and water;
(ii) facility of cleaning;
(iii) provision for mounting a camera (this can take the form of a stud 10 mm long with a $\frac{1}{4}''$ BSW thread on to which an extension could be screwed if required);
(iv) resistance to the elements;
(v)   sympathy with the environment.

(WJEC)

15. To enable an article to be labelled a 'good design' it has to fulfil certain general requirements.

Write down the most important of these requirements at the head of columns and list the subdivisions under each.

(WJEC)

16. Design a related set of graphic signs for indicating various sports in an Olympic complex.

The signs should clearly represent the activities in such a way as to be comprehensible to a number of nationalities.

The activities to be represented are:

(i) swimming, (ii) cycling, (iii) high jump, (iv) diving.

List *six* stages you would employ in making any *one* sign, and assume the signs are to be made from black acrylic sheet 3·5 mm thick mounted on acrylic rectangles 300 mm × 40 mm.

(WJEC)

17. List the questions you would ask and some of the conclusions you would draw before considering solutions, if asked to design a non-electronic method of selecting random numbers up to 50,000. Your solution would eventually be used in an outside public place before a crowd of approximately 50 people.

(WJEC)

18. Lumberjacks usually find they have to sharpen their chain-saws when out in the forest away from a vice.

Design a lightweight, portable clamp to hold the guide-bar of the chain-saw to facilitate sharpening the chain.

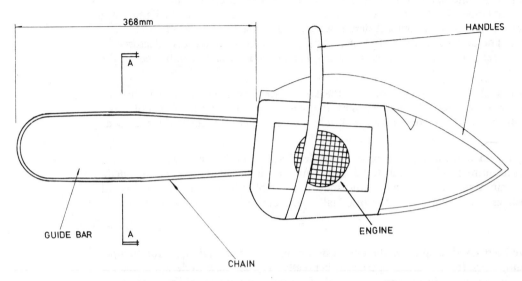

Fig. 5 Diagrammatic sketch of a chain saw

The following information is given for your guidance:

(i) a chain-saw operates by a toothed chain being driven around a guide bar;

(ii) extensions along the underside of the chain slide along a groove cut in the edge of the guide bar;

(iii) sharpening requires the use of a round file from both sides of the chain on alternate teeth;

(iv) the chain can be pulled around the guide-bar by hand;

(v) use could be made of felled trees for a rigid support or base onto which the clamp could be fixed.

(See fig. 5.)

(WJEC)

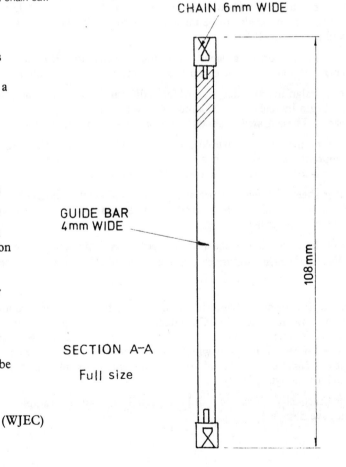

CHAIN 6mm WIDE

GUIDE BAR
4mm WIDE

108mm

SECTION A-A

Full size

19. You have been asked to consider the design of furniture for the entrance hall of a house.

You are now to design a unit which includes a seat, space for a telephone and storage for some directories. It may include space for other items at your discretion. The dimensions of a telephone directory are approximately 300 × 210mm. Remember that there is not a great deal of space in the average hall and you will therefore need a fairly compact design which uses valuable space to the best advantage. The unit should be constructed mainly of wood, including manufactured board if desired, but you are at liberty to use other materials if clearly indicated on the drawing.

On your first sheet of drawing paper, list the Design Requirements for such a unit and sketch a variety of possible solutions. Mark the one you consider most successful and develop this by means of constructional sketches which cover all aspects of the chosen design.

On your second sheet, using an appropriate scale, draw orthographic views with sufficient detail to enable the unit to be made. Full size joint details *must* be included. Add the main dimensions to the drawing and, in a suitable position on your paper and between lines 5 mm apart, letter the title Hall Seat, your name and index number.

(O&C)

20. You have been asked to consider the design of various pieces of equipment for clamping and holding work for machining operations generally. You are now to design a small machine vice which could be used particularly for light drilling and milling machine work. The vice is to be capable of holding small round material both horizontally and vertically and provision is also to be made for the vice to be bolted to a machine table. The jaw width is to be 100 mm.

On your first sheet of drawing paper, write down clearly, in *tabulated form*, the requirements that you feel are necessary for the machine vice to function successfully.

Now start to design the machine vice which will satisfy the conditions you have stated. You should begin by making clear, annotated, freehand drawings on your first sheet of drawing paper. These drawings should cover *all* aspects of the design.

State clearly the materials you would use for the different parts and suggest suitable sizes and appropriate finishes. When you consider that adequate preparatory work has been done, you may proceed to the orthographic drawing.

Take another sheet of drawing paper and provide sufficient orthographic drawings to enable the piece of equipment to be made. Include sectional drawings if you feel that they will explain details better.

Insert *five* of the main dimensions and, between lines 5 mm apart, letter the title Machine Vice, your name and index number, in a suitable position on the page.

(O&C)

21. A well-known firm manufacturing fish pastes wishes to promote its product by advertising on a range of items used in kitchens (e.g. shopping note jotters, plastic trays, aprons, tea-towels, etc). It is planned to offer such items as 'free gifts' at petrol stations. You are asked to design the motif which will appear on all the articles *and* design some of the articles. (*Note:* the number of articles included is less important than the quality of the individual designs.)

During the practical sessions you will be expected to produce a sample range of articles which you have designed.

(O)

22. Hobbies and pastimes such as coin collecting, the study of geological specimens, or the keeping of pets under particular conditions often require the designing of special pieces of equipment. Describe the making of one such piece of equipment which has involved you in the use of other materials in addition to either wood or metal.

List the design factors you had to consider before making this article.

(O&C)

23. You have been asked to consider the design of simple hand-operated machines capable of bending thin gauge metal (up to 0.9 mm) up to a right angle. You are now to design a small bending machine which can be held in a vice and which is capable of bending thin gauge sheet metal up to 100 mm in width.

Consideration will have to be given to: (a) method of holding the bending machine in a vice; (b) method for clamping the metal prior to bending; and (c) the actual method to be used for bending.

On your first sheet of drawing paper, write down clearly, in *tabulated form*, the requirements that you feel are necessary for the sheet bending machine to function successfully.

Now start to design the bending machine which will satisfy the conditions you have stated. You should begin by making clear, annotated, freehand drawings on your first sheet of drawing paper. These drawings should cover *all* aspects of the design.

State clearly the materials you would use for the different parts and suggest suitable sizes and appropriate finishes. When you consider that adequate preparatory work has been done you may proceed to the orthographic drawing.

Take another sheet of drawing paper and provide sufficient orthographic drawings to enable the bending machine to be made. Include sectional drawings if you feel that they will explain details better.

Insert *five* of the main dimensions and, between lines 5 mm apart, letter the title Bending Machine, your name and index number, in a suitable position on your paper.

(O&C)

24. Write about the design and construction of a hutch for a rabbit or guinea pig. Your answer must include references to (a) the living requirements of the animal, (b) the materials and construction to be used, and (c) preservation of the materials.

(O&C)

25. You have been asked to design and make a condiment set comprising salt, pepper, and mustard pots. State the factors you would have to consider in doing this. Explain in detail how you would make *one* of these pots. Clear diagrams should form an important part of your answer.

(O&C)

26. Elderly people often use tinned rather than fresh milk and sometimes experience difficulty when attempting to pierce the cans. The common sizes for these cans are 75 mm in diameter and 115 mm high, and 75 mm in diameter and 65 mm high. Design a device which would make piercing such cans easier for a person with limited gripping ability.

(O)

27. Some kitchen cupboard units are too high to reach. Design a stool which is easily adjusted to form stable steps which can be used to enable the higher cupboards to be reached.

(O)

28. Design a devise for chopping mint or parsley which could be sold in a high-class shop specialising in kitchen equipment.

(O)

29. A possible solution to a well-known danger to small children in the kitchen would be to have pans with detachable handles. Design such a system. During the practical sessions you will not be required to make the pans, but the handle(s) should be suitable for demonstration purposes.

(O)

30. As an 'optional extra', a firm manufacturing a small electrical coffee grinder wish to offer a wooden wall bracket to support their product (illustrated in fig. 6) when not in use. Design a suitable bracket which should be decorative as well as functional.

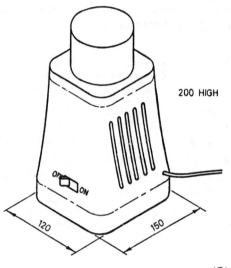

200 HIGH

120   150

Fig. 6

(O)

31. Design a cruet set which could be made in silver. During the practical sessions cheaper metals may be used to make the set.

(O)

32. Motifs (or logos) are widely used to identify the products or services of an organisation. An example is the British Rail motif shown in fig. 7.

Fig. 7

(a) Sketch and identify five well-known motifs.
(b) Sketch a motif which would be suitable for a company that specializes in the production of tools for the school workshop. Explain how the motif could be produced assuming that it is to be used on:

either, (i) the company's notepaper;
or,   (ii) the company's transport fleet.

(O)

33. Fig. 8 shows a crown top of a type frequently found on the top of bottles containing soft drinks.

(a) Design a wall-mounted bottle opener to be made from mild steel.

(b) Describe how you would heat-treat the bottle opener so that when in use wear would be minimal.

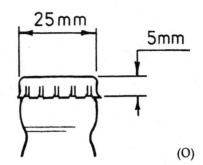

Fig. 8

(O)

34. Coffee tables vary considerably in size, shape, materials used and methods of construction. Three tables are illustrated in fig. 9.

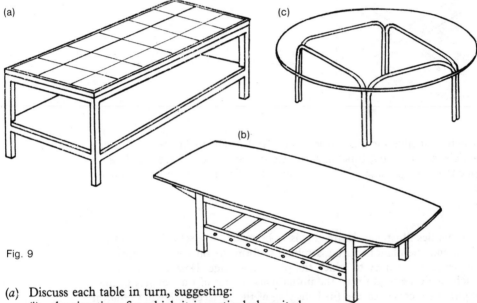

Fig. 9

(a) Discuss each table in turn, suggesting:
   (i) the situations for which it is particularly suited;
   (ii) the materials from which it could be made;
   (iii) the basic constructional details.

(b) The different types of top which may be used on coffee tables each present a different problem when the fastening of the top to the frame is considered.

Choose the frame illustrated in *either* table (a) *or* table (b) and by means of notes and sketches show how you would fasten each of the following types of top to it:

   (i) solid wood;
   (ii) manufactured board faced with wood veneer or plastic;
   (iii) tiles.

(O)

35. A junior school library requires 25 adjustable book racks as in fig. 10 (over) in order to store Ladybird books. They are to be made from accurately sized 18 thick lipped and veneered chipboard. The K.D. (knock-down) fittings shown are to be used to join the shelves and ends. A drilling jig is required to locate accurately the ⌀6 and ⌀10 holes in the ends and shelves. For the holes in the vertical ends the jig is to be set to lines squared across the face at the appropriate intervals.

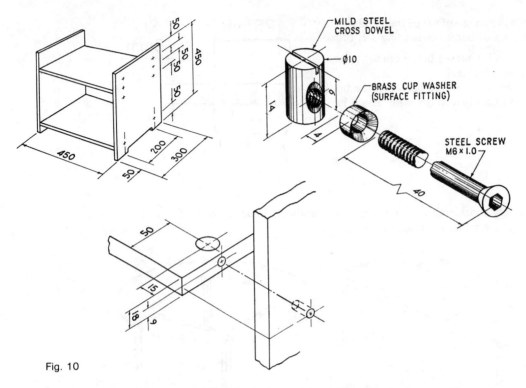

Fig. 10

Design a jig which is suitable for this purpose. Give full details for its manufacture, indicating materials, construction, functional dimensions and finish. Credit will be given for simplicity of design, ease of manufacture, ease of operation and the economic use of materials.

(L)

36. A number of the puzzles illustrated in fig. 11, is to be made for a school fund-raising sale. Five notched and one plain bar are assembled to form the puzzle. Its success depends on the degree of accuracy to which the pieces are made. Design a simple dual purpose jig which would be used for (*i*) the initial marking out of the notches in the pieces, and (*ii*) guiding a chisel for the final shaping of the surfaces following removal of the waste by sawing.

(L)

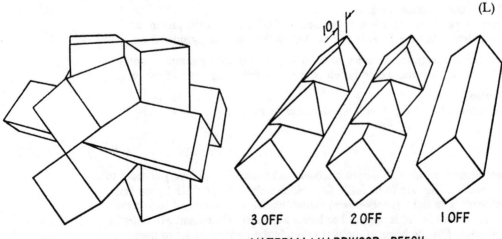

3 OFF   2 OFF   I OFF

MATERIAL: HARDWOOD - BEECH

91 LONG × 25 SQUARE

Fig. 11

37. Some electrical components are attached to the panel by means of a slotted threaded ring, as shown in fig. 12.

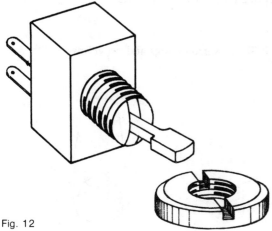

DATA:

Switch/spindle protrudes	30
Thread diameter	10
Ring diameter	18
thickness	5
Slots – width	1.3
depth	1.5
Bevel	0.5 × 45°

Fig. 12

Design a tool to tighten the ring to the following specification. It must

(a) fit the slots either side of the threaded hole of ø10,
(b) allow a 30 long switch lever or spindle to protrude through the hole,
(c) be of material and in a condition to enable it to be used without wearing.

Present your answers in the form of a large annotated sketch. Give full details for its manufacture, including materials, construction, functional dimensions and finish. Credit will be given for simplicity of design, ease of manufacture, ease of operation and the economic use of materials.

(L)

38. The school electronics society requires 250 injection moulded h.d. polyethylene radio component knobs to suit a 'D' cross-section spindle. A suitable form of knob is shown in fig. 13.

Design a mould for the production of these components on the school injection moulding machine ensuring that you detail materials, construction, functional dimensions and finish. Credit will be given for simplicity of design, ease of manufacture, ease of operation and the economic use of materials.

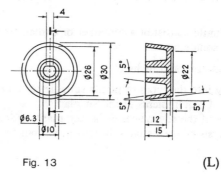

Fig. 13

(L)

39. A village church requires a few brackets which can be hung from one or two round-headed screws permanently driven into the wall. The brackets will be used to support vases or pots of flowers during festivals.

Using materials of your choice, design a suitable bracket. Include all constructional details and show particularly how it will be hung on the wall.

(O)

40. The committee of a sailing club wishes to give a small gift to a lady who has been invited to present trophies at a regatta.

Design a scarf ring suitable for the occasion and describe how it would be made.

(O)

41. The drawings in fig. 14 are of light units suited to different surroundings and providing various types of illumination.

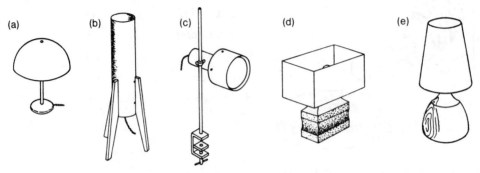

Fig. 14

Discuss each in turn, suggesting:

(i)   the materials from which it might be made;
(ii) the purpose for which it would be used;
(iii) where such a light might be found.

Select one of the light units and explain in detail how it might be made. Use notes and sketches and include details of the shade.

(O)

42. Design and make an indoor plant area for the following environment: a room 6 m × 4 m with double glazed windows from floor to ceiling extending 3 m along adjacent walls from one corner. The interior features contemporary furniture on a wooden floor.

Your design should consist of a container or containers which would occupy an area no greater than 2 square metres.

Your investigation should include:

(i)   an enquiry into the types of plants suitable for an indoor environment;
(ii) the physical requirements of indoor plants;
(iii) an account of the advantages of having plants indoors;
(iv) a full analysis of alternative solutions in various materials.

(WJEC)

43. In the home, the traditional method of storage usually consists of separate pieces of furniture or perhaps built-in cupboards, all of which may be visually unrelated.

To replace this, a modular system is required for the storage or display of items which one would expect to find in a lounge.

Design and make *three* visually related units, which fulfil the following requirements:

(i)   to house specified articles *either* hidden *or* displayed;
(ii) to allow for expansion by a method of linking with extra modules.

(WJEC)

44. Design and make a matched set of jewellery reflecting your anticipated image of the 1980's.

The set should adorn the wrist, neck and ears with each item related visually as well as by the materials employed.

(WJEC)

45. Design and make a machine for compacting wood shavings and/or sawdust for artificial fuel logs or blocks.

Your investigations should encompass:

(i)   the mechanics of compression;
(ii) methods of binding the materials and possible additives;
(iii) heat curing possibilities;
(iv) economics and possible outlets for fuels of this type.

(WJEC)

46. List the ways in which you would re-design a telephone kiosk and contents, in order to prevent or lessen damage by vandalism. Your answer should include the parts susceptible to damage and your ideas on improvements.

(WJEC)

47. In designing a table lamp for a study, show diagrammatically all the factors that need to be considered before attempting to develop a solution.

(WJEC)

48. Design a table for a modern kitchen, using the following materials in a construction of your choice:

(i)   table top of laminboard covered on one side with a plastic laminate and backed with a counter-laminate;
(ii) four legs of 65 mm diameter steel tube, which are to be satin-chrome finished (table height 750 mm);
(iii) solid teak for rails, the dimensions of which are left to your discretion;
(iv) miscellaneous materials for joints/fittings etc.

Your answer should take the form of annotated sketches, showing construction details in an exploded form, and a pictorial sketch of the completed table.

(WJEC)

49. There are continuous demands for emergency shelters for people made homeless by disasters such as earthquakes or floods.

List *twelve* design factors which would have to be taken into account in designing such shelters and illustrate some of your preliminary ideas on constructional methods and suitable material alternatives.

(WJEC)

50. Sketch two different designs for a rack to hold ten spice jars each 100 mm high × 50 mm diameter. The rack is to hang on the wall. Annotate your sketches to show suitable materials, constructions and finishes.

51. A toast-rack and 4 egg cups are required as a matching breakfast set.

  (a) Sketch *two* different designs.
  (b) Develop one of these designs into a working drawing detailing the toast rack and *one* egg cup, indicating materials, construction and finishes that would be used.

52. Furniture design

Design a school desk which can be used in any classroom as a basic working surface. The desk unit should fulfil the following requirements.

It should be:
  (a) stackable,
  (b) sturdy,
  (c) light,
  (d) washable,
  (e) *inexpensive,*
and should have (f) no moving parts.

The unit should be convenient for use by the average size pupil.

53. Visual communications

A firm, whose business is carried out in a building which contains sixteen offices, wishes to replace its intercom with a more efficient system. The reception switchboard links the offices. You are to design the switchboard which will have built in the following:

  (a) speaker
  (b) microphone
  (c) on/off switch with light indicator
  (d) sixteen numbered unit switches with light indicators.

The unit must be compact and not exceed 300 mm in any direction.

54. Design, for use in a kitchen, a stand for hot saucepans.

The stand should be so designed that it will:

  (a) suit a variety of sizes of pan,
  (b) hold the pan safely,
  (c) insulate the pan from the working surface,
  (d) not scratch or mark the working surface,
  (e) be attractive and functional,
  (f) be easy to wash and clean.

(EAEB)

55. Design a bird bath which will:

  (a) be attractive and functional,
  (b) be stable and suitable for positioning on a lawn,
  (c) hold a suitable depth of water,
  (d) be easily cleaned,
  (e) be easy and safe for birds to use,
  (f) be high enough to be out of reach of most predatory animals.

(EAEB)

56. Design a storage rack for tennis rackets to go in the School P.E. Department store room.

The rack should

(a) hold twelve rackets,
(b) should be portable,
(c) be attractive and functional,
(d) be easily stored, complete with rackets, over the winter period.

(EAEB)

57. Design a book support for use in the kitchen which should

(a) hold cookery books of various sizes,
(b) protect the books from food splashes and soiled fingers,
(c) allow the user to follow recipes and instructions as they are cooking,
(d) be easily cleaned and stored.

(EAEB)

58. Design a patio screen which could support a variety of pot plants for summer display.

Your screen should be

(a) robust in construction,
(b) decorative in itself,
(c) have a weatherproof finish,
(d) be approximately 2 metres high and 1·5 metres long,
(e) afford some privacy to the householder sitting out on the patio.

(EAEB)

59. Design a portable rack, to contain 6 video tapes, which is required by a social studies department in a school. The cassettes should be held securely whilst in transit and be easily removed for use during lessons.

(EAEB)

60. Design a visually pleasing module, providing security and display, for small items of jewellery and enamel work produced in the school workshops. Your design should incorporate the use of acrylic materials.

(EAEB)

61. Design an outdoor unit which will provide occasional seating and suitable space for bedding plants and spring bulb display.

(EAEB)

5 Introduction to tools, processes and materials

In the past, skills and processes associated with different trades and materials were often passed on as if each was completely different from any other. We now know that this is not true, and that there are many similarities between the tools and processes used with different materials. Firstly, a close look at how we work materials will show that the basic principles are the same for them all. Secondly, the tools used share many common features and can be more easily grouped together according to the work they do, than by the materials they are used with. In fact it would be impossible to decide which material many of them should be listed under. Thirdly, new tools, processes and materials are being invented every year, and new uses are continually being found for old ones. These often cut across traditional boundaries. For example, the injection-moulding of plastics is a development of the die casting of metals, and the blow-moulding of plastics, of glass blowing.

We have therefore, begun this section of the book by explaining the way in which we group together the tools we use and the principles upon which all the ways of working materials are based.

The classification of common hand tools

All the tools used to work materials can be grouped under one of four headings.

1. Marking-out, measuring and testing tools such as rules, try-squares, dividers, gauges and calipers.

2. Holding tools such as vices, cramps and jigs.

3. Driving tools such as hammers, screwdrivers and spanners.

4. Cutting tools such as saws, planes and files.

By arranging all the tools we know in this way we are able to see the similarities between tools used for working different materials. Where there are differences we should ask ourselves why they are necessary. This analysis of tool design should help us to choose the best tools to use in a new situation, and to see what is wrong when a tool is not working efficiently.

The principles of working materials

There are three main reasons why it is necessary for us to work materials. These are:
1. To change the *function* of the material.
2. To change the *properties* of the material.
3. To change the *appearance* of the material.

There are four distinct ways in which we can shape materials.

1. *Wasting.* This is where we change the shape of the material by cutting bits off it. Sawing, planing, filing and drilling are good examples.

2. *Deformation.* This is where we change the shape by bending and forming.

Forging hot metal, vacuum forming thermoplastics and bending wood veneers are good examples.

3. *Moulding and casting.* This is where we change the shape by changing the state of the material. For example, when casting metals or plastics resins we change them from liquid to solid.

4. *Fabrication.* This is where we change the shape by joining two or more pieces together by such processes as nailing, screwing, glueing and rivetting.

All the processes used in school and in industry are examples of at least one of these ways of working, and many involve two or more. For example, the blow moulding of plastics bottles consists of moulding (extruding the parison) and deformation (blowing this to shape). Making a simple wooden box is a combination of wasting (cutting the pieces to shape) and fabrication (joining them together). Laminating and bending wood veneers involves fabrication (glueing) and deformation (bending). Making a wrought iron gate involves wasting (sawing up the metal), deformation (forging to shape) and fabrication (assembling the parts).

It is important that as we learn new skills and processes we analyse them, and understand both how and why they work. This analysis will help us to see the similarities and the differences between different situations and materials, so that when faced with a new problem we can draw upon our experience of related ones. It is not sufficient to learn to use tools and materials parrot fashion, without thinking about what we are doing.

Safety

Attention to safety is the most important thing in any workshop, and everyone must learn the following simple safety rules before beginning any practical work.

1. Dress safely to avoid getting caught in machines or on the many snags around workshops. The best way to prepare for a practical lesson is to take off your jacket, roll up your sleeves and put on an apron. Long sleeves are very dangerous. Long hair must be tied up so that it cannot fall forward and get caught, jewellery must be removed and ties must be safely tucked in.

Always wear the correct protective clothing. Take special care to protect hands, eyes and feet. Soft shoes must not be worn in a workshop. Broken toes are one of the commonest industrial injuries.

2. Move safely to avoid bumping into people and things or tripping up. Never run or play in a workshop and do not play tricks on people. Carry tools and materials safely. Sharp tools must be held so that they cannot cut anybody, hot materials should not be carried about and long lengths of material must be handled carefully to avoid poking them into anyone.

3. Act safely. Never work alone or without permission in a workshop. If you had an accident there would be no one there to help you. Never misuse tools or improvise. Always

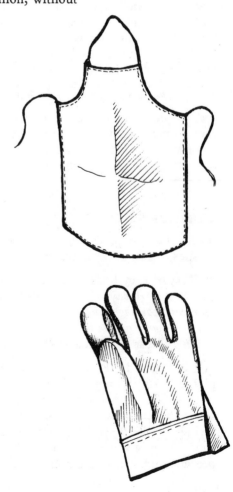

read instructions carefully and follow them. Never put down anything hot except in a clearly labelled hot area. Take special care to guard against heat, dangerous liquids, fumes, dust and electric arc flashes.

4. Machine safety. There must only be one operator on a machine at a time. Never use a machine without permission and correct training. Use all guards and safety equipment provided. Never reach across or go behind a machine. Never leave chuck keys in. Never machine work held in your fingers. Never adjust or clean a machine without switching it off at the isolator. Never remove swarf with a cloth or your bare hands.

5. Report all accidents, breakages and faults however small, so that a qualified person can decide what action is needed. This applies equally to first aid for people and repairs to faulty or broken equipment which might become dangerous. For example, a loose or split hammer shaft could result in the head flying off.

6. Keep yourself and the workshops clean and tidy. Do not allow tools, materials or waste to litter benches, machines or the floor, as this bad habit causes accidents such as tripping-up, heavy items falling on your feet and things falling into moving machines. Always wash your hands thoroughly to avoid skin disease and avoid spilling oil, chemicals, etc. onto your clothes.

Never break a safety rule. If in doubt ask.

Safety pays. An accident could change your life by causing permanent injury to yourself or a lifetime of regret for injuries caused to someone else. There is no replacement for a lost hand or eye.

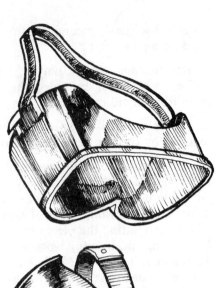

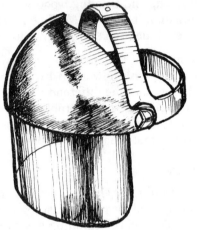

Plastics safety

There are extra precautions to remember when using plastics, paint, acid pickles and any other chemicals.

1. Respiratory hazards. Never work without adequate ventilation. *Always switch on the extractor fans before starting any work causing fumes.*
Always switch on the dust extractor when machine sawing or sanding. Wear a face mask when sawing or sanding G.R.P.

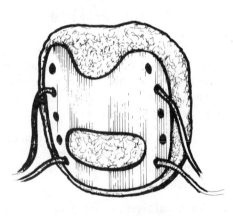

2. Eye hazards. Protect your eyes from dust, particles of plastic waste and organic liquids. Always wear safety glasses. *The catalyst used for curing polyester resins is especially dangerous to the eyes* (e.g. when embedding or laying-up G.R.P.). It must only be used under the supervision of a teacher and using a special dispenser to prevent squirting of the liquid.

If catalyst gets into your eyes, wash immediately with water or a 2% aqueous solution of sodium bicarbonate and see a doctor without delay, taking with you details of the catalyst.

3. Skin hazards. Catalysts and resins can cause dermatitis (a skin disease) and skin irritation. Protect your clothes. (Disposable plastic aprons are available.) Use barrier cream to protect your hands. For messy jobs wear disposable plastic gloves. After handling use only proper skin cleaning creams not brush cleaner, etc. Wash thoroughly immediately after using resins and catalysts. Glass fibre can irritate the skin so cover your hands and arms when handling it. *Do not* allow molten plastics to touch the skin – they stick and have a high heat capacity.

4. Fire and explosion hazards. Many plastics materials are highly flammable – keep them away from naked flames. Catalysed resin produces heat and can cause fire if not handled safely. Do not throw containers or cloths with uncured catalysed resins on them into waste bins.
Catalyst and activator must never be mixed together – they might explode.

6 Classification of common hand tools (1) marking-out, measuring and testing tools

The chart names the common marking-out, measuring and testing tools usually found in the school workshop, and shows with which materials they are usually used. Where tools with different names fulfil the same function on different materials, they are shown on the same line. This is followed by sketches of these tools together with brief notes about them.

Wood	Plastics	Metal
Rule and straight edge ──────────►		►
Try-square ──────────►◄────		Engineer's try-square
Mitre-square ──────────►		X
Sliding bevel ──────────►		►
Marking gauge ──────────►◄		Odd-leg calipers
Mortise gauge	X	X
Cutting gauge	X	X
Panel gauge	X	X
Marking knife ◄────────		Scriber
Pencil	Wax crayon/felt nib pen	Pencil
Wing compasses ──────────►◄		Spring dividers
Dovetail template	X	X
Spirit level ──────────►		►
Winding strips	X	X
Trammels or beam compass ──────────►		►
X	◄	Centre punch
X	◄	Dot punch
◄────────	◄	Inside calipers
◄────────	◄	Outside calipers
◄────────	◄	Centre square
X	◄	Micrometers
X	◄	Surface plate
X	◄	Surface gauge
X	◄	Vee blocks
X	◄	Angle plate
X	◄	Radius gauges
◄────────	◄	Drill gauge
X	◄	Wire and sheet gauge

Use of symbols

 Wood   Metal   Plastics

The symbols above are used in the following chapters. They show which sections apply to which materials. This enables students studying one material at a time to choose the relevant sections within a chapter, while students following a combined materials course will easily see where tools and processes are relevant to more than one material.

Steel rule. This is used to measure length and, as a straight edge, to test for flatness. It is marked in millimetres and made in 150, 300, 500 and 1 000 mm lengths.

Marking knife. This is used to mark lines on wood, usually across the grain. A knife cuts a thinner and more accurate line than a pencil. It is nearly always used with a try-square. To use the marking knife, hold it like a pencil and cut with the long point of the blade. The blade is of tool steel with a hardwood or plastic handle.

Scriber. This is used to mark lines on metal and plastics. Hold the scriber like a pencil. When using a scriber or marking knife make sure that the point is pressed into the angle between the try-square and the material. The point is made of tool steel and has a 30° point angle.

Try-square. This is used to test that one surface is square (at 90°) to another, and for marking-out lines square to the face-side or face-edge. Woodworkers' try-squares have a carbon steel blade and a wooden stock, sometimes with a brass face, while engineers' try-squares have a carbon steel blade and stock.

Using the try-square. For testing, hold the work up to the light, put the stock against a true face, and slide it down until the blade touches the edge being tested. If no light shows under the blade, the work is square.

For marking-out, place the marking tool on the mark first, slide the square along until it touches the marking tool, and then mark the line. In this way the line is marked exactly where it is wanted.

Marking gauge. This is used to mark lines parallel to the face-side and face-edge along the grain.

A panel gauge is a large marking gauge.

A cutting gauge has a cutter instead of a spur for marking lines across the grain from accurately prepared end grain, and for cutting veneers.

Setting the gauge to size. Put the zero of the ruler against the stock, and slide the stock along the stem. When the spur is against the correct mark lightly tighten the thumbscrew. Check the setting, adjust if necessary, and tighten the thumbscrew.

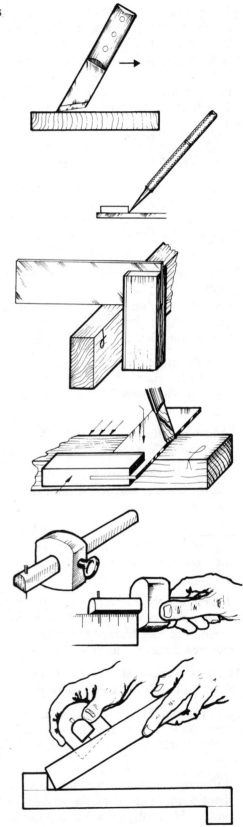

Using the gauge. Hold with the thumb and first finger round the stock, and the other three fingers round the stem. Press the stock firmly against the face-side or face-edge, and lower the spur point until it trails on the wood. It will then mark a line as it is moved. Try to mark one continuous line. To make gauging easier, hold the wood in the vice or against the bench hook.

Mortise gauge. This is used to mark double lines parallel to the face-side and face-edge. Its main use is to mark the thickness of mortises and tenons.

Setting the gauge to size. Set the spur points to the width of the chisel or cutter to be used (because chisels, etc. vary in size and should be chosen first). Set the stock and hold the gauge as for a marking gauge.

Setting a mortise or marking gauge to the middle of a piece of wood. Set the gauge as near as possible to the middle of the wood.
Gauge a short line from each side of the wood. Adjust the gauge until the marks are exactly on top of each other. Gauge from face-side or face-edge.

The thumb or pencil gauge is used to draw pencil lines parallel to a face-side or face-edge where a gauge line would show on the finished job. Cut out of scrap-wood as required.

Odd-leg calipers are used to mark lines parallel to a true edge and to find the centre of a bar, mainly in metalwork.

Setting the calipers to size. Put the stepped leg on the zero end of the ruler and adjust until the scriber point is against the correct mark.

Using the calipers to mark a line. Rest the stepped leg on the edge of the metal. Take care to keep the calipers square to the edge or the line will not be the correct distance from the edge.

To find the centre of a bar. Set the calipers to the approximate centre and scribe arcs from several points around the edge. Adjust the calipers and repeat until the required accuracy has been obtained.

Centre punch. This is used to mark the centres of holes to be drilled. It has a 90° point angle.

Dot punch. This is used to locate the centres of circles, radii and arcs when marking out, and to witness mark scriber lines which are to be cut to. It has a 60° point angle.

Witness marking. Dot punch marks are very carefully made about 5 mm apart along the scriber line to prevent it from being rubbed off, and to act as a guide when filing. File

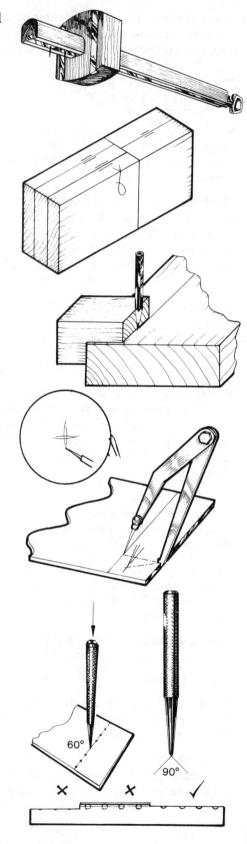

until half of each witness mark has been removed. If more than half remains the work is oversize, if less than half remains you have filed off too much.

Spring dividers and wing compasses are used to mark out circles and arcs, and to step off equal lengths along a line. Wing compasses are heavier and have a positive lock which makes them better for use on wood where divider points tend to try to follow the grain.

Beam compasses or trammel heads are used to mark large circles.

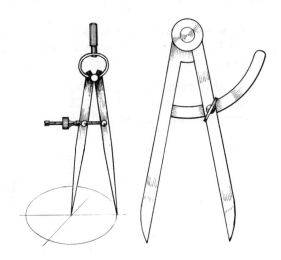

Mitre square. This is used to mark out angles of 45° and 135° and for testing mitres. A mitre is a bevel which slopes at 45°. Use it as you would a try-square.

Sliding bevel. This is used to mark out angles which are not at 90° to a true edge, and to test two flat surfaces meeting at any angle other than 90°. The bevel is set with a protractor and it is then used as for a try-square. Carpenters' bevels have a hardwood stock and tool steel blade.
Engineers' bevels are smaller and made entirely of tool steel.

Winding strips are used to test the face-side of a piece of wood for twist or winding. Because the face-side is the first part of the wood to be trued up, there are no accurate edges from which to test with a try-square, and so winding strips are used to show whether the wood is flat. To use, look along the top edges of the winding strips to see if they are parallel.

Inside and outside calipers. Outside calipers are used to measure the outside diameters of tubes and round bars. Internal diameters are measured with inside calipers. Outside calipers can also be used to check the thickness of materials, for example the thickness of the walls of a tube.

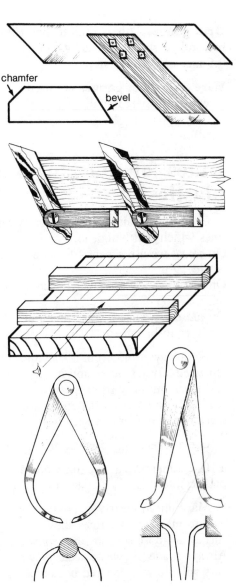

Centre square. This is used to find the centre of round work. Draw two lines approximately at right angles to each other. The centre is where they cross.

Radius gauges are used like a try-square to test the accuracy of small radii and fillets. Each blade shows the exact internal and external curves for a given radius.

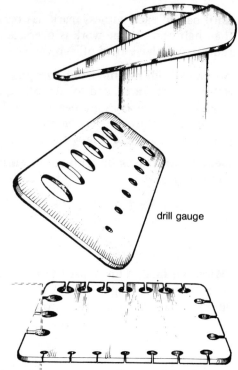

drill gauge

radius gauge

Drill gauge. This is used to find the diameter of round rod and twist drills, usually from 1 mm to 13 mm in either 0.5 mm or 0.1 mm steps.

Wire and sheet gauges are used to measure the thickness of wire and sheet metal.

Rules for marking-out wood, metal and plastics

1. On all materials we have ways of distinguishing between construction lines and lines which will be cut to.
On *wood*, we use a pencil for construction lines, and a marking knife for lines to be cut to.
On *metal* we use a scriber for construction lines and witness mark lines to be cut to.
On *plastics* we use a wax crayon or felt nib pen for construction lines and a scriber for lines to be cut to.

2. We always work from a *true edge* when marking out to ensure accuracy.
On *wood*, always plane and mark a face-side and face-edge on each piece of wood, and mark out only from these.
On *metal and plastics* file and mark a first true edge and a second true edge and mark out only from these.

3. Use a try-square to mark lines across the grain at 90° to the true edges.

4. Use a marking gauge (on wood and plastics) or odd-leg calipers (on metal and plastics), to mark lines parallel to the true edges.

5. Mark out as clearly as possible to avoid mistakes. Use marking blue (a type of dye) to make scriber lines show up on bright metal. Use chalk rubbed onto the surface to make scriber lines show up on black mild steel and rough surfaces. Always shade the waste accurately and clearly. Chalk lines, witness marks and saw cuts will show up on red hot metal.

Stages in marking-out and preparing the edges of metal

(A similar procedure is suitable for plastics and wood sheet material of all sizes.)

Stage 1.
File test and mark the first true edge on one long edge. Test for flatness with a straight edge and for squareness across the edge with an engineer's try-square. Finish by drawfiling. Mark with one straight line.

Stage 2.
File test and mark the second true edge on one short side, at right angles to the first true edge.

Test for squareness to the first true edge, flatness, and squareness across the edge with an engineer's try-square. Finish by drawfiling.

Stage 3.
Mark to width. Put the step of the odd-leg calipers against the first true edge and mark a line parallel to it. Witness mark the line. File down until half of each witness mark has gone. Test and drawfile.

Stage 4.
Mark to length. Mark the required length with a ruler and then *either* put a try-square against the first true edge and scribe a line, *or* use odd-leg calipers against the second true edge. Witness mark, file, test and drawfile.

On thin metal, the waste would be removed with tin snips.

When using flat strip and square rod only stages 2 and 4 will be needed.

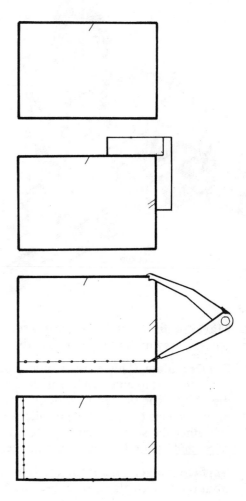

Stages in planing a piece of wood to size

(*See* Chapter 10 Planing.)

High accuracy marking-out, measuring and testing

Micrometers are used to measure with great accuracy. The commonest type is the 0 to 25 mm external micrometer shown. It measures to an accuracy of 0.01 mm.

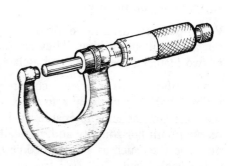

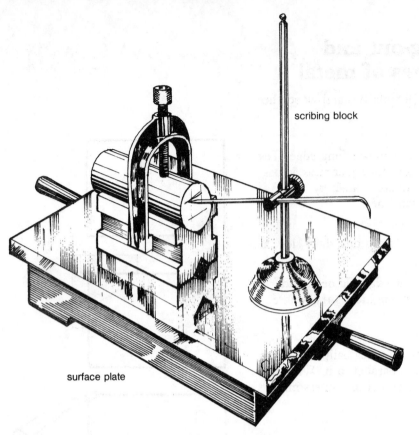

scribing block

surface plate

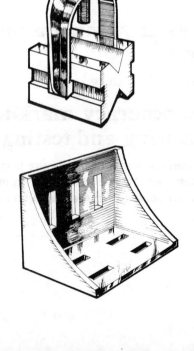

Marking out on the surface plate. This is a much more accurate way of marking out than those already described.

Surface plate. This consists of an iron casting with a very accurate flat top and a ribbed underframe to prevent distortion. The flat top provides a true surface from which measurements can be taken, parallel lines can be scribed and other flat surfaces can be tested. It is protected by a cover and light oiling when not in use.

Surface gauge. This is used to transfer measurements from the surface plate, to scribe lines parallel to the surface plate, and to test heights. The surface gauge (right) has a fine adjustment screw and the spindle and scriber can be set to almost any angle.

A scribing block simply supports a scriber and has no fine adjustment (top picture).

Vee blocks are used to hold cylindrical work for marking out and while machining. They are made in sets consisting of two matched vee blocks and a clamp (see right).

Angle plate. This is a very accurately made 90° angle used to hold work at right angles to the surface plate. It is machined on the ends to enable work mounted on it to be marked both horizontally and vertically. Work with only one true face, such as a machined casting can be mounted on an angle plate.

7 Classification of common hand tools (2) holding tools

The chart names the common holding tools found in the school workshop and shows with which materials they are mainly used. This is followed by sketches of these tools together with brief notes about them. Specialist tools used only for one type of work have been shown in the sections describing those processes.

Wood	*Plastics*	*Metal*
Carpenter's bench ———	►◄	——— Engineer's bench
Bench vice ———	►◄	——— Engineer's vice
	◄———	——— Vice jaw covers
Bench stop	X	X
Bench hook ———	►	X
Bench holdfast ———	►	X
Mitre box	X	X
G-cramp ———	►◄	
Dowelling jigs	X	X
Sash cramp ———	►◄	
X	◄———	——— Toolmaker's clamp
X	◄———	——— Hand vice
X	◄———	——— Mole wrench
X	X	Smith's tongs
X	X	Brass tongs
X	X	Folding bars
X	X	Anvil and stand
X	X	Tinman's stakes
X	X	Silversmith's stakes

Engineer's vice. The vice is bolted to the bench top so that the back jaw is just forward of the bench edge. This allows long pieces of metal to reach down to the floor while held in the vice.

Soft metal or plastic vice jaw covers are used to protect work from the diamond patterned gripping surfaces of the jaws when finish is more important than grip.

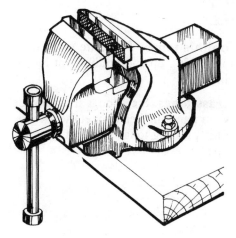

Folding bars can be made to suit the job in hand from any rigid, straight material. The sketches show the common bought and home-made types. They are used when folding metal in order to obtain a straight, neat bend, and are usually held in the vice for small scale work.

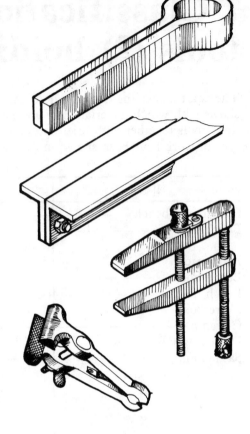

Toolmaker's clamp. These are used to hold parts together while marking out, shaping and drilling. The clamp is tightened with the centre screw until the jaws are parallel and grip the work lightly. A firm grip is then obtained by tightening the outer screw.

Hand vice. This is used for holding small and especially irregularly shaped parts while drilling, rivetting, etc. It is especially useful when drilling sheetmetal.

Mole wrench. The mole wrench can be firmly locked onto pieces of work to clamp them together, or to hold them while drilling, grinding or welding. It is now often used instead of the toolmaker's clamp and hand vice.

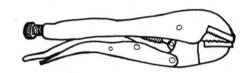

Smith's tongs. There are many different shapes of tongs for picking up and holding hot metal of all sizes and shapes.

Brass tongs. Steel tongs must not be put into acid baths when handling beaten metalwork jobs. We therefore, use brass pickling tongs either of a closed mouth or scissor type.

Woodworker's bench vice. The vice is fixed to the bench so that the top of the wooden jaw facing is level with the bench top, and is used for holding work.

Bench stop. This is used to rest wood against while planing. The height is adjusted by unscrewing the wingnut and sliding the stop up and down.

This has been developed into a surface cramping system with adjustable dogs, and a tail vice to hold material of varying lengths and widths.

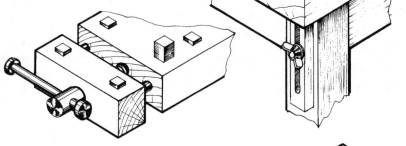

Bench hook. This clips over the edge of the bench or in the vice, and is used to hold wood while sawing. The bench hook helps you to hold the work steady, prevents the wood from splitting by supporting it under the kerf and protects the bench top. Long pieces of wood should be rested across two or more bench hooks. Left- and right-handed bench hooks are needed to suit left- and right-handed users. Bench hooks are usually held in the vice.

Mitre box. This is used to cut wood at 45° accurately. The 90° saw cut in the centre is for squaring wood accurately. Boxes can usually be made for cutting mitres at any angle, for example when making a hexagonal frame.

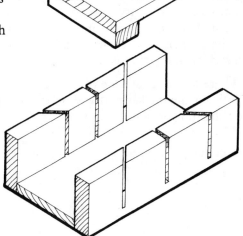

Sash cramp. This is used to hold frames, carcases and butt joints together while the glue sets and while welding large metal frames.

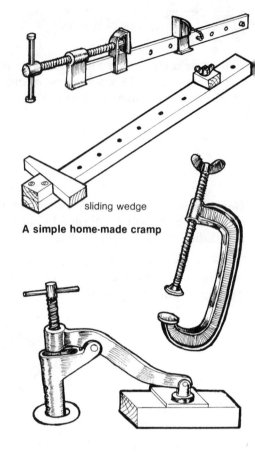

A simple home-made cramp

sliding wedge

G – cramp. This is used to hold work down onto the bench and to cramp small pieces of glued wood together. There are several different types, for example deep throat cramps to reach further in from the edge. The swivel shoe enables the cramp to grip angled pieces of wood. Common sizes go up from 50 mm to 350 mm in 50 mm steps. Protect the work with scrapwood.

Bench holdfast. This clamps work firmly down onto the bench top. The work must be protected by a piece of scrapwood.

The holdfast is particularly useful for holding down work while carving, mortising, rebating and ploughing.

Dowelling jigs are used to ensure that the holes in the two halves of a dowelled joint line up with each other. It is possible to buy adjustable jigs, but these are often expensive and difficult to use. It is therefore, often easier to make a simple jig from wood or metal to suit the job, and the design and manufacture of jigs is an interesting exercise in its own right. It is not advisable to attempt dowelled joints without using a jig.

Where legs and rails are of different thicknesses, make the jig to fit the thicker part and make a packing piece for use on the thinner one.

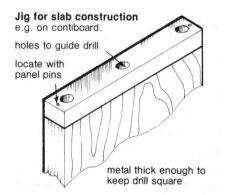

Jig for slab construction
e.g. on contiboard.

holes to guide drill

locate with
panel pins

*metal thick enough to
keep drill square*

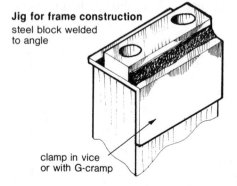

Jig for frame construction
steel block welded
to angle

clamp in vice
or with G-cramp

How to glue-up woodwork jobs

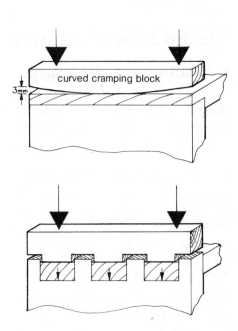

curved cramping block

3mm

1. Always protect finished surfaces from metal cramps by using wooden cramping blocks.

Make any special cramping blocks you will need. For example, convex blocks are used to make sure that the middle of a long joint is pressed together and that warped wood is straightened. Cut away blocks are used to allow pressure to be put on only in the right places, especially when cramping through dovetails and through mortise and tenon joints.

Cramping blocks must be strong enough to press the job into shape.

2. Always assemble the job without glueing, before glueing-up, to make sure that it fits together and to work out the best way of assembling and cramping it.

3. Break down the glueing of larger jobs into several easy stages.

4. Before starting, make sure that you are well organised. Lay out the parts of the job, apply glue to all parts which will touch and assemble them. If the right amount of glue has been used, a small amount will squeeze out of the joints when they are cramped up.

This can be wiped off with a damp cloth while wet or gently prised from polished surfaces with a chisel when dry.

5. Cramp up to your prepared plan and test for squareness and wind.

Testing for squareness

Measure the diagonals using a long stick or rulers. If the diagonals are unequal move the cramps sideways as shown.

Testing for wind

Look along the top edges of the job or use winding strips to see that the job is flat. If the job is twisted move the cramps up and down as shown.

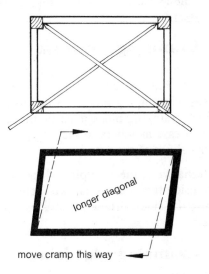

longer diagonal

move cramp this way

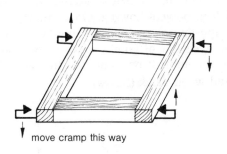

move cramp this way

Methods of cramping

1. Cramping a flat frame

Lay the cramps on a flat surface. Make sure that they are along the centre lines of the rails, and press the job down onto the bars of the cramps. Test the diagonals for squareness and across the top edges for wind.

2. Cramping a stool frame

Stage 1. Assemble the short sides first as when cramping a flat frame. Test with a try-square for squareness and across the tops of the legs for wind. A spacing bar cut from scrapwood to exactly the length of the top rail may help to keep the legs parallel. Clean any surplus glue from the mortises, and leave the job to dry.

Stage 2. When the short sides have set, assemble the long sides dry, and test. Glue-up as shown. Test the top frame for squareness and for wind, and take special care to test that the legs are in line and square. Use spacing bars if necessary.

3. Cramping a carcase

It is often necessary to cramp in two directions at once, and thought must be given to the positioning of cramps and the types of cramping blocks needed to do this. The thickness of the cramping block must be the same as the thickness of the carcase members so that the pressure is along the centre-lines of the members.

Alternatively, the cramping blocks can sometimes be placed alongside the joints as shown (below right). Since this may cause the sides to bow inwards, a spacing bar should be used.

4. Cramping edge joints

The cramps are placed alternately above and below the job to prevent bowing. Good cramping blocks are especially important to prevent bruising of the edges. Make sure that an even line of glue is squeezed out along the whole length of the joint. If necessary tap the joints flush with a hammer and wood block (below).

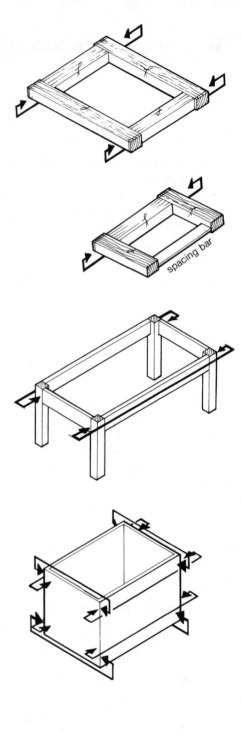

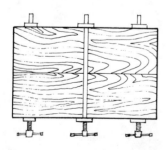

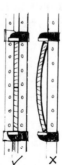

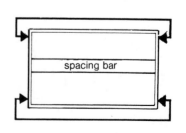

8 Classification of common hand tools (3) driving tools

The chart names the common driving tools found in the school workshop and shows with which materials they are mainly used. This is followed by sketches of these tools together with brief notes about them. Specialist tools used only for one type of work have been shown in the sections describing those processes.

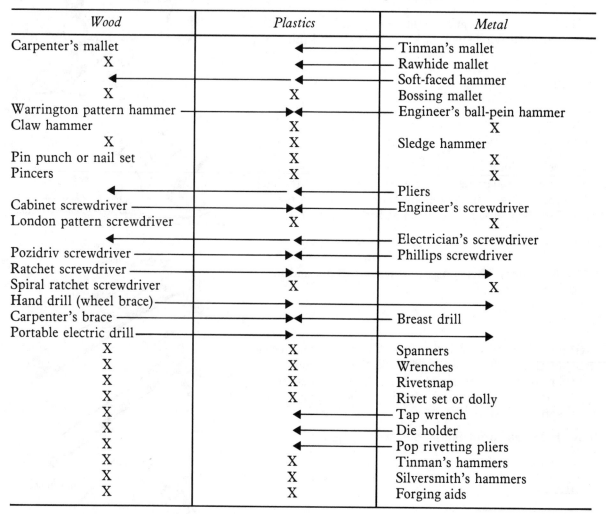

Wood	Plastics	Metal
Carpenter's mallet	◄	Tinman's mallet
X	◄	Rawhide mallet
◄	◄	Soft-faced hammer
X	X	Bossing mallet
Warrington pattern hammer ———	►◄ ———	Engineer's ball-pein hammer
Claw hammer	X	X
X	X	Sledge hammer
Pin punch or nail set	X	X
Pincers	X	X
◄	◄	Pliers
Cabinet screwdriver ———	►◄ —	Engineer's screwdriver
London pattern screwdriver	X	X
◄	◄	Electrician's screwdriver
Pozidriv screwdriver ———	►◄ ———	Phillips screwdriver
Ratchet screwdriver ———	► ———————————→	
Spiral ratchet screwdriver	X	X
Hand drill (wheel brace)———	► ———————————→	
Carpenter's brace ———	►◄ —	Breast drill
Portable electric drill———	► ———————————→	
X	X	Spanners
X	X	Wrenches
X	X	Rivetsnap
X	X	Rivet set or dolly
X	◄	Tap wrench
X	◄	Die holder
X	◄	Pop rivetting pliers
X	X	Tinman's hammers
X	X	Silversmith's hammers
X	X	Forging aids

Hammers

Warrington pattern hammer. The Warrington or cross-pein hammer is used for light nailing and general work in cabinet-making. The cross-pein is used for starting small nails held between the fingers. The shaft fits into a shaped socket and is expanded by the wedge so that the head cannot fly off.

A pin hammer is a light-weight cross-pein hammer with a long shaft for driving small tacks, panel pins and thin nails.

Using a hammer. Grip the shaft near the end and watch the nail, not the hammer. After a few taps to start the nail, take larger swings from the elbow without bending the wrist. Hit the nail with the hammer head square to it.

Claw hammer. This is used for heavy nailing, and for removing larger nails.

Ball-pein hammer. Various sizes of ball-pein hammer are used for almost all general metalwork. Smaller sizes are used for dot and centre punching, rivetting and bending, while larger sizes are used for forging. The ball-pein is used for shaping rivets.

The sledge-hammer is used for heavy forging.

Mallets

Carpenter's mallet. This is used in woodwork for striking chisels and when assembling jobs. The shaft and the mortise through the head are tapered so that the head cannot fly off. The striking faces are sloped so that they strike the chisel squarely when the mallet is swung from the elbow, while standing at a bench.

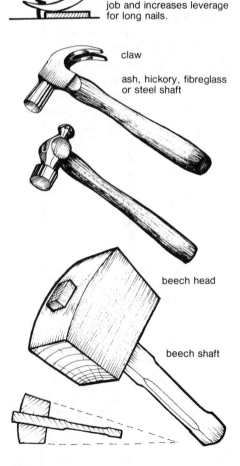

cross-pein   head of hardened and tempered forged steel

shaft of ash or hickory

wedge   shaft

scrapwood protects the job and increases leverage for long nails.

claw

ash, hickory, fibreglass or steel shaft

beech head

beech shaft

Tinman's mallet. Wooden mallets are used for shaping sheet metal without damaging the surface. The faces can be shaped for special jobs.

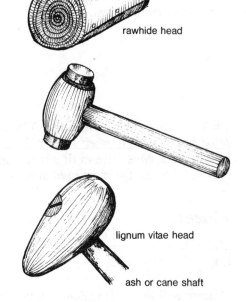

boxwood or lignum vitae head

ash or cane shaft

Rawhide mallet. This is stronger, but more expensive than a tinman's mallet.

rawhide head

Soft-faced hammer. A heavier blow can be struck without damaging the material, by using a hammer having a cast-iron head, into which are fitted replaceable faces of soft materials such as rawhide, copper, nylon and rubber. This is useful for assembling large woodwork jobs, as well as for metalwork.

Bossing mallet. This has rounded faces of different sizes and is used for hollowing out sheet metal.

lignum vitae head

ash or cane shaft

Screwdrivers

There are many types including cabinet, London pattern, engineer's, electrician's, stubby or midget, ratchet and spiral ratchet or Yankee.

It is important to keep the blades ground accurately to shape and to use the one which fits the screw exactly.

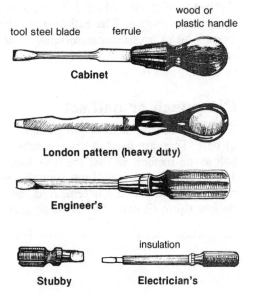

tool steel blade   ferrule   wood or plastic handle

Cabinet

London pattern (heavy duty)

Engineer's

insulation

Stubby   **Electrician's**

Straight blades. The blade should exactly fit the length and width of the slot in the screw head (right).

Common faults:

(a) A blade which is too narrow will need too much leverage to turn and will chew up the screw head.

(b) A blade which is too wide will damage the material around the screw head.

(c) A blade which is too thin may bend or break and will chew up the screw head.

(d) A blade which is too thick to touch the bottom of the slot will slip out damaging both the screw head and the surrounding material.

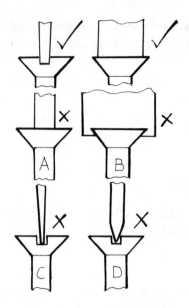

Phillips and pozidriv blades. The correct size of blade must be used as no other will fit. The sizes are identified by numbers. Most screws fit either numbers 1, 2 or 3, with number 2 being the most used size (*see* Screws).

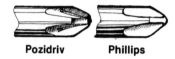

Pozidriv   Phillips

Pincers

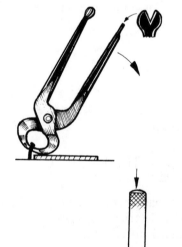

Pincers pull out nails which a claw hammer cannot grip, either because they are too small or have no head. The small thin claw on one handle of the pincers will fit under the heads of small nails and lever them out far enough for the pincers to grip. The ball on the other allows you to exert a lot of pressure comfortably. The rounded jaws roll to give leverage when pulled.

Pin punch or nail set

There are several sizes of pin punch to suit different sizes of nail. They are used to drive headless nails and panel pins below the surface, so that the hole can be hidden by filling, and so that the nails will not scratch anything. They are made from hardened and tempered tool steel, and have a hollow tip to fit over the nail head and prevent slipping.

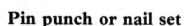

Drilling machines

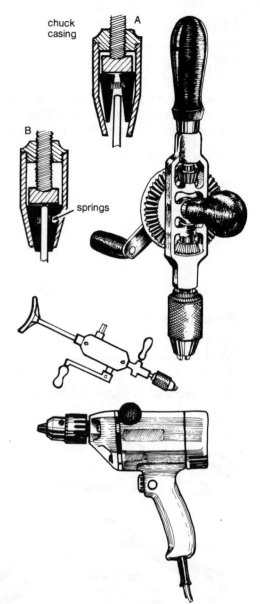

chuck casing

A

B

springs

Hand drill or wheel brace. The hand drill is used to rotate twist drills up to 8 mm diameter. The side handle can be unscrewed to allow the drill to work close against obstructions.

The chuck has three self-centering jaws to grip the round shanks of twist drills. When the chuck casing is unscrewed the jaws spring back and allow the shank of the drill to enter (A). When the chuck casing is screwed back up, the jaws close and grip the drill (B).

Breast drill. This is a large drilling machine which takes drills up to 13 mm diameter and usually has two speeds. It is used against the chest to provide extra pressure.

Portable electric drills. These are usually chosen for their chuck size and their number of speeds. Common chuck sizes are 6, 8 and 13 mm maximum drill shank diameter, and drills usually have one or two speed drives. The safest portable tools are the *double-insulated* type.

Carpenter's ratchet brace. Boring with a brace is best done horizontally because it is easier to apply pressure and to keep square. A brace holds only square-shank bits. The ratchet allows the brace to be used in corners where a full turn is not possible.

The chuck has two self-centering jaws with V-shaped slots into which the corners of the square tang of the bit fit. The spring end of the jaws fits into the slot in the chuck casing holder to give a positive drive from brace to bit. When the casing is screwed on, the taper inside it closes the jaws. The bit cannot slip round inside the chuck as can a twist drill in a three jaw chuck.

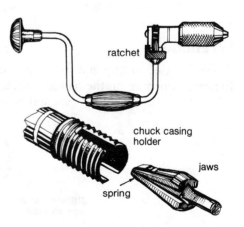

ratchet

chuck casing holder

jaws

spring

Pliers

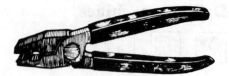

Combination pliers

These are mainly used to grip small items. Combination pliers are also able to cut wire. There are many shapes and sizes, and only some of the most used are shown here.

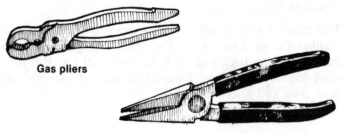

Gas pliers

Snipe or chain nose

Spanners

These are used to tighten or loosen nuts and bolts.

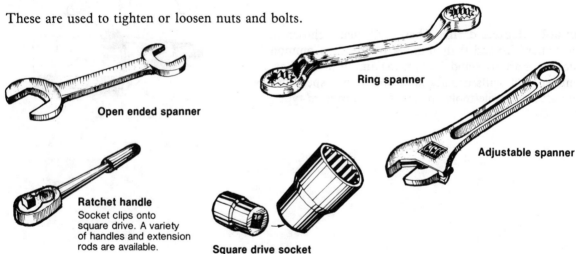

Open ended spanner

Ring spanner

Adjustable spanner

Ratchet handle
Socket clips onto square drive. A variety of handles and extension rods are available.

Square drive socket

Wrenches

These are used to grip and turn pipes and round bars. Increased pressure on the handles increases the grip of the jaws. Do not use them on nuts and bolts.

Slip-joint pliers

Stillson pattern pipe wrench

9 Classification of common hand tools (4) cutting tools

The chart names the common hand-held cutting tools usually found in the school workshop and shows which materials each is used to cut. Where tools with different names fulfil the same function on different materials, they are shown on the same line. This is followed by sketches of these tools together with brief notes about them. Specialist tools used for only one type of work have been shown in the sections describing these processes.

		Wood	*Plastics*	*Metal*
Saws	Handsaws	– rip	X	X
		– crosscut	X	X
		– panel	X	X
	Backsaws	– tenon ———————	►◄	—— Hacksaw
		– dovetail ———————	►◄	—— Junior hacksaw
	For curves	– bow	X	X
		◄—————————————	◄	—— Abrafile saw
		– coping ———————	►◄	—— Piercing
		– pad ———————	►◄	—— Pad
Snips		X	◄—————————	Straight snips
		X	◄—————————	Curved snips
		X	◄—————————	Universal snips
		X	◄—————————	Jeweller's snips
		X	Scissors	X
		X	X	Bench shearing machine
		X	◄—————————	Nibblers
		X	X	Wire cutters
Knives etc.		◄—————————	Trimming knife	X
		X	Laminate and acrylic cutters	X
		X	Hot-wire machine	X
Files	Rasps ———————————		►◄	Engineer's files
		X	◄—————————	Needle files
	General purpose files ——— e.g. surform tools		►◄	General purpose files e.g. milled tooth files
Scrapers	Hand and cabinet scrapers		Scrapers for acrylics	Engineer's scrapers
Planes	Bench	– smoothing ———————	►	X
		– jack ———————	►	X
		– try	X	X

121

		Wood	Plastics	Metal
Planes	Special – plough		X	X
	– combination		X	X
	– rebate		X	X
	– router		X	X
	– block	———→		X
	– shoulder		X	X
	– bull-nose		X	X
	– spokeshaves		X	X
Chisels	Firmer		X	Cold chisels
	Bevel-edge firmer		X	Sets and hardie
	Mortise		X	X
	Gouges-in-cannel		X	X
	-out-cannel		X	X
Drills		←————	←————	Twist drills
	Centre bit		X	X
	Jennings pattern auger bit		X	X
	Forstner pattern bit	————→		X
	Rose countersink bit	————→	←—	Rose countersink
	Flat bit		X	X
	Expansive bit		←————	Tank and washer cutter
	Dowel sharpener		X	X
	Bradawl		X	X
	X		←————	Combination centre drill
	Hole saw	————→		————→
Taps and Dies	X		←————	Taps
	X		←————	Circular split dies
Portable electric tools	Jigsaw	————→		————→
	Circular saw	————→		————→
	Belt sander	————→		X
	Orbital sander	————→		X
	Disc sander	————→		————→
	Router	————→		·X

Note. For fuller details of how to use the cutting tools shown in this chapter refer to chapter 10, Wasting-hand processes.

Saws are used for making straight and curved cuts in wood, metal and plastics.

Saws for wood
Saws for straight cuts

Handsaws are for straight cuts in large pieces of wood.

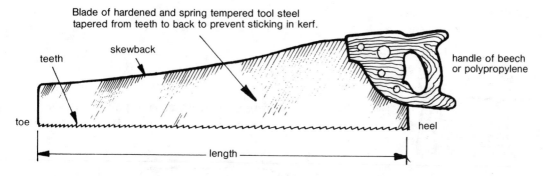

Name	Approx. length of blade	Approx. points per 25 mm	Uses
Rip-saw	700 mm	5	Sawing along the grain of large pieces of wood.
Cross-cut saw	600 mm	7	Sawing across the grain of large pieces of wood. Will also cut along the grain but not as quickly as a rip-saw.
Panel saw	500 mm	10	A fine toothed crosscut for sawing plywood, thin wood and large joints.

Backsaws are for accurate straight cuts in small pieces of wood. The back of the saw limits the depth of cut.

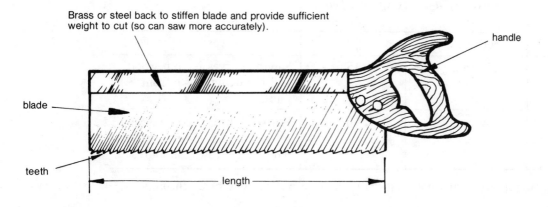

Name	Approx. length of blade	Approx. points per 25 mm	Uses
Tenon saw	250, 300 and 350 mm	14	Sawing small pieces of wood and most joints. The most used backsaw.
Dovetail saw	200 mm	20	For the smallest and most accurate work, especially sawing small dovetail joints.

Saws for curves

Bow saw.

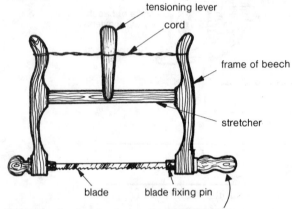

tensioning lever
cord
frame of beech
stretcher
blade   blade fixing pin

Beech handles turn to change direction of blade.

Coping saw (teeth usually point towards handle to cut as saw is pulled).

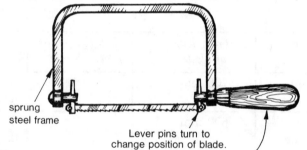

sprung steel frame

Lever pins turn to change position of blade.

Beech or polypropylene handle is tightened to tension the blade.

Pad saw.

beech or polypropylene handle

blade clamping screws

Blade length adjusted by sliding through handle.
Use shortest possible blade to
avoid breakage.

Name	Approx. length of blade	Approx. points per 25 mm	Uses
Bow saw	300 mm	10	Sawing curves in thick wood.
Coping saw	150 mm	15	Sawing curves in thin wood and removing waste from joints.
Pad saw	150 mm	10	For straight and curved cuts in the middle of large sheets where other saws cannot reach.

When making internal cuts you first drill a hole to put the saw blade through.

Saws for metal

Saws for straight cuts

Hacksaws are for straight cuts in metal. The blade is held in tension in the frame *with the teeth facing forward.*

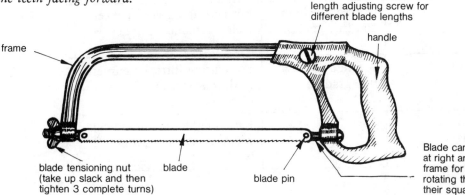

length adjusting screw for different blade lengths

handle

frame

blade tensioning nut (take up slack and then tighten 3 complete turns)

blade

blade pin

Blade can be turned at right angles to the frame for long cuts by rotating the bolts in their square holes.

Junior hacksaw is for straight cuts on small light work. The blade is held in tension by the sprung steel frame.

Blade length: 150 mm   Number of teeth: 32 per 25 mm.

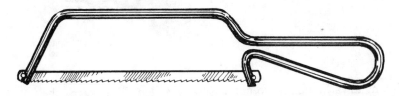

General purpose saw is for sawing most materials including wood, non-ferrous metals and plastics.

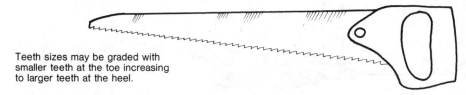

Teeth sizes may be graded with smaller teeth at the toe increasing to larger teeth at the heel.

Sheet saws are for sawing most materials including wood, sheet metal and plastics.

Blade lengths – 300 mm hacksaw blade
              – 400 mm blades with 6 and 10 teeth per 25 mm.

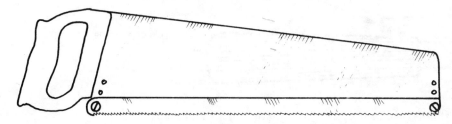

Saws for curves

Name	Approx. length of blade	No. of teeth per 25 mm	Uses
Abrafile saw	225 mm	Coarse, medium and fine grades.	For cutting curves in sheet metal, ceramics, plastics and wood.
Piercing saw	100 mm	A range of very fine grades.	For cutting intricate curves in thin or soft metal and plastics
Pad saw	Uses broken hacksaw blades.	32	For straight and curved cuts where other saws cannot reach.

Abrafile saw.

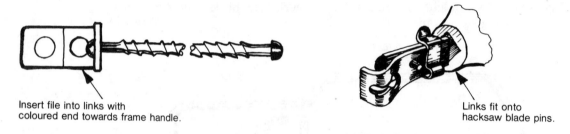

Insert file into links with
coloured end towards frame handle.

Links fit onto
hacksaw blade pins.

Piercing saw. (Teeth point towards handle to cut as saw is pulled. This keeps the blade taut.)

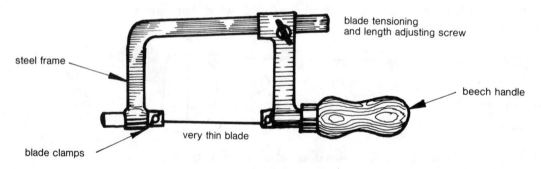

blade tensioning
and length adjusting screw

steel frame

beech handle

blade clamps

very thin blade

Pad saw. (Teeth point towards handle. Blade would bend if it cut when pushed.)

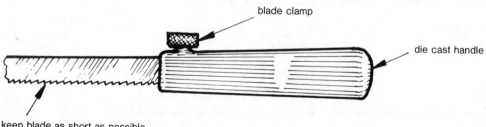

blade clamp

die cast handle

keep blade as short as possible

Saws for plastics

Saws for straight cuts

Back saws (tenon and dovetail).
Hacksaws with 24 and 32 teeth per 25 mm blades.
Junior hacksaws.
General purpose saw.
Sheet saws.

Saws for curves

Coping saw.
Abrafile saw.
Piercing saw (for intricate work).
Pad saw with 32 teeth per 25 mm hacksaw blade.

Snips or shears

These are for cutting thin sheets of metal and soft plastics.

Name	Common sizes	Uses
Straight snips	150 to 350 mm long	For straight cuts and out-side curves.
Curved snips	150 to 350 mm long	For inside curves only.
Universal snips	275 to 350 mm long	For straight and curved cuts in thicker material.
Jeweller's snips (straight and curved)	175 mm long	For small intricate work.

Straight and curved snips   Jeweller's snips   Universal snips

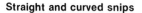

Hand-lever bench shearing machine

This is used for cutting metal sheet, strip and rod. It consists of a large pair of shears on which a system of leavers greatly increases the force which can be applied.

Nibblers

These are used for making straight or curved cuts in thin sheets without distorting the material being cut. Nibblers remove a thin strip of material. The operator's hands are kept clear of the cut and you can start a cut from inside the sheet, by first drilling a hole. For example:

Goscut. This has blades for cutting plastic laminates, hardboard, asbestos, aluminium, copper, thin mild steel, sheet etc.

Monadex is for thin sheet metals.

Wire-cutters

Side-cutting, diagonal-cutting and end-cutting nippers are used for cutting wire. Snips must not be used to cut wire because the cutting edges will be damaged.

Hot wire cutter

This is used for cutting expanded polystyrene. It consists of either a heated wire held in a fixed framework for making straight, angled and curved cuts through blocks resting on a table, or a hand-held sculpting tool which melts its way through the material.

Knives

Laminate and acrylic cutting tool

This is used for cutting acrylic sheet up to 6 mm thick and plastic laminates.

First score a line along the surface of the sheet (as in glass cutting). Then support the work with the line along the edge of the bench, and press on both sides of the line until the sheet breaks along the line.

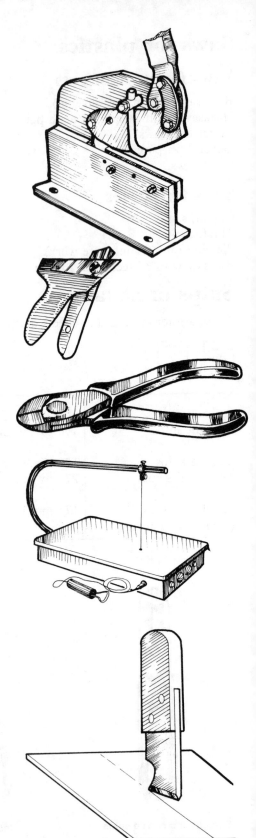

Trimming knife

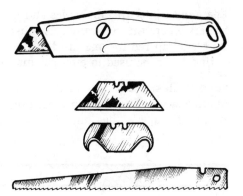

This is used for cutting thin sections of wood (e.g. when veneering and modelling), soft plastics, card, paper, floor coverings, etc., and for scoring plastic laminates.

It is available with standard, heavy duty, hooked, laminate scoring, and wood and metal cutting padsaw blades.

Files

Files are used for shaping and smoothing, mainly metal and hard plastics, but also wood.

Safety. Never use an engineer's file without a handle. The tang could stab your hand.

Common shapes (thick lines show edges with teeth).

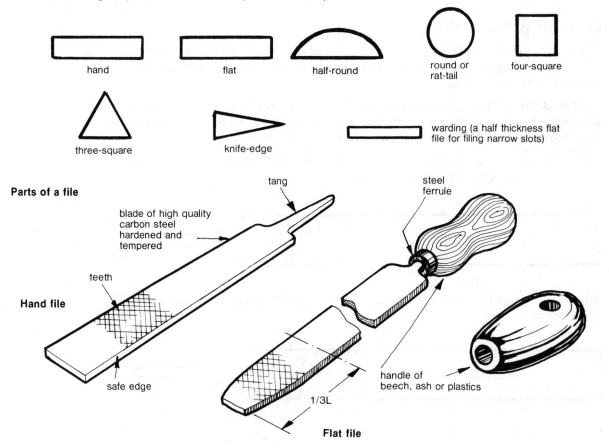

hand

flat

half-round

round or rat-tail

four-square

three-square

knife-edge

warding (a half thickness flat file for filing narrow slots)

Parts of a file

tang

steel ferrule

blade of high quality carbon steel hardened and tempered

teeth

Hand file

safe edge

handle of beech, ash or plastics

1/3L

Flat file

The *hand file* has parallel sides and one safe edge (without teeth) for filing into corners where the vertical edges must not be touched. The *flat file* has the end of the blade tapered for one third of its length and teeth on both edges like most files, so that it can be used to enlarge small openings.

Needle files. These are small precision files with round handles and fine cuts for intricate work. They have a length of 120 to 180 mm and are made in a wide variety of shapes. They must be used carefully because they are easily broken.

teeth   knurled handle

Rasps are for rough shaping of wood and other soft materials. The common sizes are 200 and 250 mm long and the common shape is half-round.

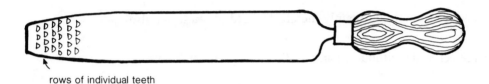

rows of individual teeth

General purpose files

There are several types of general purpose file which will file almost any material including wood, metals and plastics. They are particularly useful for filing soft materials without clogging – e.g.

1. Milled tooth files have fast-cutting teeth which do not clog easily. Common shapes are hand and half-round; common lengths are 300 and 350 mm; common grades are standard (9 teeth per 25 mm), fine (13) and extra fine (18).

Curved-tooth type (e.g. dreadnought files). The curve keeps more teeth in contact with the material when filing with large teeth.

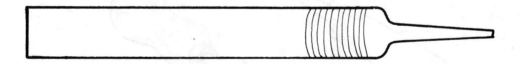

Straight-tooth type (e.g. millenicut files). These are particularly useful for shaping polyester resin.

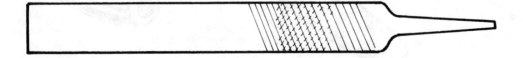

The Aven trimmatool is milled tooth. The blade has one curved-tooth side and one straight-tooth side, and can be adjusted to concave, straight or convex positions. The handle can be adjusted to file or plane positions.

2. Surform tools have individual teeth with each tooth having a hole through the blade to help clear the filings and reduce clogging. Blades are replaceable when blunt. Available with file or plane type handles.

Common shapes are flat, convex, curved and round; common lengths are 140 and 250 mm.

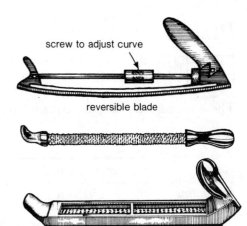

screw to adjust curve

reversible blade

Scrapers

These are used for final smoothing of hardwood, metal and acrylic plastics.

Scrapers for wood

Hand scrapers consist of a piece of hardened and tempered tool steel with the long corners burnished over to form cutting edges, which remove very fine shavings. They are used to obtain a smoother finish on hardwoods than is possible with a finely set smoothing plane, especially on cross-grained timber where a plane tears up the grain in both directions.

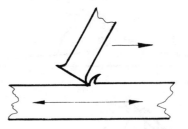

Rectangular scrapers are used for flat surfaces (common size is 125 mm x 60 mm) and *curved scrapers* for shaped work.

Cabinet scraper. This consists of a blade similar to a hand scraper held in a spokeshave-like body. It is easier and less tiring to use than a hand scraper.

Scrapers for acrylic plastics

A hand scraper as used for wood, or an old hacksaw blade with one edge ground can be used to obtain a fine finish ready for polishing, after the acrylic has been filed and rubbed down with wet and dry paper.

Scrapers for metal

These are used to remove very small amounts of metal in order to obtain very accurate flat and curved surfaces. Hand scraping has been largely replaced by surface grinding.

Planes

These are used for shaping and smoothing wood and acrylic plastics.

Bench planes

Name	Approx. length	Uses
Smoothing plane	250 mm	For cleaning up work to remove all previous tool marks and leave the surface clean and smooth. For planing end grain. Because it is small and light, this plane is popular for all kinds of general planing jobs, but its short sole will not produce a flat surface.
Jack plane	350 mm	For planing wood to size. The general purpose plane. Its greater length produces a flatter surface.
Foreplane *Jointer plane*	450 mm 600 mm	For trueing-up large surfaces and long edges. The sole is longer for accurate long work.

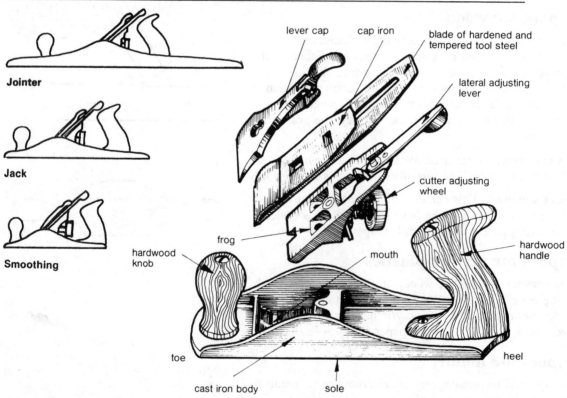

Jointer

Jack

Smoothing

lever cap cap iron blade of hardened and tempered tool steel

lateral adjusting lever

cutter adjusting wheel

frog

hardwood knob

mouth

hardwood handle

toe

cast iron body sole

heel

Main parts of smoothing plane

Special planes

Plough plane. Used to cut grooves and rebates.

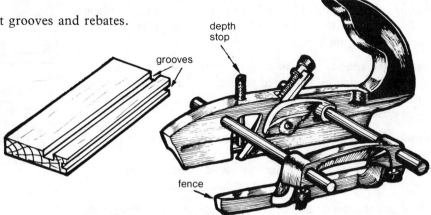

Combination plane. This is similar to the plough plane, but has a wider range of cutters including beading cutters for curved shapes, and cutters for tongue and grooved joints.

Rebate or fillister plane. This is used to cut rebates. With the blade in the forward bed, stopped rebates can be cut.

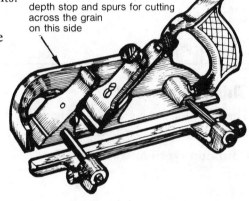

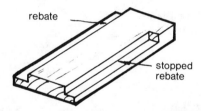

Router plane. This is used to level the bottoms of housings, halvings or other depressions parallel to the surface of the work. Remove most of the waste by sawing and chiselling first.

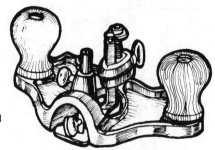

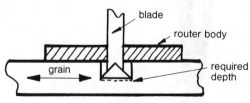

Block plane. This is used for small work including planing end grain, trimming mitres and planing chamfers. It is a low angle plane which is small enough to be used in one hand and has no cap iron.

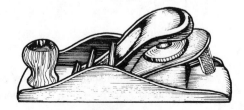

Shoulder plane. This is used for cleaning-up rebates, halvings and the shoulders of joints. It is a low angle plane and the blade is the full width of the sole to cut into corners. It has no cap iron.

Bull-nose plane. This is used to plane close up to an obstruction such as a stopped rebate. It is a shoulder plane with a very short nose which is removable to get right up to an obstruction. It has no cap iron.

Spokeshaves are used to smooth curves. There are two types
- flat faced spokeshave for outside (convex) curves.
- round faced spokeshave for inside (concave) curves.

They are sharpened and set in the same way as planes and special care should be taken to work always with the grain.

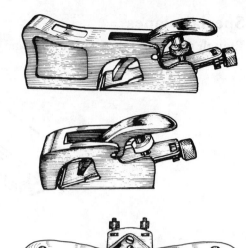

Chisels

Chisels for wood

These are for cutting and shaping wood where planes cannot be used, and especially for cutting joints.

Common types of wood chisel.

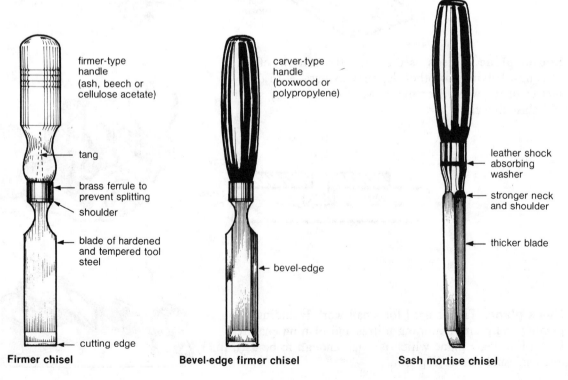

firmer-type handle (ash, beech or cellulose acetate)

tang

brass ferrule to prevent splitting

shoulder

blade of hardened and tempered tool steel

cutting edge

Firmer chisel

carver-type handle (boxwood or polypropylene)

bevel-edge

Bevel-edge firmer chisel

leather shock absorbing washer

stronger neck and shoulder

thicker blade

Sash mortise chisel

Name	Common sizes	Uses
Firmer chisel	3 to 50 mm	General purpose chisel. Strong enough for cutting with hand pressure (called *paring*) or with light mallet blows.
Bevel-edge firmer chisel	3 to 50 mm	Similar to the square-edge firmer chisel except that the blade corners are bevelled for cutting into acute corners such as in dovetails. The blade is less strong than the square-edge blade and it must be used carefully.
Sash mortise chisel	6 to 13 mm	For heavy duty work such as cutting mortises. Made to withstand heavy mallet blows and the levering-out of waste. The thick blade also prevents twisting in the mortise.

Gouges

Gouges-in-cannel are also called scribing or paring gouges.

They are ground on the inside and are used for vertical paring of concave curves, cutting mouldings, channelling and other curved paring work.

Gouges-out-cannel are also called firmer gouges.

They are ground on the outside and are used for scooping-out, e.g. cutting out finger grips and carving the inside of bowls.

Chisels for metal

Cold chisels are used to cut, shear, and chip cold metal.

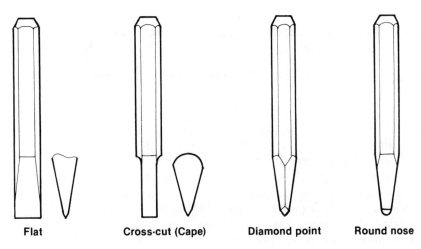

| **Flat** | **Cross-cut (Cape)** | **Diamond point** | **Round nose** |

Name	Common blade widths	Uses
Flat	6 to 25 mm	General-purpose chisel for cutting sheet metal, cleaning castings and trimming metal to size.
Cross-cut	3 to 10 mm	For cutting keyways and grooves.
Diamond point	3 to 10 mm	Square-end with a cutting edge at one corner for cleaning out sharp corners.
Round nose	6 to 10 mm	For cutting rounded grooves and cleaning out rounded corners.

Drills

These are used for cutting circular holes in most materials, including wood, metal and plastics.

Twist drills.

Straight shank drills fit into the chucks of hand and electric drilling machines. Common sizes are 1 mm to 13 mm × 0.5 mm steps and 1 mm to 10 mm × 0.1 mm steps.

Morse-taper shank drills fit directly into electric drilling machine spindles and lathe tailstock barrels. Common sizes are 10 to 20 mm × 0.5 mm steps and 21 to 30 mm × 1.0 mm steps.

Twist drills are used for drilling wood, metal and plastics, and are the most used type of drill for hand and machine drilling. Made of carbon steel or high speed steel, hardened and tempered, the smaller sizes have straight shanks to fit into drill chucks, while larger sizes have a morse-taper shank to fit directly into drilling machine spindles and lathe tailstocks. They are usually used in wood only for sizes up to 8 mm diameter, because the larger sizes leave a ragged hole. The flutes are too fast for adequate chip ejection making frequent clearing necessary. Masonry drills are twist drills with hard cutting lips brazed onto the nose.

Rose countersinks are for countersinking holes in wood, metal and plastics for screw and rivet heads.

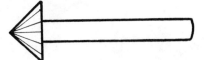

Light-duty pattern for hand drills

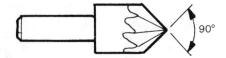

Heavy-duty machine countersink

Combination centre drill. This is used for starting holes on the lathe where centre punching is not possible and for drilling holes into which lathe centres will fit. The pilot drill makes a small hole to prevent the work resting on the point of the centre because the friction caused would burn the point off.

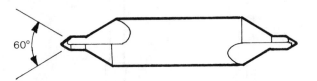

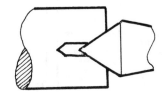

Cutting large holes in metal and plastics

Tank and washer cutter. This is used in a brace and will cut holes of any diameter from 25 mm to 125 mm diameter in metal, rubber and plastics. The pilot drill makes a small hole in the centre while the blade scrapes a circular groove until the waste is removed in the shape of a washer.

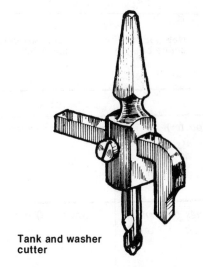

Tank and washer cutter

Hole saw. This is used in an electric drill and will cut holes from 19 mm to 75 mm diameter. It works in a similar way to the tank cutter and removes a washer. The hole saw can have interchangeable cutters which fit into one arbor (right), or separate cutters each with its own arbor and pilot drill.

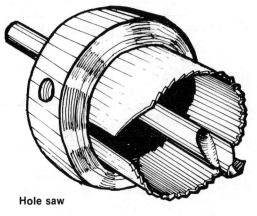

Hole saw

Common types of woodboring bit

Bits have a square tang to fit into a brace. (*See* Driving tools.)

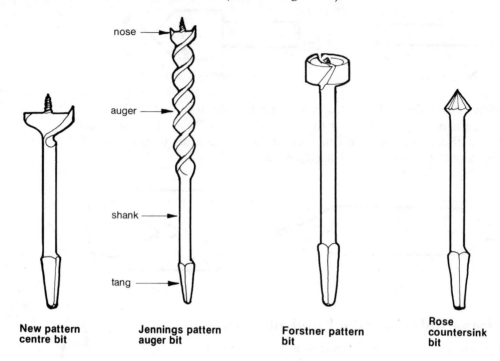

New pattern centre bit	**Jennings pattern auger bit**	**Forstner pattern bit**		**Rose countersink bit**

Name	Approx. sizes	Uses
New pattern centre bit	6 mm to 55 mm	For boring shallow holes in wood. Not suitable for deep holes because, (a) it has no auger to carry away waste and (b) it tends to wander off centre because it has no parallel sides to guide it in the hole.
Jennings pattern auger bit	6 mm to 40 mm	For boring deep holes in wood. It is one of several types of auger bit which work in the same way as a centre bit, but have a cylindrical auger to remove the waste and guide the bit in the hole.
Forstner pattern	10 mm to 30 mm	This bit is guided by its rim and not by a centre point. It will therefore bore clean, accurate, flat bottomed holes and overlapping holes in wood. It will also drill acrylic.
Rose countersink bit		Countersinking for screw heads in wood, plastics and non-ferrous metals.

Further types of woodboring bit

Expansive bits are used for drilling large diameter shallow holes in softwood. Cutters are available to give adjustment from 12 mm to 150 mm diameter.

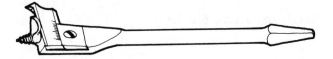

Dowel sharpeners are used for chamfering the ends of dowels to make assembling dowel joints easier.

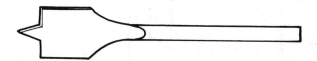

Flat bits are used in electric drills for fast, accurate drilling in hard and soft woods. They are used at the highest available speed and with only moderate pressure. Locate the point on the wood before switching on and wait for the drill to stop before withdrawing it from the hole. The usual sizes are 6 mm to 40 mm.

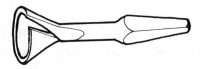

Bradawl. This is used for making small holes in wood to start screws and nails. To use it press the blade into the wood with the cutting edge *across* the grain so that it cuts the fibres and does not split them. Then rotate it from side to side while continuing to push it into the wood until the hole is the required depth.

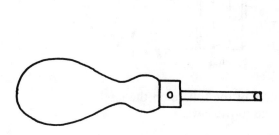

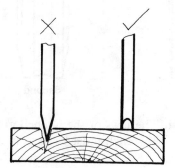

Taps and dies

These are for cutting threads in metals and acrylic plastics.

Taps

These are for cutting internal threads. They are held in a tap wrench and are made from hardened and tempered carbon or high speed steel.

Taper tap. This is used to start the thread in the tapping size hole. It tapers from no thread to full thread over two thirds of the thread length, with a short length of full thread at the top and can be used to completely thread holes through thin material.

Second tap. This is used to deepen threads started by the taper tap. It tapers for the first few threads only and can be used to finish threading holes drilled right through thicker material.

Plug tap. This is used to cut full threads to the bottom of blind holes and to thread right through thick material. It has no taper, but only a short chamfer to locate it in the hole.

The second tap is often left out of sets of taps and dies.

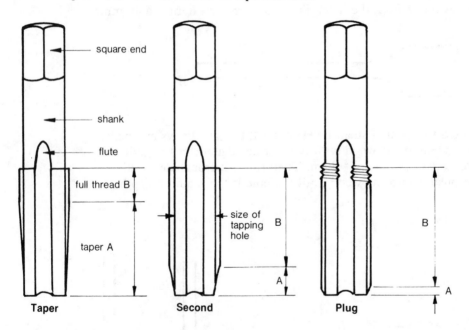

Tap wrench. The jaws of the wrench grip the corners of the square on the tap. The correct size wrench must be used to avoid damage to the jaws.

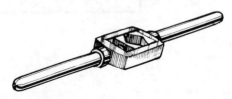

Circular split dies

These are for cutting external threads. They are held in a die stock and are made from hardened and tempered carbon or high speed steel. The first few threads are tapered on the side of the die which has the size stamped on, to assist in starting to cut the thread. The split enables the die to be opened slightly when taking the first cut, and to be closed for a second cut if the thread is too tight when screwed into the internal thread.

Die holder or stock. The circular split die fits into the die stock with the tapered side of the thread (shown by the writing on the die) on the open side of the stock, and the split in line with the centre screw. The centre screw is tightened to open the die to its full size and the side screws hold the die in the stock. To reduce the size of the die, slacken the centre screw and tighten the side screws.

10 Ways of working materials (1A) wasting–hand processes

This chapter explains how the most important cutting tools shown in chapter nine work, and gives advice on their correct use. Each section should therefore be used together with the parallel section in chapter nine.

Sawing

Principles of sawing

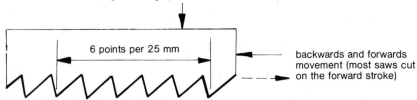

Notes.

1. It is important to select the correct shape and number of teeth per 25 mm for the type and section of material to be sawn.

2. Points per 25 mm are calculated by inclusive reckoning, so that on the example above there are six points per 25 mm although only five complete teeth are within the limit lines.

3. *Set.* Alternate teeth are bent to left and right to make the cutting edge slightly wider than the blade thickness. This prevents the saw blade from jamming in the cut or *kerf*.

Sawing wood

Tooth shapes.

Rip-saw teeth are for cutting along the grain.

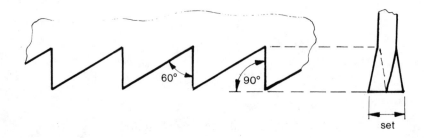

Cross-cut saw teeth are for cutting across the grain.

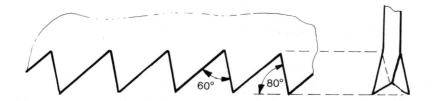

Rip-saw teeth are used only on the rip-saw, and have flat chisel-like cutting edges which remove small shavings. Rip-saw teeth cannot be used for cutting across the grain because they will tear the grain fibres instead of cutting them cleanly.

Cross-cut teeth are used on cross-cut, panel and back saws, and have knife-like cutting edges with needle points which cut the fibres at the sides of the kerf before crumbling the wood in the middle to sawdust. Cross-cut teeth will also cut along the grain, but more slowly than rip-saw teeth.

Sawing Metal

Choice of correct hacksaw blade.
You need to know:

1. Length of blade. The common sizes are 250 mm and 300 mm.

2. Type of blade. This can be made from either high speed steel or low tungsten steel. High speed steel blades are *all-hard* (hardened all over); low tungsten steel blades can be *all-hard* or *flexible* (hardened on the teeth only). Flexible blades do not break as easily as all-hard blades, but all-hard blades saw more accurately.

3. Number of teeth. At least three teeth must always touch the metal when sawing or teeth will be broken off.

Common numbers.
32 teeth per 25 mm – for metal less than 3 mm thick.
24 teeth per 25 mm – for metal 3 to 6 mm thick.
18 teeth per 25 mm – for metal more than 6 mm thick. (This is the best blade for general purposes.)

Soft materials require blades with larger teeth to prevent clogging.

Notes.
1. The teeth point forward and cut on the forward stroke.

2. The blade is held in tension in the frame.

3. The depth of cut is limited by the distance between the blade and the frame – usually about 100 mm.

With the blade turned through 90°, long cuts can be made provided that they are within the frame depth of the edge of the metal.

Set. To make the cutting edge slightly wider than the blade thickness, in order to prevent jamming in the kerf:

either   the teeth are set alternately to left and right with one straight tooth between each bent tooth;

or the teeth are set in a wavy line with several teeth bent one way and then several the other.

A new blade will not fit into a kerf started by an old blade which has lost some of its set. If a blade breaks, start a new cut from the other side with the new blade.

Sawing plastics

Any fine toothed saw can be used to saw soft or hard plastics provided that the work is well supported close to the kerf, and the minimum amount of pressure is applied. Take care not to let the saw slip and scratch the surface. For plastics, the teeth should be sharpened with the leading edges sloping farther backwards than for cutting wood.

How to saw

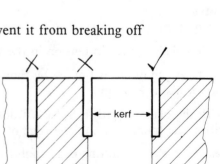

bench hook
gripped
in vice

1. Arrange the work so that you always saw vertically.

2. Support the work firmly and as close as possible to the kerf.

3. Stand correctly and grip the saw correctly.

For straight cuts at the bench:

The *grip* – thumb and first finger of the right hand guide the saw (left hand for left-handed). The other three fingers grip the handle.

The *stance* – left foot in line with the saw, right foot slightly behind and apart to give a firm comfortable position.

The right arm should be in line with the saw (reverse for left-handed).

For curved cuts at the bench:

The *grip* – both hands grip the handle.

The *stance* – feet apart. Stand squarely in front of the job.

4. When starting, use the thumb to guide the blade as it is drawn back to start a small cut. Start cutting at a low angle on a corner with as many teeth as possible in contact (at least three).

5. When sawing, use the full length of the blade. Use long steady strokes (one per second) and release the pressure on the return stroke. The spare hand is used to grip the other end of the hacksaw frame (and occasionally the other end of the tenon saw back when sawing joints).

6. When finishing a cut, support any waste material to prevent it from breaking off before it is cut cleanly through.

7. Sawing to the line. Where a sawn finish is required, saw on the waste side of the line and leave the line just showing with no waste between the line and the kerf.

Where a planed or filed finish is required, leave 2 mm waste between the line and the kerf.

If you saw, plane or file off the line, you have made the piece too small. Once the line has gone you cannot judge how much smaller the piece is than was originally intended.

kerf →

Planing

Principles of planing wood

The blade is a wedge which is driven into the wood. If the wedge angle is too great it will not cut, but if it is too small it will break. The wedge angle must therefore be a compromise between strength and sharpness.

The sole pressing on the wood prevents the blade from digging in too far and helps to prevent the wood from splitting.

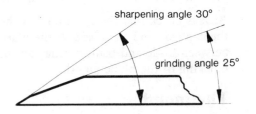

Sharpening and setting planes

Grinding angle. A plane blade is ground on one side only to an angle of 25°.

Sharpening angle. Because the tip of the grinding angle is weak and rough, it is honed down to an angle of 30° on an oilstone to give a smooth, strong cutting edge.

Sharpening leaves a small burr on the back of the blade which must be removed by rubbing the back flat on an oilstone. When the sharpening angle becomes too wide through repeated sharpening, or if the cutting edge is badly damaged, the blade must be reground.

Cutter shapes

The cutting edge of the *jack plane is slightly curved,* making the removal of waste wood a quicker and easier task, but leaving a slightly rippled surface.

Jointer and smoothing plane blades are straight across, with the corners rounded to prevent them scoring the work. They leave a flat surface.

Special planes have straight cutters with square corners except for shaped moulding cutters.

Cutter pitch

This is the angle the blade makes with the sole.

Bench planes, plough, combination and rebate planes have a 45° bed angle.

Low-angle planes (block, bullnose and shoulder) have a 20° bed angle, but because on these planes the blade is used bevel up, the effective pitch is 50°.

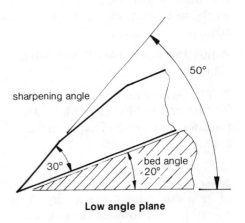

Low angle plane

A 50° pitch is particularly suitable for planing across end grain and for planing small surfaces.

The cap iron

This serves three purposes:

1. It stiffens the blade to prevent *chatter*.

2. It lifts and breaks the shaving soon after it has been cut to prevent *tearing*.

3. It guides the shaving upwards and forwards to prevent *clogging* of the mouth.

Adjusting the set of the cap iron. The edge of the cap iron is set back from the cutting edge about 1.5 mm for general work. To plane cross-grained wood or to obtain a very smooth finish, the set is reduced to 1.0 or 0.5 mm to lift and break the shavings more quickly.

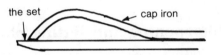

Always check that there are no gaps between the edge of the cap iron and the blade. If there are, shavings will jam between blade and badly fitting cap iron, and cause blocking of the plane mouth.

The mouth

The width of the mouth can be adjusted by moving *the frog* forwards or backwards with the adjusting screw, after loosening the clamping screws.

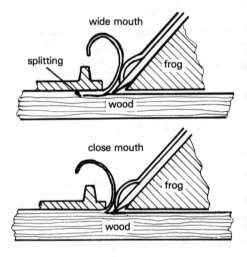

A *wide mouth* allows a thick shaving to be taken, but the wood may split ahead of the cutting edge, causing a thick shaving to either break away or clog the mouth. In either case, the surface of the wood will be torn.

A *very close mouth* will allow the plane to take only a very fine shaving without clogging, but will leave a good surface on the wood by preventing splitting ahead of the cutting edge.

Adjusting the blade. Before using a plane always look along the sole to check:

1. *The depth of cut*
The blade should stick out by a distance equal to the thickness of a sheet of paper. Adjust if necessary with the cutter adjusting wheel.

2. *Long cornering*
Make sure that the blade sticks out equally along the whole of its width. Adjust if necessary, by moving the lateral adjusting lever towards the long corner (the one sticking out furthest) to level the blade.

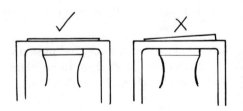

Planing awkward grain

To obtain a good finish on wood that has an awkward grain you must:

1. Have a sharp blade.

2. Have a closely set and well-fitted cap iron.

3. Set a close mouth.

4. Set the protruding blade as finely as possible.

5. After planing, finish with a scraper if necessary.

How to plane

1. Before planing:
Always check which way the grain of the wood runs and plane in the direction which smooths it down.

Always look along the sole of the plane and check that the blade is correctly set. (*See* Sharpening and setting.)

Support the work firmly, preferably flat on the bench top against the bench stop. Work held in the vice tends to slip.

2. When planing:
If the wood is twisted, plane off the high corners first. Press down on the toe of the plane at the start of the cut and on the heel at the end. Take special care not to slope the ends of the wood downwards, or to rock the plane.

Stand correctly and grip the plane correctly.

Stance. Stand in a position where you can plane without leaning over the bench; with the bench on your right if you are right-handed and on your left if you are left-handed.

Stand comfortably with your left foot parallel to the wood being planed (right foot if left-handed). Your weight should be on this foot at the end of the cut and your shoulder should be in line with the cut.

Grip. Thumb and first finger of right hand guide the plane; the other three fingers grip the handle (left hand for left-handed person). The other hand grips the knob.

When planing narrow edges, grip the toe of the plane instead of the knob and use the fingers as a fence.

Check frequently for flatness and squareness with straight edge and try-square or winding strips. It is easy to plane off too much. If necessary, use candle wax to lubricate the sole of the plane so that it slides over the wood more easily.

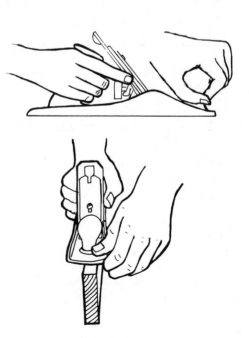

Stages in planing a piece of wood to size

1. Plane, test and mark the face-side.

Test for flatness with a straight edge and for twist (or wind) with winding strips. Aim the face-side mark towards the face-edge.

2. Plane, test and mark the face-edge.

Test for flatness with a straight edge and for squareness to the face-side with a try-square.

3. Gauge to width.

Put the stock of the marking gauge against the face-edge. Shade the waste

Plane to width, finishing when the gauge line is just visible all the way round.

4. Gauge to thickness.

Put the stock of the marking gauge against the face-side. Shade the waste

Plane to thickness, finishing when the gauge line is just visible all the way round. This line will be removed later during cleaning-up.

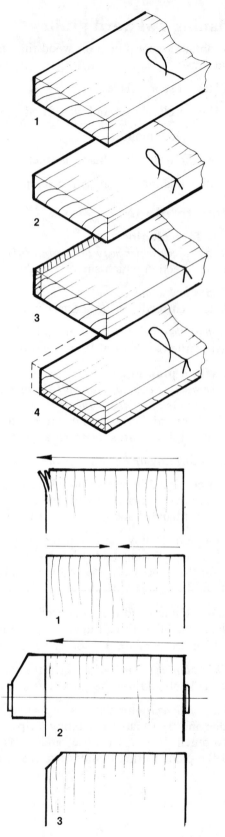

Planing end grain and the edges of man-made boards

Planing all the way across splits the wood.

This can be overcome in four ways:

1. By planing to the centre from each side on a wide board.

2. By clamping or glueing a block of scrapwood to one edge and cutting off its corner. You can then plane all the way across.

3. By cutting off a corner where this will not spoil the finished job.

4. By using a shooting board.

Planing plastics

Some plastics, particularly the edges of acrylic sheet, may be planed *with a very sharp and finely set plane.* The procedure for this is the same as for planing the end grain of wood because planing all the way across can result in chipped corners. Because acrylics chip easily, set the cap iron and mouth as closely as possible.

Suitable planes are bench planes (smoothing, jack and jointer) and low angle planes (block, shoulder and bull-nosed). (*See* Planing end grain and man-made boards.)

Plastics can often be more readily filed to shape. (*See* Filing plastics.)

Filing

Principles

Each tooth like a miniature cold chisel takes a separate cut and material is removed as fine particles (filings). The amount of material removed depends on the type and grade (or cut) of the teeth.

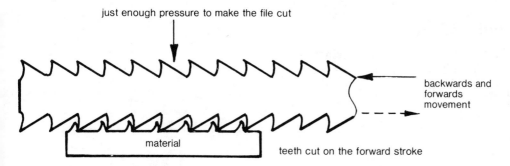

just enough pressure to make the file cut

backwards and forwards movement

material

teeth cut on the forward stroke

Common types of tooth

Single-cut files have one row of teeth cut an angle of 80°. They are particularly good for soft materials which tend to choke (pin) double-cut teeth, and for getting a smooth finish.

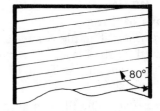

80°

Double-cut files have one row of teeth at 80° and a second row at 60°. They are general purpose files and are particularly good for medium and hard metals, and plastics.

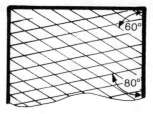

60°

80°

Curved tooth files e.g. dreadnought files are used for rapid removal of soft metals, such as copper and aluminium, and fibrous materials, such as wood and glass fibre, without clogging.

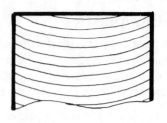

Rasps have individual teeth and are used for cutting wood and other soft materials. Rasps clogg easily as there is no clearance to help remove waste.

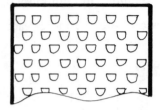

Common grades (or cuts) of teeth

Rough	approx. 20 teeth per 25 mm
Bastard	approx. 30 teeth per 25 mm
Second-cut	approx. 40 teeth per 25 mm
Smooth	approx. 60 teeth per 25 mm
Dead smooth	approx. 100 teeth per 25 mm

Common lengths of file

Measured from the shoulder to the end, these are: 100 mm, 150 mm, 200 mm, 250 mm and 300 mm.

Files are ordered by:

1. Length of blade.

2. Shape of blade.

3. Type of teeth.

4. Grade or cut of teeth.

How to file

1. Ways of filing.

(a) *Crossfiling*. The file is moved across the work using the full length of the blade. This is used for rapid removal of waste material, and for filing to a line but does not leave a smooth surface.

(b) *Drawfiling*. The file is moved sideways along the work and is used to obtain a smooth finish after cross-filing, but it does not remove much material.

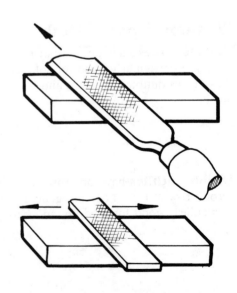

2. Holding the file.

(a) *Crossfiling* for a right-handed person (reverse for left-handed).

The *right hand* grips the handle with the thumb along the top. The *left hand*, for light filing, grips the end between the thumb and the first two fingers, but for heavy filing presses down on the end with the ball of the thumb. For accurate flat filing rest the thumb of the *left hand* on the middle of the blade, and the fingers on the end, to balance the file.

Stance. The left foot should be in line with the file, and the right foot slightly behind and apart, to give a firm comfortable position. The right arm must be in line with the file (reverse for left-handed). Rock the weight of the body from the back to the front foot as the file moves forward.

(b) *Drawfiling.* Grip across the blade, with one hand, each side of the work as close to the work as possible, placing thumbs against one edge of the blade, first fingers on top to balance it, and the other fingers against the other edge.

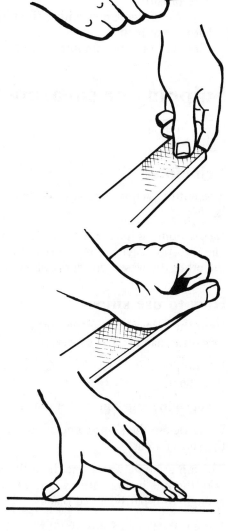

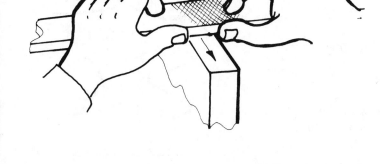

3. Support the work as close as possible to where you are going to file, usually in the vice, with the minimum amount of metal projecting. Thin sheet can be held in a filing block or pinned to a wood block.

4. When filing:

Use the full length of the blade.

> Press down on the file, push forward without rocking, and lift at the end of the stroke. Use just enough pressure to make the file cut.
> Work evenly across the whole surface.
> Use rough or bastard-cut files to remove waste almost to the line; finish with second-cut or smooth files.
> Test the surface for flatness and squareness frequently.

5. Cleaning the file. Small pieces of material become trapped in the teeth of the file. This is called *pinning*. It causes bad scratch marks on the surface being filed.

Remove these by brushing across the blade with a file card (a stiff short-bristled wire brush).

Remove difficult pins with a file pick (a pointed piece of brass). Do not use a hard metal point.

Finally, to reduce pinning when finishing a surface, rub chalk onto the file.

Snipping or shearing

Principles

The cutting action is a *shearing action* and the cutting angle is 75°.

Check. Some snips are left- or right-hand cutting only. In one direction such snips will tend to cut over the line, in the other the waste will curl away easily.

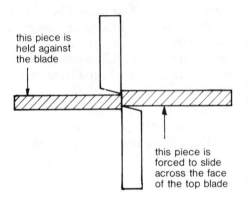

this piece is held against the blade

this piece is forced to slide across the face of the top blade

How to use snips

Hold the snips with the base of the thumb and the fingers round the handle, and squeeze.

Do not put any fingers between the handles. You could trap them.

To open the snips, push them forward into the work.

Do not close the snips completely except at a corner or at the end of a cut.

To stop accurately at a line, hold the nose of the snips level with the line before cutting. You cannot stop accurately enough with partly-closed blades.

For accuracy, in cutting complex shapes, first remove most of the waste, and then cut to the line.

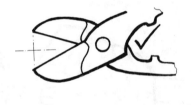

Outside curves.
1. Remove waste to within 5 mm of the line.

2. Cut exactly to waste side of the line.

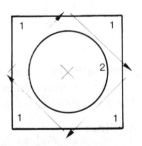

Inside curves.
1. Drill a hole in the centre.

2. Work outwards in a spiral to the final line.

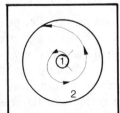

Cutting threads

Principles

Threading means cutting external threads with a die.

The diameter of the rod being threaded must be the same as the required screw diameter.

The end of the rod is tapered to the core diameter for a length equal to the screw diameter to help start the die.

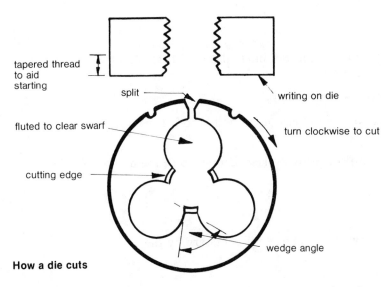

tapered thread
to aid
starting

split

writing on die

fluted to clear swarf

turn clockwise to cut

cutting edge

wedge angle

core dia

screw dia

How a die cuts

Tapping is cutting internal threads with taper, second and plug taps.

Clearance size hole – to allow a plain or threaded rod to slide straight through, drill a hole slightly larger than the core diameter.

Tapping size hole – to prepare a hole for tapping, drill slightly larger than the core diameter. (Recommended clearance and tapping sizes are given overleaf.)

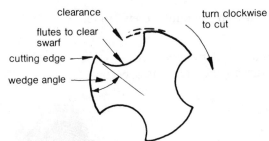

clearance

flutes to clear
swarf

cutting edge

wedge angle

turn clockwise
to cut

How a tap cuts

Cutting lubricants for threading

mild steel	thread cutting grease
aluminium	paraffin
copper	paraffin
brass	none
cast iron	none
plastics	none or cold water

Tapping and clearance drill sizes

Thread size	Tapping	Clearance
M2	1.6 mm	2.5 mm
M2.5	2.1 mm	3.0 mm
M3	2.5 mm	3.5 mm
M4	3.3 mm	4.5 mm
M5	4.2 mm	5.5 mm
M6	5.0 mm	6.5 mm
M8	6.8 mm	8.5 mm
M10	8.5 mm	10.5 mm
M12	10.2 mm	13.0 mm

How to cut threads

General points.

1. Because the die is adjustable and taps are not, cut the internal thread first and then adjust the external thread, to give a good fit.

2. Use the correct cutting lubricant. (*See* the list above.)

3. When starting, press down on the tap or die to make it cut and keep it square to avoid a drunken thread.

4. Small taps and dies (smaller than 8 mm) are easily broken. Do not force them. Remove to clean out swarf frequently.

Tapping.

5. Drill the correct tapping size hole.

6. Use the correct taper tap, held in a tapwrench, followed if necessary by the second and plug taps.

Threading.

7. Taper the end of the rod.

8. Put the correct die in a die stock with the unwritten side of the die against the shoulder of the stock and the writing showing.

9. Place the die, written side down, onto the rod.

10. For the first cut, tighten the middle die adjusting screw to open the die to its maximum size, before tightening the two outer screws to keep the die in place.

11. After cutting the thread, test the fit of the internal thread onto the previously cut external thread.

12. If it is too tight, slacken the middle screw and tighten the outer screws to close the die, before making the second cut.

13. When the thread is to size, turn the die over and screw it down, writing upwards, to complete the cutting of the final few turns which have only been partly cut by the tapered section of the die.

Drilling

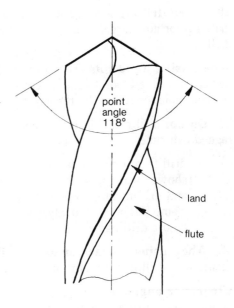

Principles of the twist drill

The V-shaped *chisel edge* in the centre of the drill nose does not cut the material being drilled because the drill speed at the very centre is zero. It is simply forced into the material by the pressure put onto the drill.

The *cutting lips* should be seen as two chisel or plane blades which remove a shaving (known as swarf) as they revolve. They do all the cutting by a wedge action.

The *flutes* act as a conveyor to carry away the swarf from the lips. They do not cut at all.

The *land* or leading edge of each flute is made the exact diameter of the drill, while the rest of the flutes are made slightly smaller to reduce friction. The land helps to keep the drill straight in the hole.

Cutting angles

Point angle – 118° for general purposes.
        – 140° for plastics which can be cut with a knife (usually thermoplastics).
        – 60° for plastics which cannot be cut with a knife (usually thermosetting plastics).

Note. To prevent thin sheets of any material breaking or bending when drilled, ensure that the whole length of the cutting lips is in contact with the sheet before the chisel edge breaks through. This often involves using a drill with a bigger point angle than that recommended for normal drilling of the material. Drills ground to a 140° point angle for thermoplastics are useful for all thin materials.

How to drill

1. Support the work firmly and safely. Never hold work in your fingers when using any powered drilling machine. (*See* Holding tools.) Many plastics will crack unless well supported.

2. Make sure that you will not drill through into anything except scrap wood.

3. Make sure the drill is tight in the chuck. On a key-operated chuck, check with the key in at least two of the three holes. Never leave a chuck key in the chuck. Always close the safety chuck guard if fitted.

4. Centre punch metal before drilling, but not wood or plastics.

5. Keep drills sharp.

6. Apply just enough pressure to make the drill cut. Too much pressure can break drills; too little can cause rubbing which blunts them. Use a slow feed on plastics to avoid overheating. *Select the correct speed and cutting fluid* if needed.

7. Withdraw the drill frequently to remove swarf and prevent binding.

8. Reduce the pressure as the drill breaks through, or it may jam and break.

9. If the drill starts off centre, stop immediately and tap the centre over to the correct position with a centre punch or small round nose chisel.

10. When drilling a large hole in metal or plastics, first drill a pilot hole larger than the chisel edge of the large drill.

When using wood bits drill to the full size in one step because the screw point cannot centre the drill over an existing hole, or screw the bit into the wood.

11. Do not drill right through wood as this will leave a ragged exit hole;

either   drill from one side with a bit until the screw point shows through, reverse, locate the point in the hole, and drill from the other side,

or   clamp scrap wood firmly against the exit hole side before drilling.

12. When using a brace or hand drill it easier and more accurate to drill horizontally than vertically.

Clearance angle. There must be the correct clearance behind each cutting edge to allow the cutting lips to penetrate the material. This is 12° for general purposes and 15° to 20° for plastics.

Chisel point angle. The angle between the chisel point and the cutting lip is always 130°.

Principles of the new pattern centre bit and Jennings bit

1. The *screw point* pulls the bit into the timber.

2. The *spurs* scribe the diameter of the hole. This cuts through the grain fibres in advance of the cutters to prevent splitting.

3. The *cutters* lift the chips and pass them up the *twist or auger*.

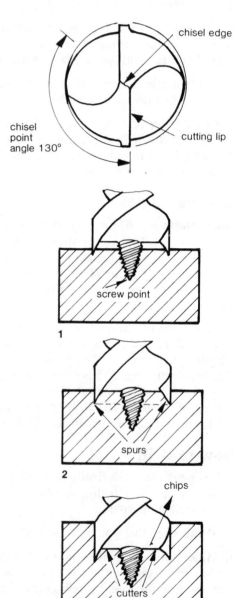

156

Chiselling

Chiselling wood (1) paring

Principles of paring. Paring is chiselling using hand pressure only. (Compare with principles of planing wood.) The wedge shape of the cutting edge is driven between the fibres of the grain.

Paring with the grain splits the wood instead of cutting it unless a very thin chip is taken, and it is difficult to control the thickness of the chip removed. Therefore, a plane should be used instead whenever possible.

Paring across the grain gives a clean cut because wood does not split across the grain, and the fibres separate and curl away easily, provided that the sides of the cut have been sawn first to prevent splintering.

Paring across the end grain also gives a clean cut.

How to pare

Horizontal paring. Hold the chisel in the palm of the hand, rest the other hand against the bench if possible, and guide the blade through the clenched hand.

Vertical paring. Hold the chisel like a dagger, rest the other clenched hand on the work, and guide the blade with the first finger and thumb. When chiselling vertically always work on a protective chiselling board.

Using a mallet. If too much effort is needed to cut using hand pressure, use a mallet. When using a mallet, always clamp the work down and always position the chisel with both hands before striking it with the mallet.

Chiselling wood (2) mortising

Principles of mortising. Mortising is cutting rectangular holes in wood using mallet blows to drive the chisel into the wood.

Cuts are made across the grain. The wedge shape of the cutting edge moves the chip sideways as it cuts.

How to mortise

General points.
1. Cut the mortise before the tenon, because it is easier to adjust the width of the tenon to fit the mortise than vice versa.

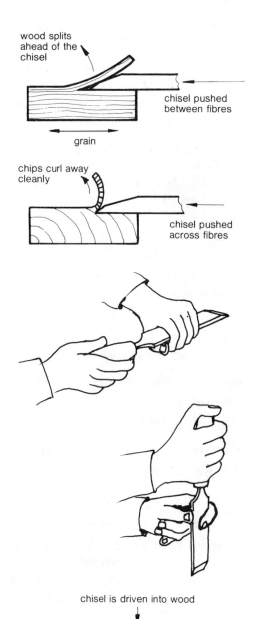

wood splits ahead of the chisel

chisel pushed between fibres

grain

chips curl away cleanly

chisel pushed across fibres

chisel is driven into wood

grinding angle pushes against wood and moves chisel horizontally

chip is cut off

grain

2. The width of the mortise and tenon should be chosen to match the available widths of mortise chisel – usually 6, 8, 10 and 12 mm.

3. When mortising near the end of a piece of wood, leave extra waste on the end to help prevent splitting, and to enable the ends to be sawn off square after glueing.

4. When mortising thin wood, clamp scrapwood on each side to prevent splitting, or clamp it in the vice making sure that it is well supported underneath.

5. Use both hands to locate the chisel correctly before striking sharply with the mallet once only.

6. Always cut across the grain. Chiselling along the grain splits the wood and leaves the finished mortise with ragged sides and irregular width.

Starting to mortise.
7. Press the chisel into the wood along the ends of the mortise to make a shallow cut. This helps to prevent accidental splitting beyond the line, especially when removing waste.

8. Start cutting in the middle of the mortise and take small bites, working to one end of the mortise, with the grinding angle facing in the direction of the cuts. (*See* Principles of mortising.)

9. Leave 5 mm waste at the end so that the end of the mortise will not be damaged during cutting.

10. Repeat 8 and 9 from the centre to the other end.

11. Repeat as necessary to reach the required depth, levering out loose waste. Do *not* try to lever out partly loosened waste, as this splits the wood.

12. If mortising right through, cut half-way from each side.

Finishing.
13. Cut the waste at each end of the mortise back to the line, taking small bites.

Grinding and sharpening chisels

Firmer chisels – for general purposes the wedge angles are the same as for a plane
– grinding angle is 25°.
– sharpening angle is 30°.

Mortise chisels – for heavier work the wedge angle can be increased to strengthen it.
– grinding angle is 30°.
– sharpening angle is 35°.

Chiselling metal

Principles. The cutting edge is a wedge which is driven into the metal. The angle depends on the hardness of the metal being cut. For example, with mild steel use 60°, brass and copper use 45°, and aluminium use 30°.

Safety. The head is left soft where it is struck by the hammer because if two hard surfaces were struck together they might shatter, causing dangerous chips to break off and fly across the room.

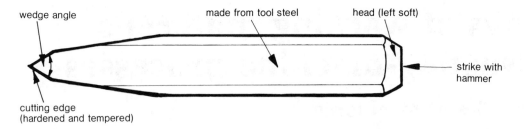

wedge angle

made from tool steel

head (left soft)

strike with hammer

cutting edge
(hardened and tempered)

This soft head will mushroom after repeated use, leaving a dangerous rough edge which might cut your hand or cause pieces to break off and fly across the room. Therefore:

1. Keep the head ground to its correct shape.

2. Protect your eyes.

How to chisel metal

1. Always chisel on a soft metal block (e.g. cutting face of anvil, chiselling block).

2. Grip the chisel firmly in one hand with thumb and fingers clenched round it.

3. Place the cutting edge on the work, and strike with the hammer held in the other hand.

4. Watch the cutting edge *not* the head of the chisel or the hammer.

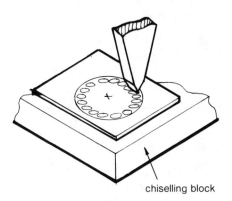

chiselling block

Cutting.

1. Place the cutting edge on the cutting line (leaving a small amount for filing to the finished size).

2. Cut lightly along the line to start the cut.

3. Repeat using heavier blows to complete the cut.

4. Cut from both sides if necessary.

5. When cutting internal shapes, drill a series of holes just inside the line, and cut through the waste between them to remove most of the waste quickly.

Finish by chiselling and filing.

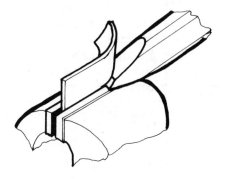

Shearing.

1. Clamp the metal in the vice with the cutting line just showing above the jaws.

2. Hold the chisel with the cutting edge at 30° to the cutting line and one side of the wedge angle resting on the top of the vice jaw.

3. Strike with the hammer to shear the metal just on the waste side of the line.

Chipping is the removal of waste metal from a surface, e.g. removing rivet and bolt heads, and cleaning up castings.

11 Ways of working materials (1B) wasting-machine processes

The principles of machining

A machine tool is any power-driven machine used to cut and shape materials. Industrial machines are basically the same as school machines, but they are usually larger and more complicated. Industry uses machine tools to produce smooth, accurate surfaces.

Machining is done by removing chips from the material, using either cutting tools or abrasives, mounted on a machine tool. The chips produced can range from fine dust when polishing or sanding to continuous thick swarf from a lathe tool which is cutting steel.

In the chart below we have arranged the most used types of machines into three groups according to the type of cutter used on each (single-point, multiple-point and abrasive). We have then explained briefly how each machine and each type of cutter works.

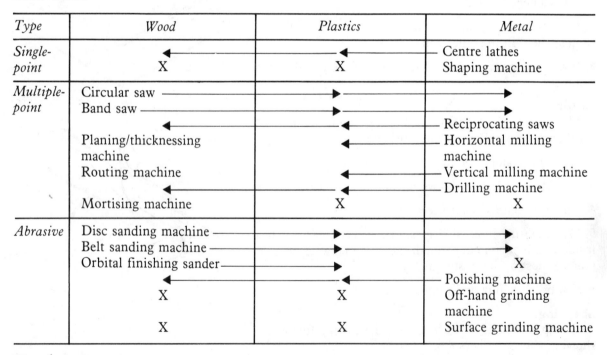

Type	Wood	Plastics	Metal
Single-point	X	X	Centre lathes Shaping machine
Multiple-point	Circular saw Band saw Planing/thicknessing machine Routing machine Mortising machine	X	Reciprocating saws Horizontal milling machine Vertical milling machine Drilling machine X
Abrasive	Disc sanding machine Belt sanding machine Orbital finishing sander X X	X X	X Polishing machine Off-hand grinding machine Surface grinding machine

The chart shows the similarities between machines used for different materials, even where names differ, and also those used for only one material.

Single-point cutting

1. Turning – Centre lathe (wood, metal, plastics).

A single-point cutting tool is moved against work revolving in a centre lathe. The tool is hand-held on a wood turning lathe and mounted in a toolpost on a metal turning lathe. Plastics are turned on a metal turning lathe. A lathe produces cylindrical shapes.

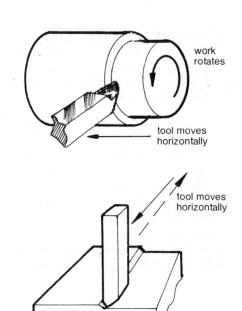

work rotates

tool moves horizontally

2. Shaping – Shaping machine (metal).
A single-point cutting tool moves in a straight line across a block of metal, cutting on the forward stroke, and sliding over the metal on the return stroke. The work is moved the width of one cut sideways after each forward stroke.

A shaper produces flat surfaces, vee-grooves, slots, keyways, etc., and is used only for one-off metal shaping jobs.

tool moves horizontally

work moves in steps

Multiple-point cutting

1. Horizontally rotating cutters –
Planing/thicknessing machine (wood)
Horizontal milling machine (metal, plastics)
Circular saw (wood, metal, plastics)

In all these machines, the work is moved against a horizontally rotating cutter with at least two cutting points. Circular saws cut material into strips and planers produce flat surfaces on wood, while horizontal millers do the same on metal and plastics, and in addition cut grooves, rebates and more complex shapes.

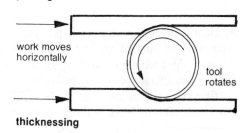

planing

work moves horizontally

tool rotates

thicknessing

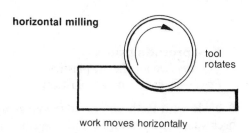

horizontal milling

tool rotates

work moves horizontally

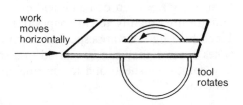

circular sawing

work moves horizontally

tool rotates

2. Vertically rotating cutters –

Drilling machine (wood, metal, plastics)
Routing machine (wood, plastics)
Vertical milling machine (metal, plastics)
Mortising machine (wood)

In all these machines, the cutter revolves vertically. In the drilling and mortising machines the revolving tool moves down against a stationary workpiece to make a hole. In the vertical milling machine the work moves against the revolving cutter, while the router is hand-held and is moved across the surface of the work as the cutter revolves. The miller and router both produce grooves, rebates, chamfers, etc. The vertical milling machine can also be used as an accurate drilling machine for cutting holes too large for drilling and to make flat surfaces.

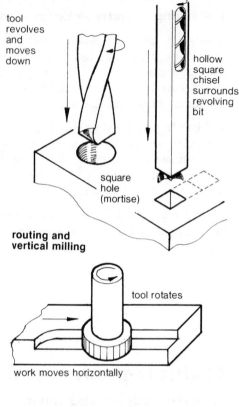

drilling　　**mortising**

tool revolves and moves down

hollow square chisel surrounds revolving bit

square hole (mortise)

routing and vertical milling

tool rotates

work moves horizontally

3. Band saws (wood, metal, plastics).

The work is pushed against a continuous band with teeth on one edge, which is rotating round two or more wheels. Band saws usually cut vertically, but for heavy metal cutting they sometimes cut horizontally. They are able to cut both straight lines and curves in most materials.

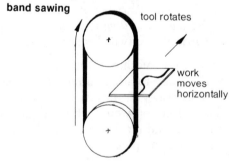

band sawing

tool rotates

work moves horizontally

4. Reciprocating saws –

Jig saw (wood, metal, plastics)
Power hacksaw (metal, plastics)

A blade with teeth on one edge moves up and down or backwards and forwards, and is pushed against the work. The power hacksaw is mounted horizontally and makes straight cuts. It is mainly used for cutting lengths of metal to size. Jig saws can be hand-held or mounted on a stand, and are used mainly to cut shapes out of sheet material. Hand-held jig saws are especially useful for cutting large holes because they can be started in a small drilled hole at any point on a sheet, and for cutting sheets too large for the bandsaw.

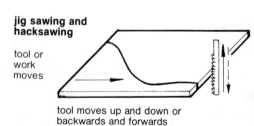

jig sawing and hacksawing

tool or work moves

tool moves up and down or backwards and forwards

Abrasive cutting

1. Vertically rotating abrasive wheels –
Disc sanders (wood, metal, plastics)
Off-hand grinders (metal)
Surface grinding machines (metal)
Polishing machines (wood, metal, plastics)

Disc sanding machines use suitable abrasive sheets mounted on a backing disc or flexible pad. Polishing machines use abrasive compounds (polishes) applied to cloth mops. Grinding machines use wheels made from abrasive powders cemented together into discs. The workpiece is pressed against the abrasive cutter and a small amount of material is removed. These machines are mainly used for cleaning-up and finishing work. The surface grinding machine is a precision machine which grinds hard metals to an accurate smooth finish.

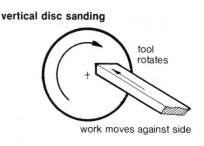

vertical disc sanding

tool rotates

work moves against side

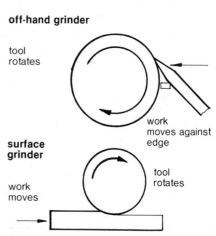

off-hand grinder

tool rotates

work moves against edge

surface grinder

work moves

tool rotates

2. Horizontally rotating abrasive wheels –
Disc sanders (wood, metal, plastics)
Orbital finishing sanders (wood)

Horizontally rotating disc sanders are usually hand-held. They are moved across surfaces which are too large to press against a mounted vertical disc.

Orbital finishing sanders have an abrasive sheet mounted on a soft rectangular pad which is rotated by a cam. This rotates it in a way which has the same effect as lots of miniature sanding discs held perfectly level, and makes it possible to produce a very smooth surface.

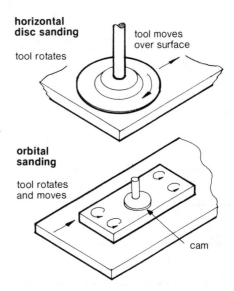

horizontal disc sanding

tool moves over surface

tool rotates

orbital sanding

tool rotates and moves

cam

3. Belt sanding machine.
A continuous abrasive band rotates over two rollers and is supported between the rollers by a pressure pad.

The machine can be hand-held for sanding large surfaces, or mounted either vertically or horizontally on a stand, so that small workpieces can be pressed against it.

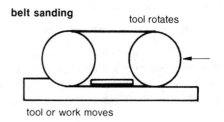

belt sanding

tool rotates

tool or work moves

163

The cutting action of machine tool cutters

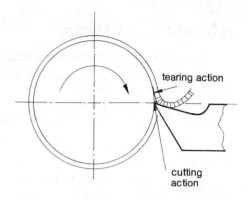

tearing action

cutting action

Single-point cutters

Although we have shown the action of lathe tools here, the same rules apply to other machine tool cutters, regardless of whether the tool or the work moves, or whether we are machining a flat surface (as when shaping), or a rotating cylindrical surface (as when turning). Multiple-point tools should be seen as a series of single-point tools.

The cutting action consists of the cutting edge of the tool forcing its way into the material and tearing away a strip by a wedge action. If a heavy roughing cut is taken, most of the chip presses behind the cutting edge and is torn off before the cutting edge reaches it. This leaves a rough surface which is cleaned up by the extreme tip of the tool immediately afterwards.

On a light finishing cut only the second part of the action operates leaving a much smoother surface.

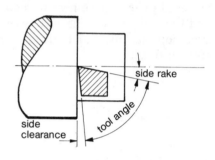

side rake

side clearance

tool angle

Tool angles. No cutting tool will work unless *clearance angles* are provided to allow the cutting edge to reach the work. Without them it will only rub against the surface.

In addition the correct tool angle is needed for the material being cut and this is obtained by varying the *rake angles*.

These angles are shown below.

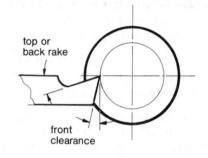

top or back rake

front clearance

	Rake angles	Clearance angles
Aluminium and nylon	30-40°	10°
Brass	0°	10°
Mild steel	15-20°	8°
Cast iron	0°	6°
Tool steel	10°	6°

Side clearance allows the cutting edge to advance freely without the heel of the tool rubbing.

Front clearance allows the tool to be fed freely into the work.

Top rake is the backward slope from the cutting edge, and controls the cutting action and chip formation.

Side rake increases the keenness of the cutting edge.

The *tool angle* or angle of keenness is the shape of the wedge which actually penetrates the metal. For example, this is approximately 62° for mild steel. This can be compared with the wedge angles of hand tools in chapter ten where for example, the angle for cutting mild steel with a cold chisel is 60°.

The softer the material being turned, the smaller the tool angle needed to prevent the tool from breaking. The smaller the tool angle, the more easily the tool will cut. The tool angle is therefore a compromise between strength and ease of cutting.

Materials (such as aluminium) which stick to the tool, need increased rake to help prevent sticking. Materials (such as brass) which produce chips instead of swarf, do not need any top rake and have a flat top, or even a slight negative rake.

Multiple-point cutters

Multiple-point cutters have each tooth carefully designed to give the correct clearance and rake angles, in the same way as single-point tools, and each tooth removes a separate chip. Details of the twist drill which is an example of a two-point cutter are given in chapter ten and a milling cutter is shown below.

Each tooth has a strong wedge angle, and a short land with just enough first clearance to prevent rubbing (about 3°), to give maximum support to the cutting edge. Each tooth would have a positive rake for milling steel or aluminium and a negative rake for brass, as on a lathe tool.

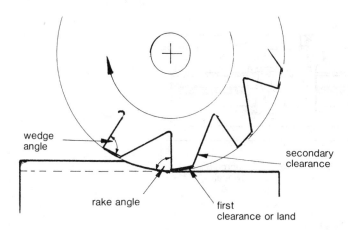

Abrasive cutters

Most abrasive cutting is done with grinding wheels. These consist of millions of grains of very hard abrasive known as the grit, glued together in a bonding material known as the matrix and cast into the required shape. Both the size and the type of the abrasive grains, and the type and the strength of the matrix can be varied to suit the materials being ground. A wheel with a soft matrix is used to grind hard materials and vice versa.

The grit provides thousands of minute cutting points on the circumference of the wheel. When these become worn down and clogged with metal particles the wheel is *dressed* with either a diamond point, or a star wheel dressing tool which has several very hard toothed wheels. The dressing tool is pressed against the revolving wheel to true it up and expose sharp new abrasive grains.

Safety. When using the off-hand grinding machine make sure that the tool rest is set to centre height, and that the gap between the wheel and the rest is as small as possible. Otherwise work could be carried down between the wheel and the rest, causing damage to the wheel and the work, and possible injury to the operator.

On most machines the rest can be set at any required angle for grinding tool shapes. Always wear safety glasses when grinding. Whenever possible grind on the circumference of the wheel because the wheel is less able to withstand side forces and the side of the wheel is difficult to dress.

Similar abrasive grits bonded to paper or cloth, or cast in a flexible matrix are used to make the abrasive discs and pads used on hand-held sanding and grinding machines.

The centre lathe

The centre lathe is used to turn accurate cylindrical and conical shapes, to cut flat surfaces across the end of pieces of material and to bore holes.

Parts of the lathe

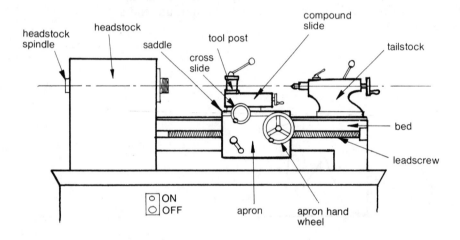

Mounting work in the lathe

Three jaw self-centring chuck. This is a quick and easy way of holding round and hexagonal shapes. Once removed work can be put back in the chuck with reasonable (but *not* perfect)accuracy. Its main uses are, therefore, for one-setting operations and preliminary work such as centre drilling, before mounting between centres.

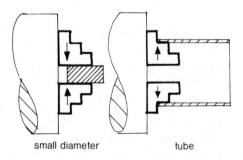

small diameter   tube

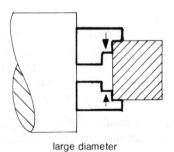

large diameter

The three jaws are moved together by a scroll, and the curve of the grooves on the back is different on each. Therefore, they are numbered and must always be replaced in order. There are two sets of jaws. One is for holding large diameter work, and the other for small diameters and gripping the inside of hollow work.

Always clean and lightly oil the spindle and chuck threads before mounting the chuck. Tighten the chuck using hand pressure only.

The four jaw independent chuck. The four jaws are moved independently one at a time. This allows a much stronger grip to be exerted on the work, and the jaws are reversible so that one set can be used for all sizes of internal and external gripping. Work can be set-up very accurately, but cannot easily be put back once removed. It can be used to hold round, square or irregular shapes, and for drilling and boring off set holes.

The face-plate. The face of the plate has a series of holes and radial slots so that irregular shaped work, such as castings, can be bolted onto it.

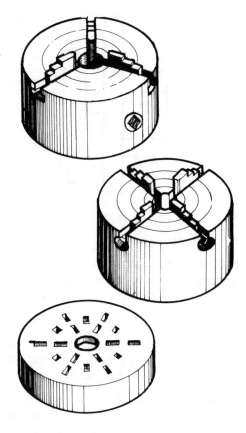

Centres. Lathe centres can be put into the headstock spindle or tailstock barrel. (*See* Combination centre drill.)

The headstock centre turns with the work and is not subject to friction. It can therefore be left soft, and is known as the live or soft centre.

The *tailstock centre* remains stationary while the work rotates. This causes friction, and so the centre must be hardened and grease must be used to lubricate it. It is known as the dead or hard centre.

On a *revolving centre*, the centre is mounted in a bearing which allows it to rotate with the work to prevent friction.

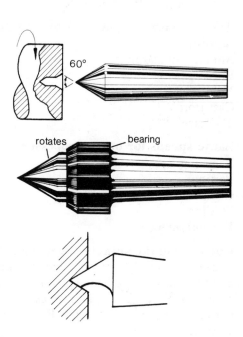

On a *half centre* part of the centre point has been ground away so that the tool can cut up to the centre hole of the work while it is being supported by the tailstock.

Turning between centres
The main advantages of turning between centres are that the work can easily be removed and replaced accurately, and that the whole length of the work can be machined simply by turning it round in the lathe.

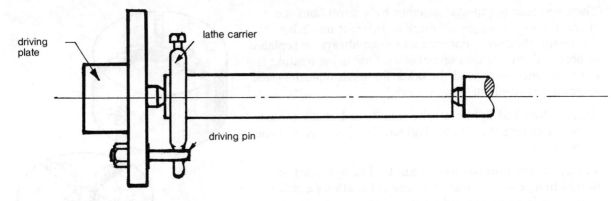

driving plate

lathe carrier

driving pin

To set up work between centres:

1. Centre drill the ends of the workpiece.

2. Screw a driving plate and pin onto the headstock spindle. Put a soft centre into the end of the headstock spindle and a hard or revolving centre into the tailstock.

3. Clamp a lathe carrier onto the work.

4. Mount the work between centres, lubricating the hard centre if used with grease. Make sure that the work turns freely but without any slackness.

Choosing the correct lathe speed.
The softer the material being turned the faster the lathe speed. For a heavy roughing cut, the lathe speed is slower than for a light finishing cut.

Average cutting speeds in metres per minute for turning.

Aluminium and nylon	300 m/minute
Brass	90 m/minute
Mild steel	30 m/minute
Cast iron	20 m/minute
Tool steel	15 m/minute

Lathe speeds for other processes.

Knurling	1/3 cutting speed
Parting	1/3 cutting speed
Centre drilling	Full speed
Drilling	3/4 cutting speed
Using form tools	1/2 cutting speed

Calculating the spindle speed in R.P.M.
Because cutting speeds are calculated in metres per minute and the speed of the lathe spindle is measured in revolutions per minute, it is necessary to convert the cutting speed to the correct R.P.M. for the diameter of work being turned.

$$\text{Spindle speed (in R.P.M.)} = \frac{\text{Cutting speed in m/minute} \times 100}{\pi \times \text{diameter of work in millimetres}}$$

Lathe tool shapes

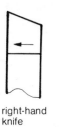 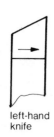   

right-hand knife   left-hand knife   round nose   parting   form

Round nosed tools give a smoother finish than pointed tools, but larger cuts can be taken with a pointed tool. A knife tool is necessary to turn to a sharp shoulder, and can be used to take roughing cuts. It must have a slight radius at its tip, produced by using a slip stone, to prevent the extreme tip from burning or breaking off and to improve finish.

When roughing with a knife tool set it to give the correct approach angle as shown, with the tool angle trailing, so that swarf is directed away from the work, and so that it will swing safely out of the way without digging into the material if the tool comes loose.

Right-hand knife tools can be used to face off the right-hand end of a bar, to cut to a right-handed shoulder, or to cut along the work from right to left.

Left-hand knife tools can be used to cut to a left-handed shoulder or cut along the work from left to right.

Round nosed tools can be used to cut in either direction and to cut to left- or right-handed shoulders where a radiused corner is wanted.

Parting tool. *See* parting off.

Form tools can be specially ground to produce any required shape, such as the curved top of a turned screwdriver handle.

Setting up lathe tools

The correct height for general purposes is to set the tool at centre height as shown.

Always support the tool in the toolpost, as near to the cutting edge as possible. A large overhang increases the risk of vibration or chatter, causing poor finish, inaccurate work and the risk of tool breakage. A tool which is set too *high* will simply rub against the work without cutting. A tool which is set too *low* will dig into the work and try to go underneath it. This may bend the work or break the tool.

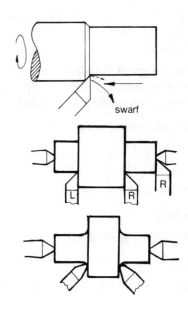

swarf

Setting up lathe tools

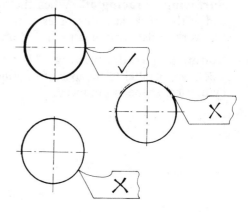

169

Cutting fluids. The main functions of a cutting fluid are:

1. To cool the work and the tool by carrying away the heat generated by friction during cutting.

2. To lubricate the point of contact between the work and the tool to reduce friction.

It also helps to prevent welding of the chip to the tool and tool breakdown, improves surface finish, gives some protection against corrosion and washes away the swarf.

The correct cutting fluids are:

Aluminium	none, soluble oil or paraffin
Brass	none
Mild steel	soluble oil
Cast iron	none
Tool steel	soluble oil

Soluble oil is a mixture of one part soluble oil to lubricate and ten parts water to cool the work. This makes a white milky suds.

Getting a good finish.
The factors which combine to give a good finish to a piece of work when making a final finishing cut are:

1. A high cutting speed.

2. A slow tool feed, ensuring that the tool moves uniformly without any stops or starts.

3. A round nosed tool.

4. A light cut.

5. A highly polished tool.

6. The correct lubricant.

All these factors should be checked before taking the final cut.

Lathework processes

Surfacing or facing off. When the tool moves across the end of the work, at right angles to the axis of rotation of the work, a flat surface is produced on the end.

Sliding or parallel turning. When the tool moves sideways, parallel to the axis of rotation of the work, a cylindrical shape is produced.

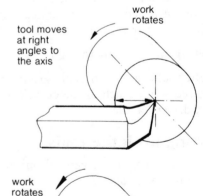

work rotates

tool moves at right angles to the axis

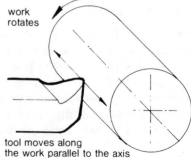

work rotates

tool moves along the work parallel to the axis

Taper turning. When the tool moves along the work, at an angle to the axis of rotation, a conical shape is produced.

(a) *To turn a very short chamfer* use a form tool.

(b) *To turn a short taper* rotate the compound slide to the required angle, tighten the clamping screws, and move the tool with the compound slide handle. The maximum length of taper which can be turned is limited to the length of feed on the slide.

(c) *To turn a long gradual taper* offset the tailstock or use a taper turning attachment. The work must be mounted between centres for this.

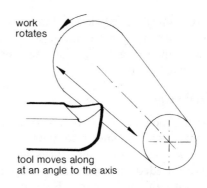

work rotates

tool moves along at an angle to the axis

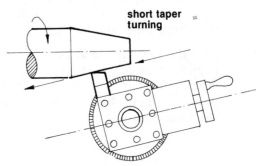

short taper turning

Drilling in the lathe. This is more accurate than drilling on a drilling machine. Because it is not possible to centre punch work held in the lathe before drilling, we use a centre drill instead.

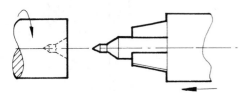 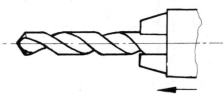

Boring

When a single-point tool is used to turn inside an existing hole the process is called boring. Special care is needed in measuring the depth of the hole and plotting the position of the tool accurately. Light cuts only should be taken if using a long unsupported boring tool.

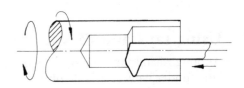

Parting-off

A narrow tool is fed into the work, exactly square to the axis, to cut it to the correct length and face it off at the same time.

The tool is offset to the left so that you can part off as close to the chuck as possible. The sides of the tool taper 1° or 2° from the cutting edge to the back to prevent the tool jamming in the groove. The sides also taper 2° from top to bottom and the tool has a front clearance of about 5°.

The top rake is 5° for steel and aluminium, flat for cast iron and 2° negative for brass. The cutting edge slopes so that the workpiece is cut off cleanly, and the pip remains on the spare material where it is faced off.

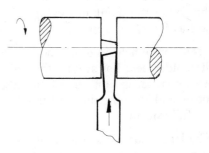

171

The tool must be fed slowly and smoothly by hand. Withdraw the tool frequently and move it slightly sideways before feeding in again so that the groove cut is slightly wider than the tool.

Knurling

Knurling tools are used to *press* (not cut) a diamond or straight pattern of lines into metal, usually to provide a grip. Two very hard steel wheels mounted in a swivelling head are needed to make a diamond knurl, but only a single wheel for straight knurling. Fine, medium, and coarse knurling tools are available. Oil should be used to lubricate the wheels when knurling steel.

Feed the tool into the work and adjust it until the impression made by the wheels is equal and even from left to right. Then increase the pressure until a full knurled print is being made on the metal, and slowly move the tool along the work.

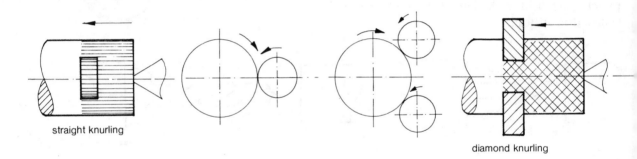

straight knurling

diamond knurling

Using taps and dies in the lathe

Although hand taps and dies should not be used in the lathe under power, it is helpful to use the lathe as a means of ensuring that threads are cut square.

Taps can be held in the tailstock chuck or in the usual tap wrench with the tailstock centre located in a centre hole in the end of the shank of the tap. Use taper, second and plug taps as for hand tapping.

Dies can be held in a tailstock die holder or in the usual die holder held flat against the end of the tailstock barrel. A short taper is first turned on the end of the work to help locate and start the die, and the first cut is made with the die fully open.

The lathe must be switched off and the spindle must be out of gear, so that the chuck can be rotated by hand using the chuck key as a handle. Use the same cutting lubricants as for hand threading. Always cut the internal thread first if possible, so that the external thread can be adjusted to fit it.

172

12 Ways of working materials (2) deformation

Laminating

When two or more layers of any material are bonded together to form a single thicker section, the process is called laminating. It is usually used to obtain material which is longer, thicker or wider than is available in one piece (such as in plywood and block board making), to obtain shapes which could not be cut from one piece (such as curved beams), or to obtain materials with improved properties (such as the stability of plywood or the heat and water resistance of Formica).

Laminating and bending wood

Thin strips of wood can be bent to curved shapes, but unless they are fixed to a frame they will spring back to their original shape when released. This problem is overcome by laminating several layers together. While the glue between the laminates is wet they can be bent to shape, but if they are held in a curved shape and pressed together until the glue has set, the laminates will no longer be free to move and they will retain the curved shape.

Timbers for laminating and bending.
Strips up to 3 mm thick of either natural or man-made timbers can be bent. All the laminations must be of equal thickness to obtain a smooth curve, and where they are difficult to bend, slight damping of what will be the outer curve of each lamination will help bending. Laminates must not however be glued wet, and if damping is used the laminates are cramped in the former overnight to dry in their new shape, before being glued in the usual way.

More expensive decorative woods can be used for the outside laminates, with cheaper materials used inside, provided that this does not leave an unsightly edge. Alternatively, layers of contrasting colours can be used to give a striped pattern to the edges.

The main laminating timbers are:

Veneers: thin decorative veneers 1.5 mm thick and constructional veneers 3.0 mm thick.

Plywood: thin plywood up to 3 mm thick especially 1.5 mm thick mosquito ply for tight curves.

Solid wood: naturally pliable timbers up to 3 mm thick, e.g. ash, elm, beech, oak, sycamore, birch, African mahoganies.

Hardboard: oil-tempered hardboard can be bent and pinned to a shaped framework.

Glues. Most types of wood glue, except impact and animal glues, can be used. P.V.A. glue is cheap, easy to use and does not stain the wood, but will not withstand high stresses, heat or moisture. It is, therefore, suitable for most indoor work. Synthetic resin glues such as cascamite are more expensive and require mixing, but produce a stronger, moisture resistant and almost colourless joint.

Curing is slow because the laminations are partly enclosed by the former, but the glue will usually set overnight at room temperature.

Avoid putting on too much glue as it is difficult to remove when dry and blunts cutting tools.

Ways of bending

1. Rigid formers.

(a) *Solid wooden formers*. The simplest way to make mating formers is to cut the required shape from a solid block of wood. This method is suitable for small or simple shapes such as salad servers and sledge runners. Allowances must be made in the design of the former for the thickness of the laminates to be used. The surfaces which press against the laminates must be smoothed, either by careful cleaning up, or by covering them with rubber or cork. These coverings also give some flexibility to allow for slight inaccuracies in the former or laminates.

(b) *Built up wooden formers*. Larger rigid formers are built up from softwood slats screwed onto blockboard or softwood rails. There is no need to fit slats together accurately. Stiff cardboard can be used to cover the slats and bridge the gaps when laminating thin veneers which might be marked by the slat edges.

To avoid the need to make accurately matched male and female formers we can hold single shapes, such as curved chair seats and backs, in place on built up formers with thick strips of wood held by G-cramps. Alternatively, put the whole job into a vacuum forming envelope. (*See* Flexible formers.)

2. Flexible formers.

(a) *Flexible steel bands*. Where rigid formers are difficult to make or to use, flexible spring steel cramping bands are used. The examples right show, first the use of a flexible female former with a solid male former to form a stool leg frame and secondly, the use of flexible male and female formers. The male former is mounted on a sheet of block board with steel angle brackets, and the female former and the laminates are cramped onto it with G-cramps and blocks. This method enables complicated shapes to be set up quickly and all the parts are reuseable.

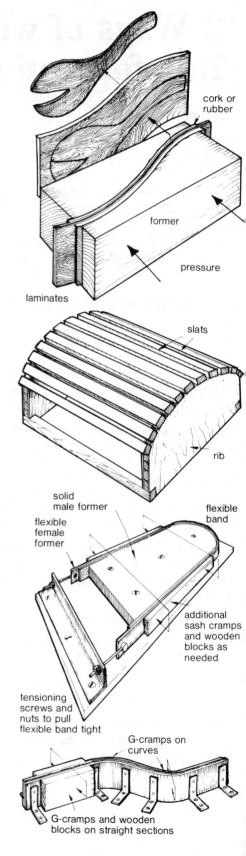

cork or rubber

former

pressure

laminates

slats

rib

solid male former

flexible female former

flexible band

additional sash cramps and wooden blocks as needed

tensioning screws and nuts to pull flexible band tight

G-cramps on curves

G-cramps and wooden blocks on straight sections

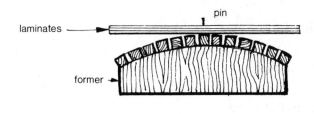

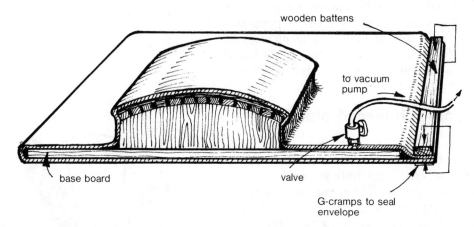

b) *Vacuum forming envelope.* This allows laminates to be shaped easily using only one former, and makes possible the forming of complicated shapes which would be difficult to cramp in any other way. It is also useful for veneering both flat and curved surfaces. A built up wooden former is made, waxed and covered with paper to prevent glue sticking to it. The laminates are located on the former with staples or panel pins and covered with a further sheet of paper to keep glue off the bag. The work is placed in the envelope and the air is sucked out so that atmospheric pressure on the bag presses it onto the laminates, thus pressing them to the shape of the former. Pressure is equal over the whole shape, however complicated. Care must be taken to prevent the bag being pulled up between laminates and former as the air is sucked out. Drying time is the same as for other methods of laminating.

Stages in laminated bending

1. *Make the former* or clean and wax an existing one. Cut polythene sheet or paper to prevent surplus glue from sticking to it and tape in place.

2. *Cut the laminates to size* allowing 25 to 75 mm extra on the length for movement of one layer over another and for trimming. Allow about 5 mm at the sides.

3. *Assemble the job dry* to make sure that the laminates are the correct size and will bend to the shape of the former. If damping is needed leave the damp laminates cramped up overnight. Check that cramping arrangements work.

4. *Glue the laminates* evenly and without excess glue, stack them in the correct order.

5. *Position the laminates carefully in the former and gradually tighten the cramps* starting in the middle so that excess glue and air bubbles are squeezed out.

6. *Leave to dry overnight.*

7. *Remove, mark out and cut to shape.* Wear safety glasses when cleaning up as dry glue is brittle and fragments may fly about.

Laminating thermosetting plastics

Making plastic laminates. Layers of paper or cloth are impregnated with thermosetting resins and forced together under high pressure in a heated press.

Plastic laminates such as *Formica* consist of sheets of paper soaked in phenol formaldehyde with the patterned surface made by printing the design on the top sheet of paper and soaking it in a clear resin such as melamine formaldehyde. Laminates such as *Tufnol* used for electronic circuit boards and electrical switchgear consist of either fabric or paper soaked in phenol formaldehyde.

Laminating glass reinforced plastics (G.R.P.)

Glass fibre mat is embedded in polyester resin to produce a strong hard-wearing material commonly known as fibreglass. This can be used to make almost any shape and size of construction from cars, caravans and boats to chair seats, trays and toys. Weight for weight, glass reinforced plastics are stronger than steel, and other important properties include high tensile and compressive strength and excellent corrosion resistance.

The resin provides the shape, colour and surface finish and the glass fibre mat the strength. The resin must be mixed with a catalyst or hardener to make it set and an accelerator or activator to speed up the reaction time. If both catalyst and accelerator are to be added to the resin *they must never be mixed together* as they might *explode*. Many resins can be bought pre-accelerated and this is more convenient and safer than mixing accelerator yourself.

Mould making. Most G.R.P. mouldings are made by laminating on a mould and the quality of this is one of the most important factors in getting a good result. The side of the finished product which is in contact with the surface of the mould will come out smooth and the other side will show the rougher texture of the mat. On a female mould the lamination is built up on the inside of the mould, and the outside of the product will be smooth (e.g. on a canoe), while on a male mould the lamination is on the outside, and the inside of the product will be smooth (e.g. on a tray or a fishpond lining).

Since the surface of the completed moulding will be an exact copy of the mould surface it is important to obtain a good finish on the mould.

The first or master mould can be made from almost any material available, and wood, plasticine, plaster and clay are commonly used. The finished moulding can be made from this or from a fibreglass mould taken from this master mould. It is often easier to make the master mould as an

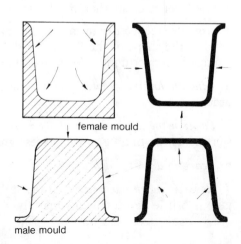

female mould

male mould

exact model of the finished product, and then to take a fibreglass mould from it, than to build a negative mould. Fibreglass moulds may also be better for repeated use and are easier to store.

Important points to remember when designing a mould are that you must:

1. Be able to get at all parts of the mould with brush, resin and glassfibre.

2. Be able to remove the finished job from the mould. Therefore, the mould must have tapered sides.

3. Avoid sharp corners. They are weak spots and are often difficult to laminate without trapping air bubbles.

4. Avoid large flat surfaces as they usually become curved. Make all surfaces large convex curves to increase strength and improve appearance.

Stages in laminating

The lay-up of glass fibre can be a very messy job, and it is therefore very important to be well organized and to work carefully.

Protect your hands with barrier cream or by wearing disposable polythene gloves, and your clothes with an apron.

1. Prepare the mould. Porous moulds such as wood and plaster must be sealed with several coats of french polish or special sealers.

Non-porous moulds such as fibreglass, perspex, glass and metal, and sealed porous moulds must be polished with three coats of non-silicone wax and/or coated with a release agent.

2. Cut-up sufficient glass-fibre mat for all the layers. This consists of strands of glass about 50 mm long stuck together into a mat with a binder. When polyester resin is added it dissolves the binder, allowing the strands to become a loose mat, which will then follow the shape of the mould.

There are three common grades or weights of mat – 300 gms, 450 gms and 600 gms, per square metre.

Two thicknesses of 450 gm mat are strong enough for most purposes. Allow a 25 mm overhang round the edges and a 25 mm overlap where two pieces in the same layer join. Use the smallest possible number of pieces and avoid waste. Simple paper patterns can be made to work out the number and shapes of pieces needed.

3. Gel-coat the mould. Gel-coat resin is the first layer of a G.R.P. lay-up and it must provide a smooth, glossy, hard-wearing, waterproof surface. So that it does not run off the mould before it cures, it is a *thixotropic* (thick) paste.

Mix the gel-coat resin with colour pigment if required and catalyse it. Brush it evenly all over the mould to a maximum thickness of 1 mm. Leave it to cure until it will not stick to the fingers when touched although it is still tacky (usually about 30 minutes).

4. Lay-up glass fibre. Mix pre-accelerated lay-up resin with colour pigment if required. You will need approximately $2\frac{1}{2}$ times as much resin as glass fibre mat by weight.

Brush a thick coat of resin onto the cured gel-coat using a stiff bristled brush. Lay the first layer of mat in position and stipple it into the resin. Do not brush as this will pull the mat to pieces. Stipple until the mat softens and curls up, resin rises up through all parts of the mat, and all air bubbles have been released. Do not add more resin unless you have to.

Continue stippling on layers of resin and mat, without waiting for previous layers to dry, until the required thickness is reached.

A smoother rough side to the lamination can be achieved by using a very fine glass fibre surface tissue for the final layer, and/or by pressing a sheet of polyester film onto the surface to squeeze out excess resin and air bubbles. Leave the polyester film on until the lay-up has cured and then peel it off.

5. Leave the lamination to cure and then remove it from the mould. The complete job can most easily be removed from the mould when it is still rubbery or 'green'. Complete curing takes at least 24 hours. Clean up equipment immediately using brush cleaner to dissolve off the resin.

6. Trim to shape. This can be done with a sharp knife while the job is still green, or using wood and metalwork tools after it is completely cured. Trimming is often done while the job is still on the mould, using the mould edge as a guide.

Using continuous rovings. These are continuous strands of glass fibre made into a string which can be wound into cylindrical shapes such as lampshades, or used to reinforce lay-ups. Rovings are used in the proportion of seven parts glass fibre to three parts resin, by weight.

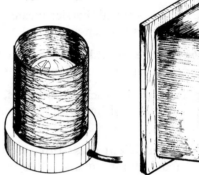

Using clear resin. To produce laminates through which light can shine as in lampshades and skylights we use a clear lay-up resin. This can be tinted using translucent colour pastes.

Shaping thermoplastics

There are two types of bend, single curvature and double curvature.

In *single curvature bending*, thermoplastic sheet, usually acrylic, is heated until pliable and bent to shape over simple formers. The sheet is formed in one direction only and this is a simple operation.

In *double curvature bending*, the sheet is formed in two directions to make such shapes as dishes, trays, lamp shades and covers. This is more difficult and requires special equipment. The usual methods are press-forming, blow-moulding and vacuum forming.

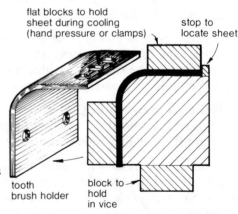

flat blocks to hold sheet during cooling (hand pressure or clamps)

stop to locate sheet

tooth brush holder

block to hold in vice

simple former for single bends

Single curvature bending

Design of formers. To obtain an accurate bend a simple former must be made to support the sheet during cooling. It must be smooth because the softened plastic will be marked by any blemishes. Formers are usually made from wood, but pieces of pipe will also be found useful for larger curves.

It is bad practice to try to form a sharp square bend in thermoplastics as this can overstretch and weaken the material. You should design radiused corners when using plastics.

It must be possible to put the heated plastic onto the former and shape it quickly. The jig must be designed to slightly over-bend the curve, because during cooling it will spring back a little.

Heating for bending.

Strip heater. This is used where only a narrow strip is to be heated across the sheet in order to form a small curvature bend. It is a single electric element enclosed in a box which has a slot above the element.

The sheet is placed over the slot so that a strip is heated. If the sheet supports can be adjusted for height, the width of the strip heated can be varied to suit the thickness of material and sharpness of bend. The higher the supports, the wider the strip heated. The sheet should be turned over at intervals to ensure even heating.

Oven and infra-red heaters. Where a wide strip is to be heated, it is necessary to either put the whole sheet in an oven or under infra-red heaters. Even heating of the sheet is important. Take care to protect the sheet from damage during heating.

Bending should not be attempted until the sheet is heated right through and completely flexible.

3 mm thick acrylic should be heated to 160/170°C for 20 minutes.
6 mm thick acrylic should be heated to 160/170°C for 30 minutes.

Heating to 180°C will damage the sheet.

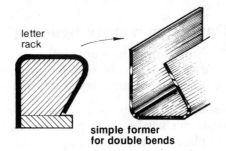

letter rack

simple former for double bends

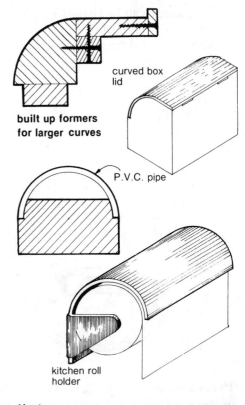

curved box lid

built up formers for larger curves

P.V.C. pipe

kitchen roll holder

Heaters

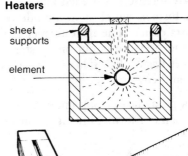

sheet supports

element

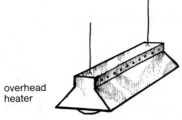

overhead heater

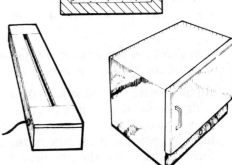

Double curvature bending

To form in two directions, it is necessary to make an accurate former of the required shape and to exert considerable pressure on the softened plastic.

Vacuum forming is used to shape thin sheets because they would not stay hot long enough to be taken from the oven and placed on the former. (*See* Vacuum forming.)

Thicker sheets can be shaped by press-forming or blow-moulding. For both of these the sheet is heated in an oven or under infra-red heaters and then placed on the former for shaping.

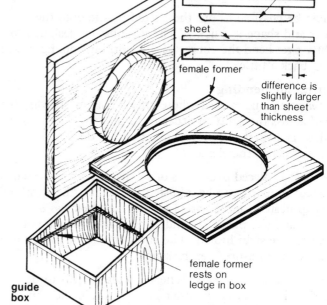

male former

sheet

female former

difference is slightly larger than sheet thickness

female former rests on ledge in box

guide box

finished dish

Press forming. In the first example shown here, the sheet of thermoplastic is softened and then placed on top of the female former, which is in a guide box to make lining up of the parts easier. The male former is placed on top of the sheet and pressure is put on by standing on top of it until the sheet has cooled. This is a very good way to make small dishes and covers.

Once a guide box strong enough to stand on has been made, pairs of formers to fit it can be made from 12 mm ply.

The sheet and formers are always cut to fit the box so that locating the hot sheet is easy.

An alternative method is to make an accurate male former with a simple ring former to press down the sheet. This is a good method for making larger lids and covers. A small taper is needed to make sure of the easy removal of the finished shape, and the ring must be larger than the male former to allow for the thickness of the sheet.

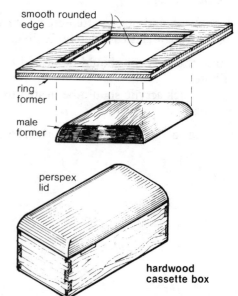

smooth rounded edge

ring former

male former

perspex lid

hardwood cassette box

Blow moulding

There are three main types of blow moulding. In the simplest, *free blowing*, a sheet of softened thermoplastic is clamped into a jig and air is blown in to inflate it to a dome shape. In the second, *blowing into a mould*, the softened sheet is blown into a female mould instead of into space, so that the shape of the finished bubble can be controlled. This method produces shapes such as stereo unit lids and food containers, and is an alternative to press forming. The third method, *extrusion moulding*, is used in industry to mass produce plastic containers of all shapes and sizes from bottles to barrels. Either rigid or squeezee containers can be made simply by varying the types of granule used. This process is a mixture of two processes, extrusion and blow-moulding. Details of this process will be found under 'Extrusion' in chapter thirteen.

Free blowing.

1. Cut a piece of thermoplastic (usually acrylic) to fit the jig, and heat it in an oven until soft.

2. Quickly clamp it into the jig and inflate gently.

3. Allow the shape to cool before reducing pressure, and removing from the jig.

4. Trim to shape using bandsaw and sanding machine or hand tools. Polish the edges.

Blowing into a mould. The stages are similar to those of free blowing. The mould must be made to the high standards already described for other forming processes.

Materials for blow moulding. Most thermoplastics can be blow-moulded. In school, free blowing and blowing into a mould are most often done with thin acrylic sheet. In industry polyethylene, polystyrene and P.V.C. are widely used for extrusion blow moulding (*See* page 197).

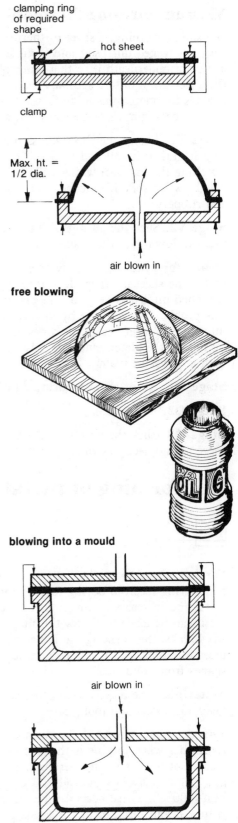

clamping ring of required shape

hot sheet

clamp

Max. ht. = 1/2 dia.

air blown in

free blowing

blowing into a mould

air blown in

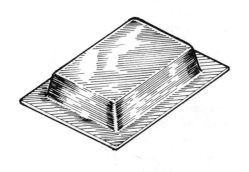

Vacuum forming thermoplastics

In vacuum forming, a sheet of thermoplastic held in a clamp is heated until soft and flexible, and the air is sucked out from underneath it so that atmospheric pressure forces the sheet down onto a specially made mould. This process enables thermoplastics to be formed into complicated shapes such as packaging, storage trays and seed trays.

Stage V1. Clamp the sheet across the top of the box and heat it until it is soft and flexible. This can be judged by watching the material which will start to sag under its own weight when soft. If touched with a stick it will feel soft and rubbery.

Stage V2. Suck the air out of the box so that the sheet is pressed down over the shape of the mould.

Drape forming. The disadvantage of vacuum forming is that if the sheet is drawn deep into the box it will be stretched until it is very thin in places. In drape forming this problem is overcome by forcing the mould upwards into the hot sheet before the air is sucked out. This is done by raising the platen, and can only be done on a machine with a moveable platen.

Stage D1. As for vacuum forming (V1).

Stage D2. Raise platen.

Stage D3. Suck the air out of the box. It can be seen that there are no deep drawn sections.

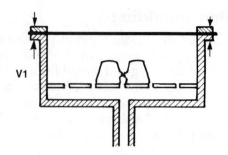

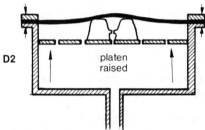

vacuum

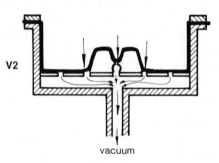

platen
raised

Hot forming of metals – forgework

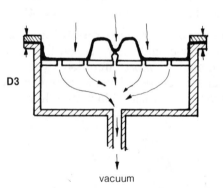

vacuum

Forging is used to produce strong, tough shapes. The hammering received during forging refines the grain of the metal and increases its toughness. By correct forging the grain can be made to follow the shape of the job without any breaks, thus making the job stronger. It is also often more economical in materials and quicker than machining shapes from solid steel.

Materials. The metals most often shaped while hot are black mild steel and tool steel.

Correct heat. One of the most important things to remember when forging is that the metal must only be worked at the correct temperature. For example, mild steel at a bright red/yellow heat (1 200°C) and tool steel at red heat (900°C). These heats can be reached either by heating with a gas-air torch or in a blacksmith's hearth.

Tools for forging

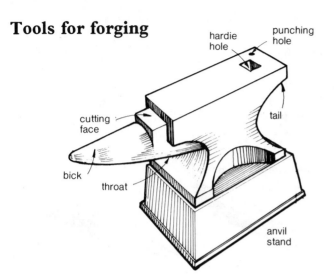

hardie hole

punching hole

cutting face

tail

bick

throat

anvil stand

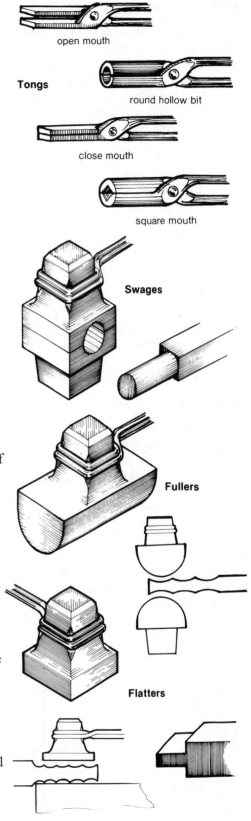

Tongs

open mouth

round hollow bit

close mouth

square mouth

Swages

Fullers

Flatters

Anvil. This is made from mild steel with a hardened steel working face welded onto it. It is mounted on a cast-iron anvil stand to raise it to a good working height.

The bick is used for forming curves, the cutting face for cutting metal with a chisel or rough work which might damage the main working face, and the working face for general forming. Part of one edge is rounded for making radiused bends. The hardie hole is used to mount various forging aids (hardie, swage, fuller) and the punching hole when making holes.

Tongs. These are used to pick up and hold short lengths of hot metal. A pair must be chosen which grips the metal firmly. Some of the most used shapes are shown here.

Hammers. Ball-pein hammers are used for most general forging. They are usually from $\frac{1}{2}$ to 1 kg in weight. A sledge hammer is used for heavy work. (*See* Driving tools.)

Swages. These have semi-circular grooves which are used to finish-off metal to a circular shape. The bottom swage fits into the hardie hole while the top swage is struck with a hammer. Several pairs of different diameters are needed.

Fullers. These have a smooth rounded shape and are used when necking down large sections of metal as the first stage of forging a shoulder, or for making rounded grooves and corners. The bottom fuller fits into the hardie hole while the top fuller is hit with a hammer. This process is a good example of how forging squeezes the fibres of the metal into a new shape without cutting them.

Flatters. These are used to smooth the surface of the metal after other processes. The metal is trapped between the flatter and the anvil, and the flatter is struck with a hammer.

Forging processes

The most important thing to remember here is that the hottest part of the metal will bend most easily. The temperature should, therefore, be controlled very carefully by a combination of heating and pouring on water to keep cool the parts which are not to be forged. Do not try to forge metal which is too cold as this will result only in hammer marks on the metal and bad shaping.

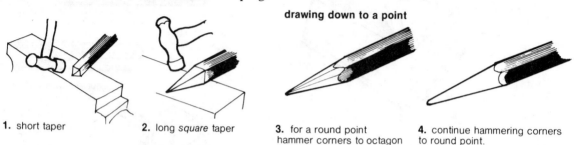

drawing down to a point

1. short taper

2. long *square* taper

3. for a round point hammer corners to octagon

4. continue hammering corners to round point.

Drawing down. This reduces the cross-section of the metal by increasing its length. For heavy jobs, swages, fullers, or flatters may be needed, but on light sections it usually consists of forging a tapered point or a shoulder on the end of the metal.

Bending. The simplest bend is to form a radiused bend on the curved edge of the anvil. A square bend needs extra metal to be added to the corner to avoid over-thinning through stretching. This is done by *upsetting* the metal. Only the metal being upset or bent must be hot during shaping, the rest being kept cool by pouring on water.

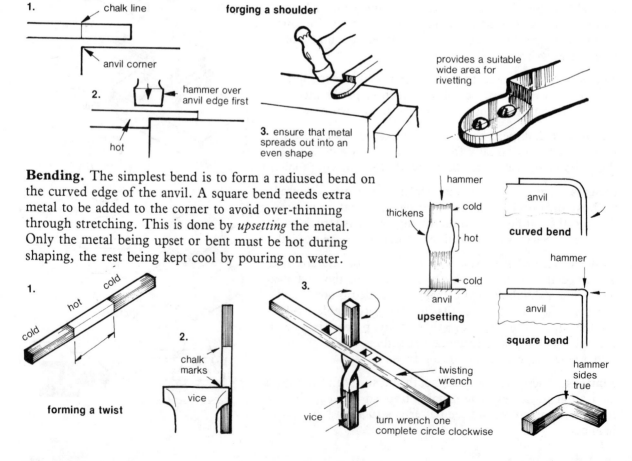

1.

chalk line

anvil corner

2.

hammer over anvil edge first

hot

forging a shoulder

3. ensure that metal spreads out into an even shape

provides a suitable wide area for rivetting

hammer

thickens

cold

hot

cold

anvil

upsetting

anvil

curved bend

hammer

anvil

square bend

hammer sides true

1.

cold

hot

cold

forming a twist

2.

chalk marks

vice

3.

vice

twisting wrench

turn wrench one complete circle clockwise

Forging an eye. It is important to follow the stages shown. Unless a right angle is formed first, and the eye by bending the end outwards from this, a P-shape will result.

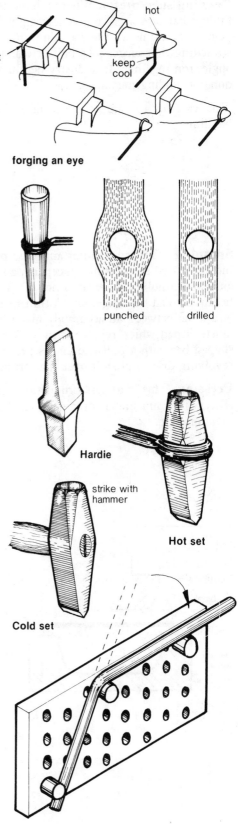

forging an eye

Punches. These are used to punch holes through the metal instead of drilling them and is another good example of how to shape rather than cut the grain fibres. It is done by placing the metal over the punching hole and hammering the punch into both sides of the metal in turn until it breaks through. A small pilot hole is often drilled to make punching easier.

Drifts. These are used to enlarge, tidy up, or change the shape of holes, for example, from round to square. They have a large taper and no handles.

punched   drilled

Heavy duty chisels for forgework.
Hardie. This is a chisel which fits into the hardie-hole on the anvil. To use, either lay the hot or cold metal on the hardie and strike the metal with a hammer, or trap the metal between the hardie and the correct set, and strike the set with a hammer.

Wedge angles of 30° (hot) or 60° (cold), because hot metal is softer and easier to cut.

Hardie

strike with hammer

Hot set: Used to cut hot steels and wrought iron on the anvil.
A heavy duty chisel fitted with a wooden or metal handle.
Used on the cutting face of the anvil or with a hardie.
Wedge angle of 30°.
Not hardened and tempered because hot metal would re-soften it.

Hot set

Cold set: Used to cut cold metals on the anvil.
Similar to the hot set.
Wedge angle of 60°.
Hardened and tempered.

Cold set

Cold forming of metals

Simple bends. Thin sections of metal can be bent cold, usually after annealing (softening). Black mild steel can be bent without annealing, but bright mild steel would probably crack in tight bends.

Simple jigs can be made where several pieces must be bent to the same shape. An adjustable jig can be made by drilling holes in a thick steel plate, and turning pegs of any required diameter to fit.

Bending sheetmetal. Where a long bend is to be made folding bars are used to give a straight line. Bend a small amount at a time all the way along the bend to avoid over-stretching. For larger jobs bolt or clamp two lengths of angle-iron together. In industry bending of sheetmetal is done on folding machines.

Take care not to damage the surface of the sheet during bending.

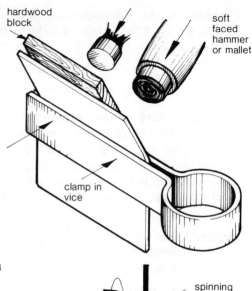

Spinning. This is an important mass production process in industry used for making saucepans, and stainless steel and aluminium hollow-ware. It is not often used in school because it can be dangerous. A thin metal disc is mounted in a lathe between an accurately made former and a tailstock pad which revolve with it. A heavy steel finger-shaped bar with a polished end is pressed firmly against the revolving disc to push it over the former.

Pressing. This is a mass production process used to make all types of thin metal containers, car body panels, heating radiators, etc.

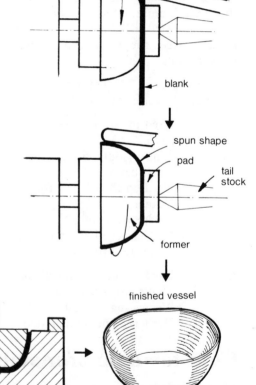

Beaten metalwork

Malleable metals such as copper, brass, gilding metal and silver can be shaped, after annealing, into container shapes such as jugs, bowls and vases. There are several ways of working these materials, the most used ones being hollowing, sinking and raising, all of which are usually followed by planishing. More advanced work usually involves a combination of these processes and fabricating, where shapes such as cylinders and cones are folded from flat sheet, silver-soldered along the seams and then soldered to each other. For example, a tankard might be made by folding and soldering a cylinder, raising it to shape and soldering on base, plinth and handle.

Sinking. This is a method of thinning the centre of a piece of metal to form a shallow tray with the edge of the metal being left almost untouched.

Marking-out. On the annealed and cleaned blank, draw a pencil line to mark the width of the lip which is to be left round the tray.

Method. The simplest method is to make a wooden block as shown, cut to the cross-section required, and with two pins to limit the width of the lip.

Hold the annealed metal against the pins and hammer with a sinking hammer just inside the pencil line. A gradual depression should be made all the way round the tray. Hammering is repeated as many times as necessary gradually moving away from the line, and annealing and cleaning frequently. This is a slow and difficult process.

Hollowing. This is a simpler process used to make shallow dishes. The metal is thinned so that the diameter of the finished dish is again approximately the same as that of the blank used.

Marking-out. After annealing and cleaning, draw concentric rings in pencil round what will become the inside of the dish and a radial starting line.

Method. Using the smaller face of a bossing mallet and a leather sandbag, work round the outside line and then each line in turn, working towards the centre. Anneal and clean as necessary. After each round of hollowing, use the large face of the mallet to true up the shape and remove any wrinkles in the edge of the bowl. You must get the bowl as smooth and even as possible at each stage.

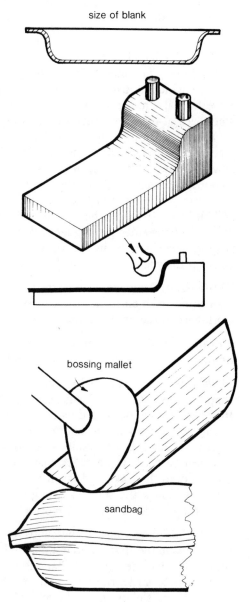

size of blank

bossing mallet

sandbag

Raising. This is a way of making taller shapes by bending up the sides of a blank. It is the opposite of hollowing and sinking where the centre of the blank is pushed down. During raising the thickness of the metal is increased as the circumference of the vessel is reduced. *The blank must first be hollowed to turn the sides inwards.*

Marking-out. Draw concentric circles about 10 mm apart and a radial starting line on the outside of the hollowed shape of the job. Use a flat-faced planishing hammer unless the centre will show the diameter of the base of the finished vessel.

Method. The metal is placed on a raising stake and struck with a raising hammer or mallet (stage 1). The blow strikes the part which is just above the stake and forces it down onto the stake and into a smaller area, thus thickening it. The force of the blow must stop before the metal is trapped between the hammer and the stake, and thinned. This is repeated all the way round the circle. The job is moved to a new position on the stake and raising continues round the second line (stage 2). After the whole blank has been raised in this way, dress out any wrinkles in the edge, and anneal and clean ready for further raising. Raising gets more difficult as the sides get higher and continues in smaller steps. If the shape is uneven raise part of the way round to even up the shape.

Planishing. After we have shaped our job we finish it by planishing to smooth the surface, true up the shape and work-harden the metal so that it will keep its shape.

Marking-out. Draw concentric circles and a radial starting line on the outside of the annealed and cleaned shape.

Method. Choose a stake which curves slightly more than the shape of the job, and a flat-faced planishing hammer unless the shape of the job would cause the edges of the hammer to dig in. Both stake and hammer must be smooth and highly polished. If a flat stake is used, a curved hammer face will be needed. To check that the stake is correct, put the job onto the stake and tap it with the hammer. If the sound is hollow the stake is wrong or you are striking in the wrong place. If solid it is correct.

When planishing, start in the centre of the job and planish round inside the first circular line, then the second, etc. To make sure that the finished shape is the same all the way round always strike the same spot on the stake with the hammer, and slowly move the job in order to planish the whole surface. Every planishing mark must just touch the next one, so that the whole surface is covered evenly with no gaps, like the scales of a fish. It is important to make sure that the corner of the hammer does not dig into the surface by keeping it square to the work. Hold the end of

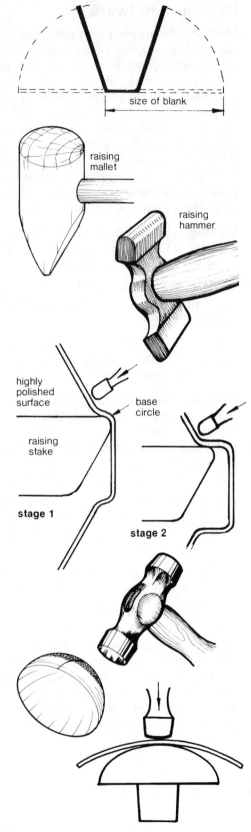

size of blank

raising mallet

raising hammer

highly polished surface

raising stake

base circle

stage 1

stage 2

the hammer shaft, and deliver the blows by moving the wrist so that they fall lightly and evenly on the work exactly over the point of contact between the job and the stake. Do not swing the hammer from the elbow or shoulder as this increases the danger of digging in.

Folding and seaming. Instead of raising deep shapes from a flat sheet we can draw the development of the nearest simple geometrical shape, cut it out, bend it and silver solder it. This is easier than raising such shapes as cylinders and cones, and the best way to make such shapes as square, hexagonal and octagonal vessels. After soldering, the basic shapes can be modified by raising and then finished by planishing if needed. The base can be a flat piece soldered on, a simple hollowed shape soldered on, or a flat piece set about 3 mm inside the seamed shape, so that the joint does not show.

To make a square corner, a V-groove is first cut with a simple scraper made from hardened and tempered silver steel, so that a neat sharp fold can be made.

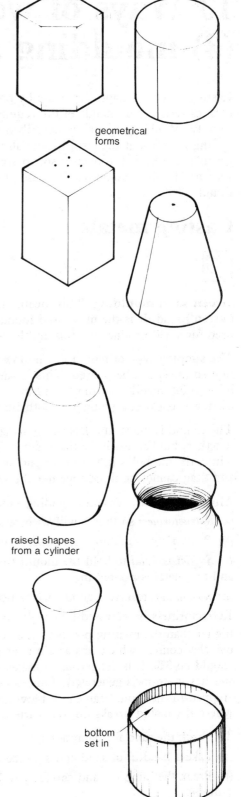

geometrical forms

raised shapes from a cylinder

bottom set in

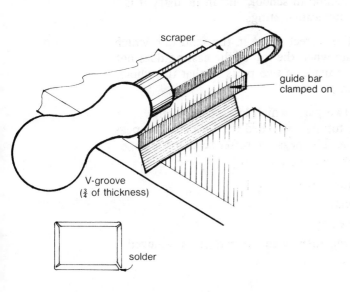

scraper

guide bar clamped on

V-groove (¾ of thickness)

solder

13 Ways of working materials (3) moulding and casting

Casting is where shapes are made by pouring molten metal or thermosetting plastics resins into moulds of the required shape and leaving the castings to solidify. Moulding originally described the process of making the sand moulds for casting metals, but the term is now also used to describe processes where plastics granules are heated to make a soft paste which can then be shaped in processes such as injection moulding. In these processes the material is never completely liquid.

Casting metals

Green sand moulding. This means simply that the mould is made from damp ('green') sand. It is the most used foundry method in school, and in industry it is used for small production runs and large or intricate castings.

The simplest type of mould is a hollow of the correct shape in the sand into which molten metal can be poured. This is adequate when the top of the casting does not have to be smooth, but most sand moulds are made in two parts so that the whole casting is enclosed, giving a smooth finish to all sides.

The mould is made in a *flask* consisting of two parts which locate accurately together, but can easily be taken apart. The top part is called the *cope* and has pegs which fit into holes in the lower part or *drag*. The pegs are offset so that the cope and drag cannot be fitted together the wrong way round.

Moulding sand. A good moulding sand must have:

(a) *Refractoriness* so that it will withstand heat.

(b) *Permeability* to allow steam and gases to escape.

(c) *Sufficient bond* to hold the mould shape together when the pattern is removed and the metal is poured in.

(d) *Smoothness* to give a good surface finish.

Refractoriness is increased by the presence of silica which fuses at a temperature higher than the melting points of the common metals. Bond is provided by a 3% to 6% clay content which acts as a binder when water is added. The moisture content should be 8%. It is dangerous to make the sand too wet because when hot metal touches it steam is generated. This can cause the metal to splash back, or when trapped in the mould can cause blow holes in the casting, or even a blow back where the mould breaks up under the pressure of the steam.

To check the sand for dampness:

(a) Take a handful of sand and squeeze it together. It should bond together.

(b) Break the lump of sand carefully in half. The edges should stay firm and not crumble.

(c) Drop the lumps onto the moulding bench. They should break up.

Improving the mould surface

There are several ways of doing this. For example:

1. Oil bound sand, such as *Petrabond,* can be used to cover the pattern or for the whole mould. It is finer than green sand and because it has no water to cause steam it can be rammed harder. This gives a very good finish to the casting.

2. A mould coating can be sprayed onto the surface after the pattern has been withdrawn.

Pattern making

Patterns can be made from any material which will give a smooth, water-resistant surface and which is strong enough to withstand the ramming of the sand around it.

Close grained, easily worked hardwoods (such as jelutong) or softwoods are usually used. Metal is used in industry for patterns which will be used repeatedly. When designing a pattern you must remember the following points:

(a) The metal will shrink as it cools. Therefore, make the pattern slightly oversize.

(b) Parts which must be machined or filed to shape after casting will need an extra machining allowance left on.

(c) All corners should be radiused and all sides tapered so that the pattern can easily be removed from the mould.

(d) There should be no sudden changes in metal thickness as this would weaken the casting.

(e) Work out how the finished casting will be shaped. It may be necessary to cast in a mounting lug to hold the work in the lathe or vice. This can be cut off after shaping.

(f) Time spent in finishing the pattern is time well spent because it is much easier to make a smooth, accurate casting than to clean up a bad casting.

Types of pattern

Flat-back patterns. These are the simplest type having one flat and one shaped side. They are moulded in one half of the flask only. (*See* Making a flat-back moulding.)

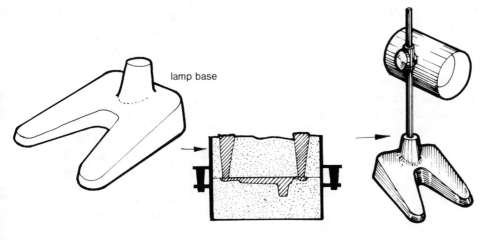

lamp base

Odd-side patterns. This type does not have a flat side and must be moulded in both halves of the flask. The parting line between the cope and the drag must be carefully chosen so that the pattern can be removed without damaging the mould.

Making a mould using an odd-side pattern is complicated because the pattern must first be temporarily supported by burying it up to the parting line in the sand-filled cope so that the drag can be made up. The drag and pattern are then carefully removed and turned over so that the cope can be broken up and remade properly with runner, riser, etc.

There are two ways of redesigning the pattern to overcome this difficulty.

Split patterns. The pattern can be made in two parts located together with tapered metal dowels. This makes it possible to build up the bottom half of the mould as with a flat-back pattern and then fit the other part of the pattern to complete the mould. Split patterns are also used when moulding shapes which are too complicated to remove from the mould in one piece. In the example shown, the problem of an *undercut* shape which could not be withdrawn in one piece has been solved by using a three-piece split pattern.

Match-plate patterns. The two halves of a split pattern can be mounted on either side of a piece of 12 mm thick plywood which fits between the cope and drag. The mould can then be made simply by filling the drag, turning the flask over, placing the sprue pins and filling the cope. The pattern can include the shapes of the gates so that these do not have to be cut separately. Match plates are a simple aid to the quantity production of castings.

Cores. These are used where internal shaping is needed in a casting. It is easier and more economical to cast in shaping than to machine it afterwards. For example, the large hole in the bracket above would only require finishing to the correct size, while to set up and drill a solid casting would be quite a lengthy task.

Cores can be made by mixing a special silica sand with a binder and ramming this into a mould to form the shape. After removal from the mould, the core is baked in an oven ready for use and carefully placed in position, resting in core prints in the mould made by the pattern. After pouring, the core can easily be broken out of the casting.

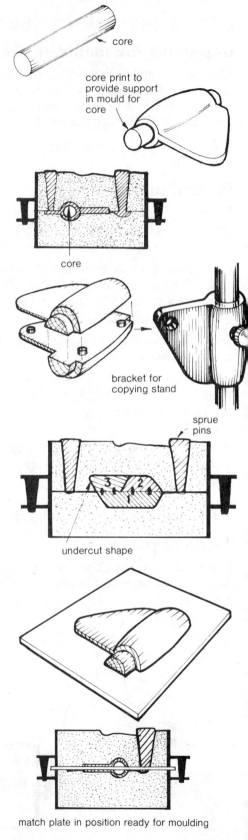

core

core print to provide support in mould for core

core

bracket for copying stand

sprue pins

undercut shape

match plate in position ready for moulding

Making a flat-back moulding

1. Put the drag upside down on a flat board. Place the pattern inside the drag, making sure that there is at least 25 mm space all round, and that there is room for the sprue pins later. Shake parting powder over the pattern to prevent sand sticking to it.

2. Riddle a covering of sand over the pattern, and fill up the rest of the drag by throwing in unsifted sand and ramming it down. Strickle (level) off the top with a straight edge to give a flat surface.

3. Turn the drag and the board over together so that the pattern does not drop out. Fit the cope. Sprinkle on parting powder. Put sprue pins in place to make the runner and riser. Riddle sand over the pattern, fill up with unsifted sand and strickle off.

4. Cut a pouring basin at the top of the runner with a lip to prevent sand or slag being washed down. Smooth all the edges especially round the top of the runner and riser. Tap loose and carefully lift out the sprue pins. Finish smoothing the edges.

5. Remove the cope and place it carefully aside. Cut gates or channels from the runner and riser to the pattern, and smooth the edges. Screw a woodscrew into the pattern, tap it all over to loosen it and carefully lift it out. Blow out any loose sand.

6. Refit the cope. Place the flask in a tray of sand and pile sand around it as a precaution against leaks between cope and drag during pouring.

Some other metal casting methods

Gravity die casting. Green sand moulding is slow and does not produce a high quality surface finish. These problems can be overcome by die casting, where the metal is poured into a cast iron or steel die. This process is only economical where large numbers of the same casting are needed.

Pressure die casting. Where very large numbers are needed, pressure die casting becomes economical. Here the metal is forced into alloy steel dies under hydraulic pressure. This enables intricate shapes such as cylinder heads to be cast accurately and automatically in die casting machines. The process is similar to the injection moulding of plastics.

Lost wax casting. This is a very old process where an expendable pattern of a shape too complicated to be withdrawn from the mould is made from wax. This is then coated with refractory material to make the mould and buried in sand.

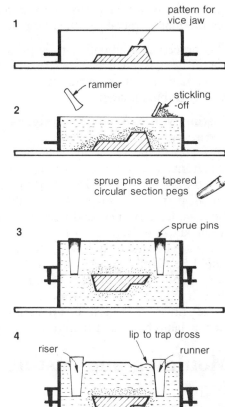

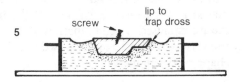

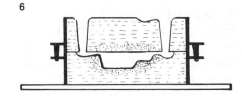

The mould is heated so that the wax melts and runs out, and the molten metal can then be poured in.

This process is used both for the production of intricate one off designs, such as jewellery and for the small scale production of parts requiring great dimensional accuracy, such as turbine blades.

Casting with expanded polystyrene patterns. This is a modern variation on lost wax casting. Because expanded polystyrene vaporizes away when hot metal is poured onto it, patterns of any shape or size can be made and left in the mould during pouring. Take care to ram the sand firmly into all parts of the shape. The mould must be well vented, and have large runners and risers so that the metal can flow in quickly, and the fumes can easily escape. Pouring must take place outside or in a well ventilated area, and the metal should be slightly hotter than usual so that it will melt the pattern and flow to all parts of the mould. This method is not suitable for precision work and does not produce a good surface finish. It is ideal for producing ornamental castings such as lamp bases and sculptures.

Moulding and casting plastics

Compression moulding. This is a way of shaping *thermosetting* plastics into such things as electrical fittings and melamine 'unbreakable' crockery. Powdered plastic is placed in the heated lower half of the mould, and the mould is closed. A combination of heat and high pressure is then used to plasticize the powder and force it into the shape of the mould.

The main materials used are melamine formaldehyde, urea formaldehyde and phenol formaldehyde.

Rotational casting. The correct amount of *thermoplastic* paste (usually plasticized P.V.C.) is poured into a hollow mould. This is then rotated on a special machine in two directions at once while being heated in an oven. The paste is spread evenly over the whole of the inside of the mould. After cooling the mould is opened and the completed shape removed. Products of this process include footballs, squeezy toys and dolls heads.

Slush moulding is a similar but simpler process now being replaced by rotational casting.

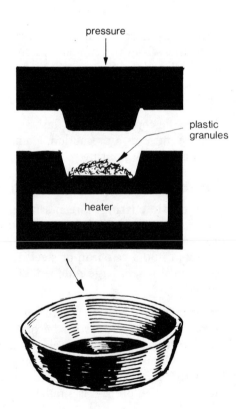

Cold resin casting with thermosetting resins. Polyester resins and epoxy resins can be cast into solid blocks which can then be used as cast, for example in making lamp bases and small statues, or they can be machined and worked with hand tools in the same way as metal castings.

Clear polyester resin can also be used for *embedding* small items, in order to preserve and display them, or to make decorative paperweights, jewellery, etc.

Instructions for the safe handling and mixing of resins have been given in the section on glass reinforced plastics, and must be followed.

Moulds for casting

These must have a smooth polished surface to give a good finish to the casting, and if needed a slight taper so that the casting can be removed after curing.

Ready made moulds can be polythene, P.V.C., glass, porcelain, waxed paper, aluminium foil and other materials. Polystyrene should not be used as it is sometimes melted by resins. To make your own mould, first make a wood, clay or plaster pattern of the required shape and finish it to the standard required on the finished casting. Seal porous patterns with french polish or a suitable sealer and then polish all patterns with non-silicone release wax or brush on release agent. This pattern is then used in one of several possible ways to make the mould.

For a complicated shape we can use flexible mould making materials such as re-meltable P.V.C., rubber latex, or silicone rubber. For a simple shape which can easily be withdrawn from the mould, we can vacuum form a P.V.C. sheet over it, lay-up a G.R.P. mould or cast a plaster mould round it.

Choice of resins for casting

Most *polyester resins* can be cast, but special casting resins and clear embedding resins are available to give the best results.

There are three problems to beware of in using these resins:

1. *Cracking.* During curing a lot of heat is given off and this reaction can cause cracking of the casting.

2. *Shrinking.* During curing the casting will shrink by at least 5%. While this often helps removal from the mould it can also be a cause of cracking around hard objects embedded in the resin, and when a new layer of resin is poured onto a layer which has shrunk it can seep down between casting and mould causing serious cleaning-up problems later.

Both these problems can be overcome by using less activator (if the resin is not pre-activated) and less catalyst, by building up the resin in layers of not more than 10 mm thick to control the amount of heat given off, or by using special resins which do not crack when made into large castings in one go.

3. *Stickiness.* A further problem is that with some clear embedding resins the surface which is left exposed to the air during curing will remain sticky. There are several ways to overcome this. A piece of *melinex* polyester film laid on the surface during curing will reduce the problem; a thin final layer of a non-sticky opaque resin, suitably coloured, can be poured on to cover the stickiness; the stickiness can be cleaned off with acetone or brush cleaner and after further drying with wet and dry paper; or a piece of felt can be stuck on to make a base.

Casting method

Almost any type of resin can be used for opaque castings. Inert fillers such as calcium carbonate (powdered chalk) can be added to economise on expensive resin and to reduce the amount of exothermic heat produced during curing. For most castings a 50:50 mix of resin and filler is suitable. Other fillers such as sawdust, metal filings and sand can be added to vary the texture and colour of the casting. Alternatively, a gel-coat containing the required finish can be put on the mould before casting.

Opaque colour pastes can be added to give the required colour.

The amount of resin needed for a casting can be worked out by filling the mould with water and then pouring it into a graduated waxed mixing cup.

The resin must be mixed and poured carefully to avoid trapping air bubbles in the casting, and to make sure that any fillers are well mixed in.

Mix the resin carefully to the manufacturers instructions and do not add more than recommended in one go.

Clear casting and embedding.

For this, clear resin must be used, but some or all of the layers can be tinted using translucent colour pastes. Special care must be taken to keep dirt out of the mould which must always be covered during curing.

Before starting to cast, coat the mould with a release agent to prevent sticking of the completed casting and set up the mould absolutely level.

1. Pour the first layer of resin into the clean, waxed mould and leave to cure.

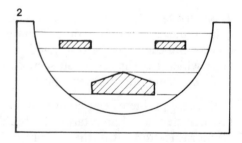

2. As soon as the first layer has gelled enough to support it, place the article being embedded in position and pour on the second layer of resin. If you are embedding a large object several layers may be needed to cover it. If embedding an object which will float stick it down with a very thin layer of resin. If embedding several objects at different levels place them on different layers of resin. Take care not to trap any air bubbles under objects.

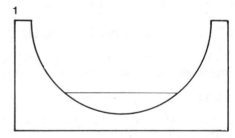

3. Pour in the final layer of resin. A translucent colour paste in this layer will appear to tint the whole casting. An opaque coloured layer will provide an attractive base to the finished job. In choosing your final layer or layers think about the problem of stickiness already discussed.

In a clear casting built up in several layers you will be able to see the joints between the layers slightly. This is unavoidable.

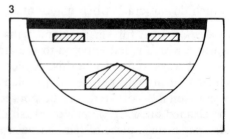

Decorative patterns can be made in the resin by mixing small amounts of opaque or translucent coloured resins and applying them in a variety of ways, such as dripping them into the still wet resin, trailing them in with a spatula, or painting them onto a dry surface before adding more clear resin.

Extrusion

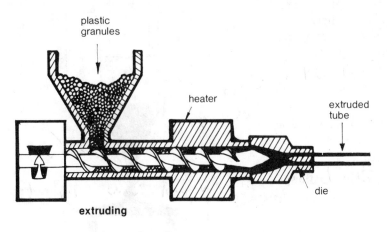

plastic granules

heater

extruded tube

die

extruding

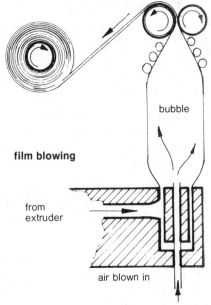

film blowing

bubble

from extruder

air blown in

This process converts granules of thermoplastic into such products as pipes, rods, mouldings and films. The granules are fed into the hopper and fall into an electrically powered rotating screw which forces them towards the die at the other end of the extruder. The pressure on the plastic is increased as it moves towards the die by the increasing core diameter of the screw and the tapered aperture leading up to the die. It is also heated to the correct temperature by the heaters surrounding the barrel so that when it reaches the die it is in a plastic state, and can be forced through it. It is then quickly cooled so that it keeps its shape.

To put plastic covering on wire, such as electrical insulation, the wire is fed through the centre of the die as the plastic is extruded.

Many schools have a pug mill in their pottery room which can be used to demonstrate a similar process.

In *film blowing* a continuous plastic tube is extruded and blown into a large bubble. This stretches the plastic into a thin film which cools and is wound onto a roller to make materials such as wide polythene sheeting for building and packaging. The bubble is blown vertically and may be 10 metres or more high.

In *extrusion blow moulding* a tube of molten plastic is extruded between the two halves of a die (1) which close sealing the ends of the tube (2). Air is blown into the tube to enlarge it to the shape of the die (3). The waste is trimmed off and the finished shape is ejected (4).

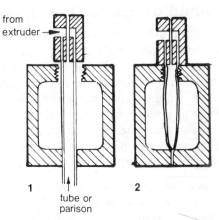

from extruder

tube or parison

1

2

extrusion blow moulding

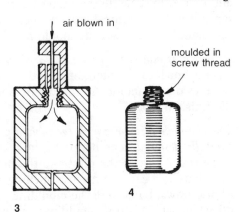

air blown in

moulded in screw thread

3

4

Injection moulding

This process is similar to extruding except that the screw is replaced by a plunger which injects a shot of thermoplastic into a mould. The mould is warmed before injecting and the plastic is injected quickly to prevent the plastic hardening before the mould is full.

Pressure is maintained for a short time (the dwell time) to prevent the material creeping back during setting. This prevents shrinkage and hollows, and therefore gives a better quality product.

When the plastic has solidified sufficiently to be removed without damage, the mould is opened and the moulding ejected. After checking that the mould is clean, it is closed and the process starts again.

In industry the process is completely automatic and is the most important manufacturing method for everyday plastic goods ranging from bottle tops, sink plugs, small containers and model kits, to bowls, buckets, dustbins, chair seats, milk crates and even small boats.

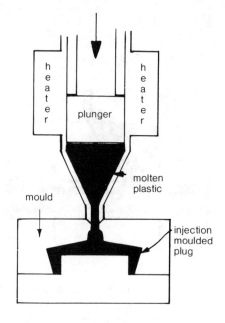

Mould design for injection moulding

Good mould design and construction is essential to successful injection moulding, and provides great scope for projects in school. A mould consists of two or more pieces in which the shape of the moulding has been cut. Steel or brass is usually used but softer materials such as plaster of Paris or epoxy resins can be used, provided they are contained in a steel box to resist the pressure of moulding. This avoids the need for machining. They must also withstand temperatures of up to 300°C.

It must be possible to open the mould and eject the moulding easily and without misusing tools. A slot can often be made along the joint line so that a screwdriver can be inserted and turned to separate the parts. Deep shapes must be tapered to help removal and an ejector pin can be built into the mould to push out the moulding if necessary.

All surfaces must be very smooth and highly polished to ensure a good finish to the mouldings and leakproof mating surfaces on the mould, so that there is no flash to clean off the finished job.

The channels through which the molten plastic flows must be carefully designed. The nozzle of the machine fits against the *sprue* which carries the plastic to the mould cavity. Close to the cavity is a *gate* – a narrow opening through which the plastic flows, but where the moulding can easily be broken off when set. Multiple mouldings can be injected from one sprue using a system of *runners* to link the sprue to the cavities, as for example when moulding all the parts of a plastic model kit in one operation. Each part is linked to the runner by a separate gate.

The sprue is usually placed along the parting line of the mould for ease of ejection, and to avoid any cleaning out problems between mouldings. Sprues, runners, and gates are round or half round in section so that they can be made by drilling wherever possible and to give a smooth flow. They must be large enough to allow quick filling of the mould.

Sharp corners and sudden changes in section must be avoided because they interrupt the flow of plastic and weaken the moulding. *Large flat surfaces should also be avoided* because the finished moulding will often not come out completely flat.

Calendering

This process is used to produce plastic sheet, packaging films, sticky tape and plastic coated fabrics and papers. Examples of products made in this way include vinyl washable wallpapers, P.V.C. leathercloth upholstery materials and plastic coated playing cards.

The machine consists of large heated rollers which squeeze softened plastic into a continuous sheet. The surface can be smooth or a pattern can be embossed on it by feeding the warm sheet through patterned rollers. If the plastic is to be bonded to a backing material this is fed through the rollers with the hot plastic. The sheet finally passes through cooling rollers.

The softened plastic can be supplied from an extruder fitted with a wide slot, or granules can be plasticized on the calender.

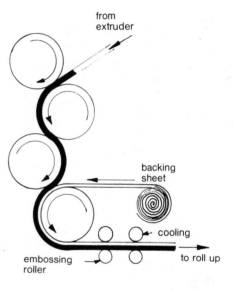

199

14 Ways of working materials (4) fabrication

In order to choose the best way of joining any combination of materials in any situation which is likely to arise, we must have a good general knowledge of methods of joining.

Joints can be classified in several ways such as temporary and permanent, flexible and rigid, and hot and cold formed. Below we have listed temporary and permanent joints, but you should also be able to list them in other ways to make sure that you know the important features of each.

	Wood	*Plastics*	*Metal*
Temporary joints	Screws ——————————————▶		——————▶
	Nuts and bolts ————————▶		——————▶
	Knock down fittings ———▶		——————▶
	Hinges, catches and ——▶ stays		——————▶
Permanent joints	Glues ———————————————▶		——————▶
	Nails	◀————————	Rivets
	Carcase joints	X	Sheet metal joints
	Frame joints	◀————————	Frame and tube joints
	X	X	Soldering
	X	X	Brazing
	X	◀————————	Welding

In the pages which follow we have given enough details of the common ways of joining for you to be able to choose the best method and use it correctly.

Nails

Nailing is the quickest way of making a permanent joint in wood. Nails cannot be removed easily or without damage, and therefore should not be used as temporary joints.

The nail punches the fibres of the wood away from the nail head. They grip the shank of the nail and resist attempts to withdraw it. The serrations round the shank, below the head, give extra grip. The treaded pattern on the head stops the hammer from slipping. Always nail through the thinner piece of wood into the thicker piece. The nail length should be about $2\frac{1}{2}$ to 3 times the thickness of the thinner piece.

Nails are sold by length, type, material and weight (not number).

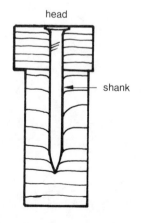

head

shank

Common types

Round wire nails have a round shank and a flat head. They are made from steel wire and can be galvanized to stop rusting. The usual sizes are from 12 mm to 150 mm long and they are used for general joinery work.

Oval wire nails have an oval shank and a narrow head which is driven below the surface. Turn the long axis of the oval shape in line with the grain to prevent splitting. They are made from steel wire and can be galvanized. The usual sizes are from 12 mm to 150 mm. Because they have no heads they do not hold the wood as firmly as round wire nails, but they are neater and are therefore used for interior joinery. The nail holes can be hidden by filling.

Standard panel pins have a thin round shank and a small head which is driven below the surface with a nail punch. The usual sizes are from 12 mm to 50 mm and they are used for strengthening joints and fixing thin sheets.

Hardboard pins have a hard square shank to penetrate hardboard without bending and a pointed head which does not need punching below the surface.

Clout nails are short nails with extra large heads for fixing roofing felt, canvas chair webbing, etc. They are usually galvanized to prevent rusting.

Hardened fixing pins are hard, round shanked nails designed to withstand persistent hammering and to penetrate bricks, etc. They should be long enough to go through the job being fixed, any plaster on the wall, and then 15 mm to 20 mm into the wall.

Staples are square for crate-making and upholstery, and round for holding wire. Square staples are usually fired in by a staple gun. Round staples are heavier and are hammered in.

Dovetail nailing. To give extra strength to a joint, drive in pairs of nails towards each other dovetail fashion.

Staggered nailing. When nailing a frame together stagger the nails across the width of the wood to avoid splitting the grain.

If the wood is brittle or tough, bore a small hole and blunt the nail point. These precautions help to prevent splitting, especially when nailing close to the end of a plank.

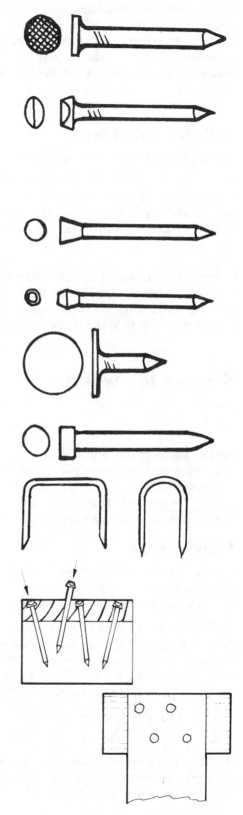

Clinched nailing. This is used to prevent nails being easily pulled out when nailing into thin wood. The process is shown right. Note that the usual rule is still used to calculate the length of the nail (3 x thickness of piece A). A convenient round bar, such as one handle of a pair of pincers, is used to help in turning the nail point back into the wood to give a strong, safe joint. Simply bending the nail over leaves a dangerous point exposed.

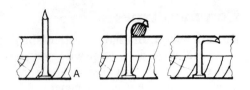

Nails for upholstery

Gimp pins are small wire nails, often of brass, with a large head used in upholstery where the nail heads will show.

Cut tacks are short, sharp-pointed, flat-headed nails, usually with a blued or black mild steel finish. They are used in upholstery where the nails will be hidden.

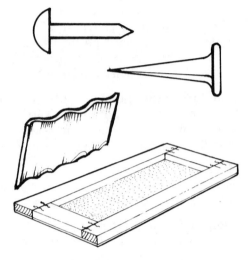

Corrugated fasteners are short strips of corrugated steel with one sharp corrugated edge, used to make crude joints in cheap work. They are hammered in across the joint lines at each corner to hold the frame together.

Screws for wood

Screws are an effective way of making a permanent or temporary joint in wood. The thread of the screw becomes enmeshed with the grain fibres to make a strong joint. Screws are stronger, neater and more accurate than nails, and can be taken out without causing damage.

Using screws

1. Select the correct length of screw. This is $2\frac{1}{2}$ to 3 times the thickness of the top piece of wood. Always screw through the thinner piece of wood into the thicker.

2. Drill the pilot hole to slightly less than the screw length. A bradawl hole may be enough in softwood, but in hardwood and for large diameter screws, use a drill equal to the core diameter. Failure to drill properly causes chewed-up screw heads and split wood.

3. Drill a clearance hole for the shank.

4. Countersink for the screw head if needed.

5. When using brass screws which easily break, screw in a stronger steel screw first to cut a thread, and in hardwood, lubricate the screw with soap or wax.

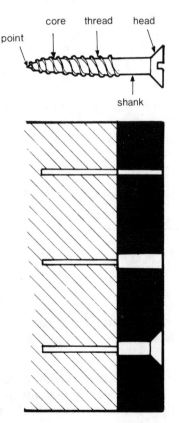

point   core   thread   head   shank

Common types of screws

Countersunk head screws are used to join wood to wood where the head has to be flush with the surface, and for fitting hinges. They are the most commonly used type.

Round head screws are used to screw thin metal fittings to wood (e.g. tee hinges and shelf brackets), and for joinery work where the head need not be flush. They are often of black japanned steel to resist rusting.

Raised countersunk head screws are less common and are used to screw fittings to wood. They are often of chrome plated brass to look attractive or plated to match fittings such as door furniture.

Twinfast screws have two threads instead of one, so that fewer turns are needed to screw them in. They have more holding power than ordinary screws, and this is especially useful for joining difficult materials such as chipboard and blockboard.

Coach screws are large heavy duty screws with a square head onto which a spanner is fitted to turn them. They are used to join large pieces of wood such as bench tops, and to screw heavy metal fittings such as vices, to wood.

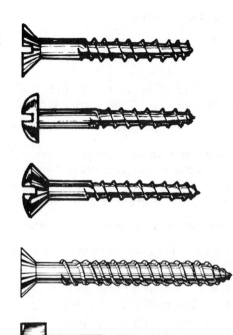

Screw caps and screw cups are used where appearance is important or where the screw must be removed frequently.

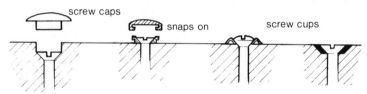

screw caps

snaps on

screw cups

Types of screwdriver slots

Straight slot. A screwdriver can slip out of a straight slot and damage both screw head and wood.

Phillips slot.

Pozidriv slot. The main advantage of Phillips and Pozidriv slots is that the screwdriver blades do not slip out of the slots so easily.

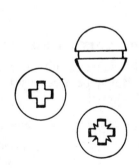

The common materials are steel and brass, and screws are often plated with chrome, zinc, nickel, or black japanning.

Steel screws are the strongest and cheapest. Brass screws look better and do not rust, but are not very strong.

The common sizes of steel countersunk screw are 6 mm to 150 mm long and 0 to 22 gauge number sizes. The gauge number indicates the diameter of the shank and the size of the head. The higher the number, the thicker the screw.

Screws are sold by:

1. Quantity (How many?)
2. Length (How long?)
3. Gauge (How thick?)
4. Material (What is it made from?)
5. Type of head (What shape? What sort of slot?)

e.g. 100, 25 mm x No. 6 steel countersunk.

Screwing into end grain. Screws will not hold in end grain without special methods being used, and nails are often better because the screw thread cuts through the grain fibres and they crumble away.

Two ways of solving this problem are shown here.

Method 1. Let a dowel into a hole across the width of the wood to provide a nut for the screw.

Method 2. Insert a rawlplug into a hole bored down the end grain. The rawlplug holds firmly in the wood and the screw holds firmly in the plug.

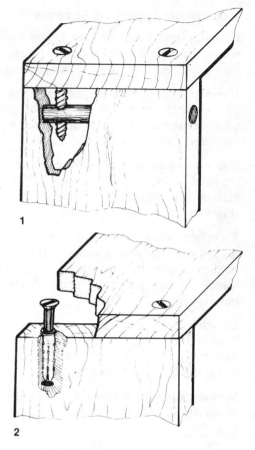

1

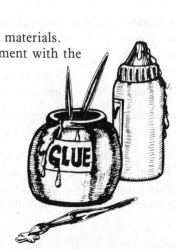

2

Glues

Choosing the correct adhesive

The following list suggests suitable adhesives for most jobs, but there are many other glues and it may be necessary to experiment when faced with an unusual combination of materials.

Acrylic to acrylic	– Tensol cements.
Acrylic to others	– It is not usual to glue acrylic to other materials. Use screws, etc. if possible, or experiment with the various types of *Bostik*.
Polystyrene to polystyrene	– Polystyrene cement.
Polystyrene to others	– Contact adhesive.
Expanded polystyrene to expanded polystyrene Expanded polystyrene to others	P.V.A., natural latex (e.g. *Copydex*), or contact adhesives used sparingly.
P.V.C. to P.V.C.	– P.V.C. cement.
P.V.C. to others	– Contact adhesive or P.V.C. cement.

Wood to wood	– a wide range of wood glues suitable for all purposes.
Wood to others	– epoxy resin or contact adhesives.
Metal to metal	– epoxy resin.
Metal to others	– epoxy resin, or contact adhesive.
Rubber to rubber	– rubber solution, contact adhesive, or natural latex.
Rubber to others	– contact adhesive or natural latex.
Leather to leather	– contact adhesives, epoxy resin or P.V.A.
Leather to others	– epoxy resin or contact adhesive.
Textiles to textiles	– natural latex.
Textiles to others	– natural latex, contact adhesive or P.V.A.
China to china or glass to glass	– epoxy resin.
China or glass to others	– epoxy resin or contact adhesive. Do *not* stick glass to wood. If the wood shrinks or warps the glass might break.

(For further details, *see* Some common glues and their uses.)

Hints on glueing

Surfaces to be joined must be clean, dry and grease free. Do not apply any finishes to the parts to be joined and remove any old paint, varnish, glue etc.

Whenever possible, slightly roughen the surfaces to be joined, to help the glue to wet the surface more thoroughly.

Plastics should be washed in warm water containing a small amount of liquid detergent, rinsed in clean warm water, and left to dry. Always *dry-cramp* the job before glueing to make sure that the parts fit, and to work-out the best method of cramping. (For details of cramping, *see* Holding tools.)

Follow the manufacturers instructions carefully. Most glues have a setting time during which pressure must be applied to hold the parts together, and a longer curing time during which the job must not be roughly handled or used.

Always check for squareness and correct assembly before the glue sets and wipe off surplus glue.

Some common glues and their uses

Scotch glue is an animal glue made from bones and hide which is used *hot* to stick wood. It is available in slab or pearl (bead) forms.

To use it, break a slab wrapped in cloth into small pieces and soak these in water overnight to form a jelly. Put the jelly and more water into the inner pot of a glue kettle, half fill the outer pot with water, and heat slowly until the glue melts into a liquid. The water in the outer pot prevents overheating. Pearl glue is ready for heating after a short soaking.

The glue is ready for use when it just runs from the brush and a thin skin forms on top. Remove the skin.

Advantages. It is cheap, does not stain wood, is very strong if the joints fit well, and there is no waste because it can be reheated several times.

Disadvantages. It must be used quickly before it cools, leaving little time to fit the job together and the job must be left in cramps overnight to set. It is not heat or water resistant.

Casein glue is an animal glue made from the curds of sour skimmed milk which is used *cold* to stick wood. It is sold as a white powder which must be mixed with water to make a thick cream and left for 20 minutes before use.

Advantages. It is heat and water resistant, but only semi-waterproof. It is very strong and can be used for several hours after mixing.

Disadvantages. It is liable to stain hardwoods and must be left in cramps overnight to set.

Synthetic resin glues are made from plastics resins and make joints in woods which are stronger than the wood itself. There are two main types.

The one shot type (e.g. Cascamite) consists of a resin and a hardener ready-mixed in a powder which must be mixed with water to make a thick cream.

The two shot type (e.g. Aerolite 306) consists of a resin powder which is mixed with water and spread on one half of the joint, and a separate hardener which is spread on the other half. The two are then pressed together and cramped. Take care not to mix up the brushes.

Advantages. They make very strong, almost colourless and waterproof joints which set in only three hours. They will fill small gaps in the joints and have a long shelf life.

Disadvantages. They stain some woods and you must mix only as much as is needed straight away to avoid waste.

P.V.A. (Polyvinyl acetate) glue (e.g. Evostik Resin W) is sold as a white ready-mixed liquid in a plastic container. It is the most widely used wood glue and is also useful for some other materials.

Advantages. It is easy to use, non-staining, strong if the joints fit well and water resistant. It has an unlimited shelf life and joints set in two hours.

Disadvantage. It is not waterproof.

Contact (impact) adhesives (e.g. *Evostik impact, Bostik, Dunlop Thixafix*) are synthetic rubbers and resins in a solvent. They are used to hold sheets of light and usually dissimilar materials together, such as Formica to a chipboard worktop and P.V.C. leathercloth upholstery to a plastics chairshell. They work because two dry films of synthetic rubber will stick under light pressure. The glue is spread evenly over both surfaces with a comb and allowed to become touch-dry, usually after about 15 minutes. One part is located over the other without allowing them to touch, and then they are pressed together. Once touched together the parts cannot be separated or moved into position.

Advantages. No cramps are needed, and this allows large difficult items to be joined.

Disadvantages. The joints are not very strong and they are not suitable for such jobs as furniture making. Once opened, the glue has a short shelf life.

Epoxy resin glues (e.g. *Araldite*) will stick wood, metal, glass, china, stone, concrete, rubber and plastics. Equal amounts of resin and hardener are mixed together, spread on very clean surfaces, and cramped together.

Advantages. They will stick almost anything.

Disadvantages. They are very expensive, and should only be used when there is no cheaper alternative. The joints are not strong enough to handle for 24 hours and do not reach their full strength for two or three days.

Resorcinol and phenol glues are considered the ultimate for high stress joints in wood. They are used mainly for such purposes as making laminated beams and boat building.

Advantages. The joints are very strong and completely waterproof.

Disadvantages. They are very expensive and leave dark brown glue lines.

Plastics cements

Joints can be made in many thermoplastics by using suitable cements containing a powerful solvent for the material being joined. Some thermoplastics (e.g. polypropylene, polythene and P.T.F.E.) cannot be cemented together because suitable solvents are not available.

Other adhesives can also be used to join plastics and to join plastics to other materials, but the joints are usually less strong than cemented joints.

Acrylic (e.g. perspex, oroglass) can be joined to itself using *Tensol* cement. Tensol No. 6 is a ready-mixed acrylic solvent which is easy to use for most purposes, but does not give a clear joint. Tensol No. 7 is a two part pack which must be mixed with care but has the advantages of making a completely clear and waterproof joint suitable for use outdoors.

Perspex is not usually stuck to other materials. Try to use screws, etc. if possible.

P.V.C. can be joined using Tensol No. 53 cement or a number of readily available P.V.C. adhesives, some of which will also stick P.V.C. to other materials (e.g. *Gloy P.V.C. repair* and *Vinyl weld*. Acetone (nail varnish remover) can be used to clean joints and remove excess glue.

Rigid polystyrene can be joined using the polystyrene cements widely sold for use with polystyrene model kits such as *Airfix*. They dry quickly and give a clear joint. Glue can be removed with acetone or carbon tetrachloride.

Soldering, brazing and welding metals

Soldering makes a permanent joint between 2 pieces of metal, by using an alloy which has a lower melting point than the metals being joined, as a 'glue'. This alloy makes the bond by forming an alloy with the base metals which are not melted during the process.

Soft soldering, hard soldering and brazing are all examples of this process, while welding works by melting the edges to be joined so that they fuse together. A filler rod of similar metal is added to fill the weld.

These joints all involve heating the metal and the higher the temperature needed the stronger will be the joint made. Where several joints are to be made on the same job, the first is made at the highest temperature and the others, in turn, at progressively lower temperatures.

The following chart shows the correct temperature, flux and filler rod for each process.

Process	Filler rod	Flux	Approx. temperature
Welding	Same as parent metal	None needed for mild steel. Depends on metal being welded.	Melting temperature of metal.
Brazing	Brazing spelter 65% copper 35% zinc (brass)	Borax (usually in a proprietory flux).	875°C
Silver soldering or hard soldering	Enamelling (81% silver plus copper and zinc)	Borax	800°C
	Hard (78% silver)	Borax	775°C
	Medium (74% silver)	Borax	750°C
	Easy (67% silver)	Borax	720°C
	Easy-flo (50% silver)	Easy-flo flux	625°C
Tinman's soldering or soft soldering	50% lead 50% tin	Active – zinc chloride Passive – resin	200°C

Fluxes

The purposes of a flux are:

1. To protect the cleaned surfaces from oxidisation during heating. Solders only stick to clean metal.

2. To break down the surface tension of the filler rod so that the solder will run into the joint.

3. To chemically clean the joint. Only active fluxes, such as zinc chloride for tin soldering, do this. Active fluxes can only be used where the job can be washed to remove surplus flux after cleaning.

Soft soldering

Soldering irons. The bit is made of copper because it has a high heat storage capacity, is a good conductor of heat and is easily wetted with solder. Soldering irons are heated in a gas soldering stove or by internal gas or electric heaters. When the gas flame turns green the copper is hot enough.

hatchett bit

straight bit

Tinning the bit before use. Heat the soldering iron to soldering temperature, quickly file the copper clean, flux it and roll it in a tin-lid full of solder, to coat it with fresh solder.

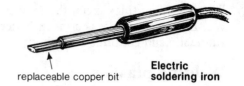

replaceable copper bit

Electric soldering iron

Stages in soft soldering a joint.

1. The joint must be clean and close fitting so that the solder will flow in by capillary action.

2. Flux the joint. Active fluxes should be used if possible as they are more effective. Passive fluxes are used for such jobs as soldering electronics components where the job cannot be washed afterwards and an active flux would corrode the metal.

3. The surfaces to be joined are tinned with a film of solder using a soldering iron. It is necessary to allow time for the job to heat up so that the solder flows from the iron to the surfaces.

4. The tinned surfaces are refluxed and pressed together. Heat is applied with either a flame or a clean hot soldering iron, to remelt the solder and join the surfaces.

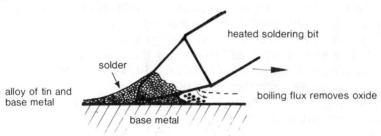

heated soldering bit

solder

alloy of tin and base metal

boiling flux removes oxide

base metal

Hard soldering and brazing

Stages in hard soldering or brazing a joint.

1. Clean the joint with file and emery cloth and make sure it fits together well.

2. Mix the correct flux to a thick creamy consistency.

3. Paint the flux onto the joint and onto the end of the filler rod.

4. Wire the joint together if necessary.

5. Heat the joint to the correct heat with a blow torch, gently at first to dry the flux.

6. Touch the solder onto the joint. If the joint is hot enough, the heat from the job will melt the solder, and it will run along the joint.

7. Remove the heat and allow the joint to cool.

Welding metals

Two pieces of the same metal are heated using either a very hot oxy-acetylene flame, or an electric arc, until the surfaces to be joined melt. At the same time a filler rod is melted into the joint to fill in the gap between the two pieces of metal. The molten pool of metal formed during welding rapidly solidifies, fusing the surfaces together. A properly welded joint should be as strong as the surrounding metal.

When welding thick metal the joint is prepared by bevelling the edges to form a vee. In industry there is a much wider range of welding processes, including automatic and continuous methods.

Welding plastics

The process is basically the same as when welding metals. Two pieces of the same material, and if needed a filler rod of this material, are heated until they soften, and pressure is applied to fuse them together.

There are two methods commonly used in school. These are heated tool welding, to fuse thin sheets up to 1 mm thick and films, and hot air welding for thicker sheets. In industry a wider range of methods is available.

In heated tool welding a tool similar to an electric soldering iron is drawn across two thicknesses of thin sheet to soften them, followed by a roller to press the joint together. Heated tool and roller can be combined into one heated roller which is wheeled across the joint.

To prevent the sheet melting and sticking to the hot roller, a sheet of polyester film such as *Melinex* is placed between the roller and the sheet being welded.

In hot air or hot gas welding a stream of hot air or gas is used to heat the surfaces being joined and the filler rod, exactly as when oxy-acetylene welding. The simplest hot air welding tools are similar to hair dryers with interchangeable nozzles and temperature control. The joint is prepared by bevelling the edges to form a vee and by cleaning them. When the material has been heated to the correct temperature, the softened filler rod is pressed into the vee to fuse the parts together. This is often done by feeding the filler rod through a tube attached to the nozzle so that it can be heated and pressed with the same tool.

Suitable plastics for welding. Only thermoplastics which do not burn or decompose when heated to their softening temperature can be welded.

Polythene, polystyrene, polypropylene, P.V.C., nylon and some acrylics are examples of thermoplastics which can be welded by both the above methods.

Rivets

Rivets are used to make permanent joints in metal, to join metal to soft materials and for joining soft materials to each other.

Solid rivets

Snap or round head rivets are used for general purposes where a flush finish is not important and countersinking would weaken the job.

Countersunk head rivets are used for general purposes where a flush surface is needed. They are the most commonly used type.

Flat head rivets are used for joining thin plates which cannot be countersunk.

Bifuracted rivets are used for joining soft materials such as leather, plastics and occasionally thin plywood.

washer

To choose the correct rivet you must know:

1. The length.

2. The diameter – 3 mm is the commonest size in school.

3. The shape of the head.

4. The material from which it is made – low carbon steel, brass, aluminium stainless steel, copper etc.

In order to work out the correct length you must know how much of the rivet shank to leave projecting, ready to be shaped into a second head.

On a countersunk rivet allow an extra 1 × the diameter of the rivet.

On a roundhead rivet allow an extra $1\frac{1}{2}$ × the diameter of the rivet.

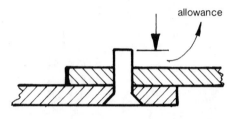

allowance

Riveting tools

The rivet set is used for setting or pressing together metal plates and making sure that the rivet is pulled all the way into the hole. The hole in the set is the same size as the rivet diameter.

The rivet snap (or dolly) is used to support the head of a round head rivet while riveting (dolly), and to finish a round head rivet to the correct shape (snap). It has a concave hole the same size and shape as the rivet head, and two are needed to complete a round head rivet.

Both set and snap can be combined into one tool and are available in several sizes to fit different rivet diameters.

Stages in roundhead riveting.

1. Drill both plates. Clean off any burrs.

2. Support the rivet head with a dolly held in the vice.

3. Swell the rivet with the flat face of a hammer until it is tight in its hole.

4. Use the ball-pein to shape the head.

5. Finish the head with the snap to make a smooth shape.

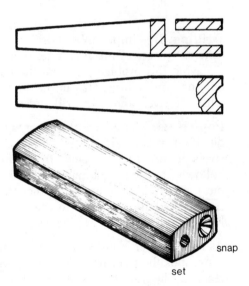

snap

set

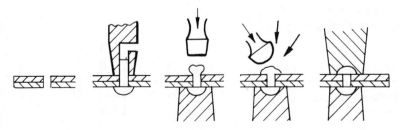

Stages in countersunk riveting.

1. Drill and countersink both plates. Clean off any burrs.

2. Put in the rivet and press the rivet and the plates together with a set. Support the countersunk head on a flat block.

3. Swell the rivet with the flat face of a hammer until it is tight in its hole.

4. Use the ball-pein to fill up the countersink.

5. Finish with the flat face and file the head smooth. A good countersunk rivet should be almost invisible.

   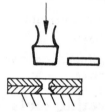

Drilling. It is impossible to drill several holes in two different pieces of metal and get them to match up exactly. To avoid this problem, drill all the holes in one piece, but only one in the other. Clean off the burrs, join the pieces with one rivet, and then drill and rivet one hole at a time.

Pop rivets. These have the advantage that they can be set quickly from one side only. They are weaker than solid rivets because they are made from soft metal and are hollow. They are used mainly for joining thin sheet metal, but they can also be used for other thin materials. Washers can be put onto the rivets to enable soft materials such as leather and rubber to be riveted.

As the mandrel is pulled through by the pop riveting pliers, it expands the rivet head. When the correct pressure is reached, the head breaks off and stays in the rivet.

Nuts, bolts and machine screws

All these fixings are usually made of steel or brass and can be coated either to rustproof the steel or to improve their appearance.

Bolts usually have either a square or a hexagonal head. They are ordered by the diameter of the thread and the length to the underside of the head. Bolts may be threaded for all or part of their length.

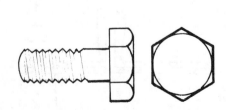

Coach bolts are used to join wood to wood or wood to other materials. They have a domed head with a square collar underneath which is pressed into the wood to prevent the bolt turning. They are usually used for strong structural woodwork.

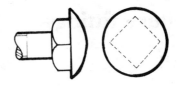

Machine screws are available in a wide range of thread diameters, lengths and head shapes.

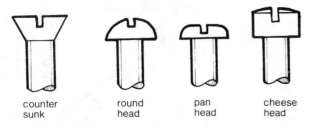

counter sunk   round head   pan head   cheese head

Nuts are either plain square, plain hexagonal, wing nuts for easy removal, or special locking nuts to prevent vibration loosening them.

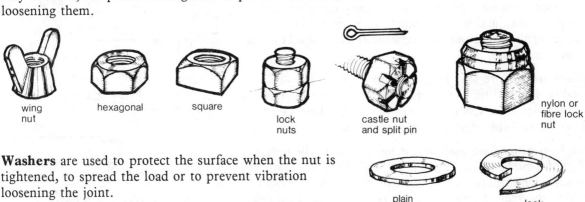

wing nut   hexagonal   square   lock nuts   castle nut and split pin   nylon or fibre lock nut

Washers are used to protect the surface when the nut is tightened, to spread the load or to prevent vibration loosening the joint.

plain washer   lock washer

Self-tapping screws are used to join thin sheets of metal and plastics, and as chipboard screws where ordinary woodscrews would cause the chipboard to crumble. They are made of hardened steel so that they can cut their own thread as they are screwed in.

Common sizes are 6 mm to 50 mm with Phillips, Pozidriv and straight slots.

Drill a tapping size hole equal to the core diameter of the screw.

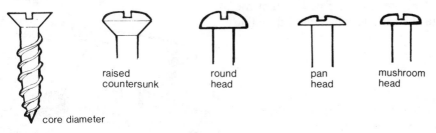

raised countersunk   round head   pan head   mushroom head

core diameter

countersunk

Furniture fittings

Hinges

The sketches show a few of the common types of hinge. There are many others.

Butt hinges are used for room and cupboard doors, small boxes and windows. They are usually made of steel, nylon or brass, and may be plated. They fit onto the edge of the wood and are usually recessed so that when the door is closed they are neat and almost hidden. The main disadvantage is that because the screws are close together and in a straight line there is a danger of splitting the wood.

Back flap hinges are used for drop-down leaves and flaps, and strong tool box lids. They are usually made of steel, nylon or brass, and may be plated. They fit onto the surface of the wood and the screw holes are spaced out for greater strength.

Piano hinges are long lengths of butt hinge. They are used on box and furniture lids. They are neat and allow the screw holes to be spread out over the whole door length. They conceal the edges of man-made slabs.

Laid on hinges are used where doors fit onto the outside edge of a cupboard and must open within the width of the cabinet, for example, when a row of kitchen unit doors fit closely together in a row. The doors can usually be opened through 180°. The hinges are usually made of plated steel.

Flush hinges are light weight hinges where one flap fits into the other when closed. The hinge is thin and does not need recessing. They are usually made of plated steel.

Tee hinges are used on shed doors, gates, and workshop cupboards. The long arm spreads the load across several planks of a tongue and grooved door, while the short arm fits onto a narrow frame or post.

Stays are used to control the opening of fall flaps and to keep lift-up doors open. They are usually fitted so that the fully open stay is at 45° to the cabinet when the lid or flap is opened to 90°.

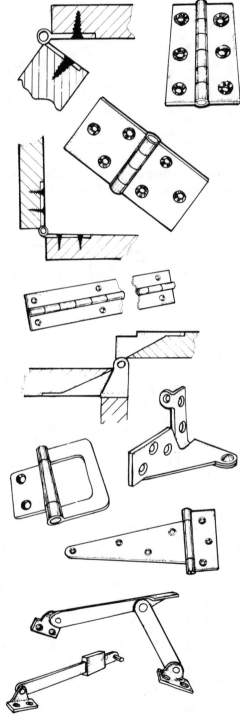

Catches

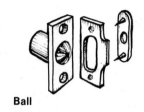

Magnetic **Ball** **Spring**

Locks

Surface fitting cupboard and drawer locks are screwed onto the inside surface of the door or drawer.

Cut cupboard or drawer locks are recessed into the door or drawer edge. The two keyholes enable the lock to be used vertically or horizontally.

Box locks are used for lift-up lids and sliding doors where a cupboard lock would pull open.

A sliding bolt in the lock engages with the hooks on the keep.

Sliding doors

So that the doors can be lifted out, the top track is twice as deep as the bottom track. To remove a door, lift it and pull the bottom outwards. The tracks can be made by cutting grooves or by using ready-made channels.

Adjustable shelves

There are many ready-made adjustable shelving systems available, but we have shown here one simple way of fitting adjustable shelves into cabinets.

1. Drill 6.5 mm diameter holes 10 mm deep into the sides.

2. Cut lengths of 6 mm diameter nylon, aluminium or brass rod, and file or face off to 20 mm long. Chamfer the ends to ease fitting.

3. File approximately halfway through for half of the peg length.

4. The shelf resting on the dowels prevents them from falling out.

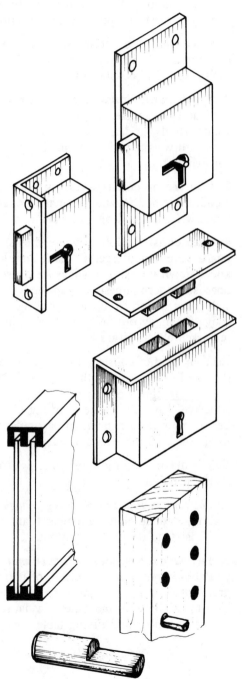

Constructions in wood

There are four types of construction in wood; carcase construction, stool frame construction, flat frame construction and slab construction. Many pieces of work contain examples of more than one type, and there are usually at least two possible constructions for any job.

1. Carcase or box construction is where planks of wood are joined to make box shapes such as cabinets, drawers, tool-boxes and bookshelves.

2. Stool frame construction is where a supporting frame is made from several legs and rails, such as in tables, chairs, stools, underframes for cabinets and frames covered with lightweight panels, as an alternative to carcase construction.

3. Flat frame construction is where several pieces of wood are joined together to make flat shapes such as doors, window frames and picture frames.

4. Slab construction is where sheets, usually of man-made boards, are joined together using simple permanent or knock-down joints. The widespread use of man-made boards, modern adhesives, and ready-made joints has caused slab construction to replace the three traditional methods above for many purposes, such as built-in furniture and self-assembly furniture kits.

Each method of construction is governed by a set of rules designed to ensure that the final product is sound and pleasing in appearance, and although modern materials and adhesives have made woodworking easier, it is still necessary to follow them. In particular there are appropriate joints for each material and purpose.

Before making each job, examine your design carefully and make sure that:

1. The construction will be strong enough. For example, if making a coffee table remember that people will sit and perhaps stand on it at some time.

2. You have not misused the chosen materials. For example, you should not joint two pieces of natural timber with the grain in one piece at right angles to the grain in the other. You must allow for movement in natural timber. (*See* Faults in timber and Fixing table tops.)

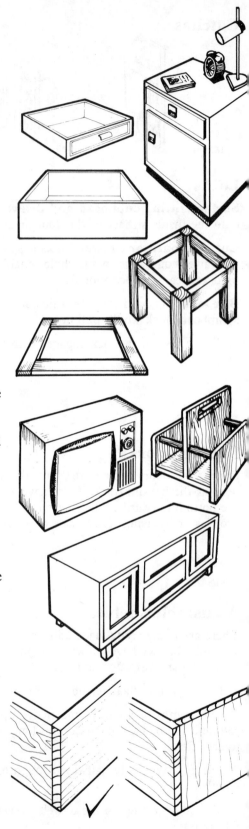

3. You have used the correct joints in the correct way. For example, a double tenon should be used to join a wide rail into a leg to avoid weakening it. A dovetail should only be pulled apart in one direction. Make sure that this is the direction which takes the smaller strain.

Many joints are designed to reduce the risk of warping. A shelf of natural timber which has been housed at both ends should stay flat, but the same shelf simply resting on brackets is likely to cup. Therefore, an adjustable shelf might be better made from man-made board.

4. It will be possible to assemble the job when you have cut the joints. It is very easy to design joints which cannot all be assembled at the same time because they go together in different directions.

Joints

On the pages which follow we have shown the most used joints, together with examples of how they are used for each type of construction.

Flat frame construction – corner joints

The sketches on this page show some of the simple joints which can be used to make a flat frame such as a flush door (right), and then some of the more advanced joints used in better quality work.

Butt joints are the quickest and simplest joints to make, but they are not very strong and must usually be strengthened by dovetail nailing, corrugated fasteners, or wood or metal reinforcing plates. On the flush door above, the ply- or hardboard panels would provide most of the strength.

Mitre joints are neater than butt joints because the end grain is hidden, but they are harder to make because the ends must be cut at 45° and fitted accurately together.

The mitre can be strengthened by nailing or by inserting veneer keys into saw cuts across the joint.

Corner halving joints are stronger than butt joints and simple to make, but still need strengthening with screws or dowels for heavier work.

Dowelled joints are neat and strong. The holes must be lined up exactly but this can be done using a dowelling jig. The dowels are coned at the ends to make them easier to drive in, and grooved to let surplus glue escape. (The making of dowel jigs is discussed in chapter 7 – Holding tools.)

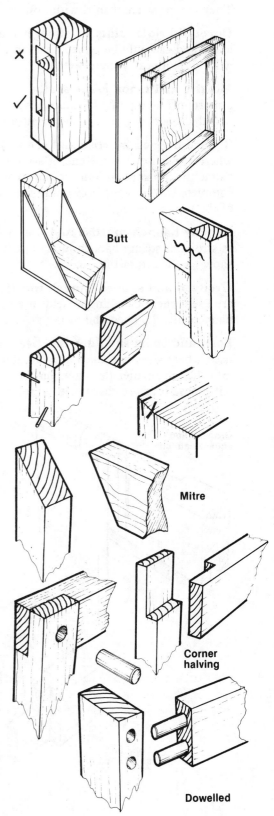

Butt

Mitre

Corner
halving

Dowelled

Corner bridle joints are strong and fairly easy to make. They can be strengthened with dowels.

Dovetail bridle joints are stronger than corner bridle joints and can only be pulled apart in one direction. They will therefore carry more weight.

Mortise and tenon joints are the strongest and most important frame joints for more advanced work such as panelled doors and frames for furniture making.

Square haunch mortise and tenon joints are used where a mortise is at the end of a piece of wood. The haunch is designed to join the rail to the leg for its complete width, while preventing the mortise breaking out of the top of the leg.

Sloping haunch mortise and tenon joints are not quite as strong as square haunch joints but the haunch does not show on the top of the leg.

Grooved and square haunch mortise and tenon joints are used where panelling is held in a frame. The square haunch fills the open end of the groove.

Long and short shoulder mortise and tenon joints are used where glass is held in a frame. The glass can be fitted into the rebate after the frame has been made, and held with loose beads so that it can be replaced if broken.

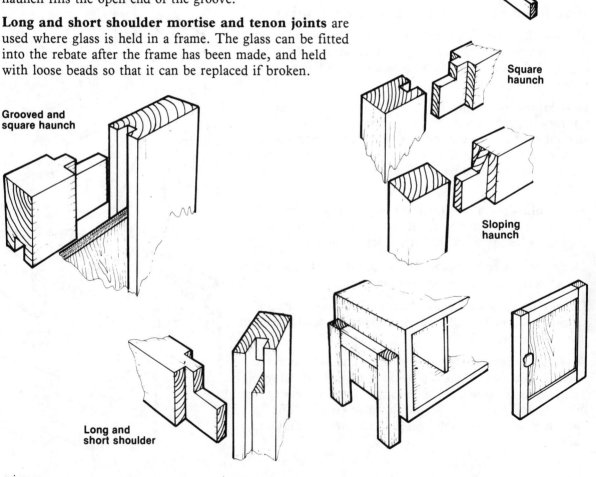

Corner bridle

Dovetail bridle

Square haunch

Sloping haunch

Grooved and square haunch

Long and short shoulder

Flat frame construction – tee and cross joints

When a flat frame has a horizontal centre rail or a vertical *muntin*, tee and cross joints are needed.

Butt joints are made and strengthened in the same ways as corner butt joints.

Tee halving joints can be strengthened by dowels or screws or by the use of a dovetail halving joint.

Dovetail halving joints can only be pulled apart in one direction.

Dowel tee joints are fairly simple to make using a dowel jig, as for dowelled corner joints.

Tee bridle joints can be strengthened by dowels.

Mortise and tenon joints are the strongest tee joints, and can be further strengthened by wedging or dowelling. This is a through mortise but a stopped mortise can be used to hide the end grain on the tenon.

Cross halving joints are the usual way of joining two rails which cross without cutting right through either piece. Alternatively, cut a through mortise in one piece, cut the other piece in half, and make a tenon on the end of each to go into the mortise, or use dowel joints.

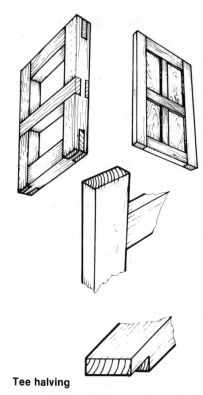

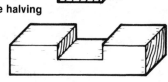

Tee halving

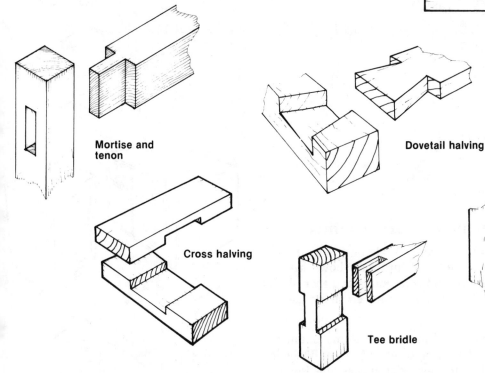

Mortise and tenon

Dovetail halving

Cross halving

Tee bridle

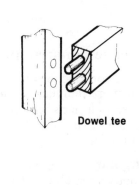

Dowel tee

Stool frame construction

All the joints shown in the preceeding section can also be used in stool frame constructions, but in addition there are special combinations of joints used where two rails join into a leg at the same level.

Square haunch mortise and tenon joints are used where rails join into the top of a leg. If two rails join at the same level the tenons are mitred so that they fit together inside the leg. The haunches will show on the top of the leg.

Secret haunch mortise and tenon joints are used where the haunches must not be seen on the top of the leg, for example where there is no stool or table top to hide them.

Single dovetail joints can be used to make frame constructions as shown below, where the rails and legs are joined in a 'box' construction.

More details of dovetails will be found in Carcase construction.

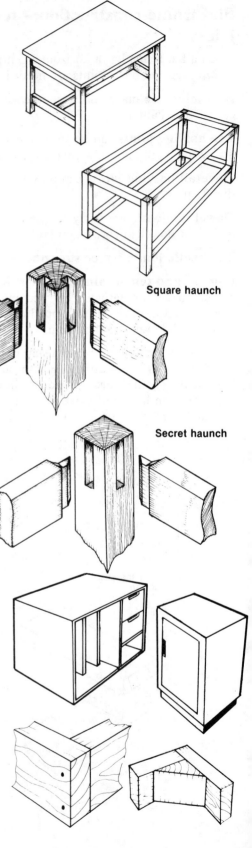

Square haunch

Secret haunch

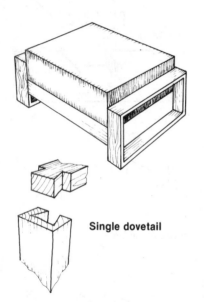

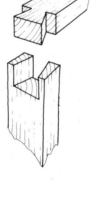

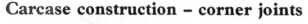

Single dovetail

Carcase construction – corner joints

Carcase constructions range from simple butt jointed boxes to the more complicated pieces of furniture shown here. This section starts with the simplest joints and then shows more advanced joints suitable for furniture making using solid timber.

Butt joints are the quickest and simplest to make, but they are not very strong, and show a lot of end grain. They are reinforced by dovetail nailing, wooden blocks glued or screwed in, or metal angle brackets.

Corner rebate or lap joints are stronger than butt joints because they increase the area being glued, and neater because less end grain shows. They are simple to make, and as the diagram shows are convenient for use with grooves or rebates as the lap hides the end of them.

Finger or comb joints are simple to make because there are no dovetail-type angles, and strong because of the large glueing area. They are often used for machine-made joints.

Through dovetail joints are the strongest carcase construction joints because they can only be pulled apart in one direction and have a large glueing area. They can also be an attractive feature if well made.

Lap dovetail joints are used where the joint must not show on one surface such as for the front corner joints of drawers, and the tops of cabinets where a smooth surface with no end grain is important. Lap dovetails allow grooves to be cut without making special dovetail joints to hide the ends.

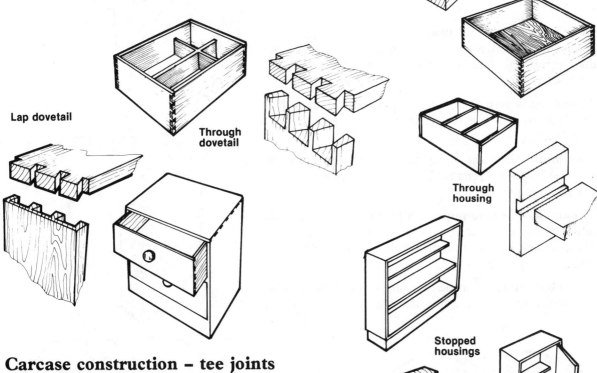

Corner rebate or lap

Finger or comb

Lap dovetail

Through dovetail

Through housing

Stopped housings

Carcase construction – tee joints

Housing joints are the most used method of fitting shelves and partitions into carcases.

Through housings are simple to make and are suitable where the two parts being joined are the same width.

Stopped housings are harder to make, but are neater because the joint does not show on the front edge. They are also used where the shelf is narrower than the side.

Dovetail housings are used to give strong joints where there is danger of them being pulled apart, as when books are wedged into a bookcase. They can be through or stopped, and dovetailed on one or both sides.

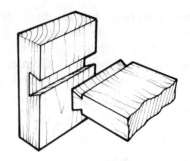

Mortise and tenon joints can be used to make a stronger tee joint, especially for fitting vertical partitions which must bear heavy weights. They can be through or stopped, but are often taken through so that they can be strengthened by wedging. Strong attractive joints can be made by using housings with tenons near the edges to help prevent warping.

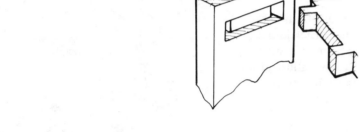

Edge jointing of solid timber.

Solid timber is often too narrow for cabinet work and it must therefore be jointed along its edges, by one of the methods shown.

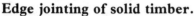

The timber is prepared by planing the edges true with a try-plane, so that they are perfectly flat and square to the face-side.

Butt joints depend on the quality of the preparation and of the glue for their strength. There are several ways of strengthening them.

Tongue and groove joints can be made using matching tonguing and grooving cutters in a combination plane, or by ploughing grooves in both pieces and inserting a loose tongue of plywood.

Dowelled joints are made by using a dowel jig on both prepared boards to make sure that the holes line up.

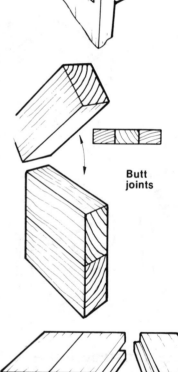

Butt joints

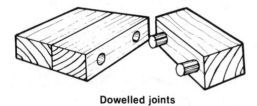

Dowelled joints

Tongue and groove joints

Joint proportions in wood

Mortise and tenon.

Length of haunch (L) = thickness of tenon.

Match thickness of tenon to the nearest mortise chisel size, usually 6, 8, 10 or 12 mm.

Length of tenon (T) = width of wood containing mortise for a through joint, and two-thirds of the width for a stopped joint.

Bridle.

Dovetail.
Mark out and cut the tails first and draw round the tails to mark the pins.

T = thickness of the wood.

The dovetail slope is 1:6 for softwood and 1:8 for hardwood. Remember the average slope of 1:7.

P = approximately $\frac{1}{4}$S.

Stages in marking out tails.

1. Before dividing up the width of the wood, leave half the width of a pin ($\frac{1}{2}$P) at each side so that the outer pins will be strong enough to resist splitting when the joint is assembled. (3 to 5 mm is usually a convenient amount to leave.)

2. Then decide on the number of tails needed and divide up the remaining shape as shown into equal spaces (S).

3. Mark out the pin widths (P) and use a dovetail template or adjustable bevel to complete the shape.

Housing.
Depth of joint (D) = $\frac{1}{3}$ to $\frac{1}{2}$ the thickness of the wood (Th), or

Halving.

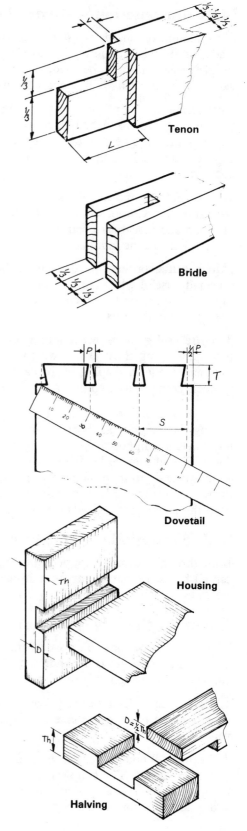

Tenon

Bridle

Dovetail

Housing

Halving

Slab construction – corner joints

Since man-made boards are stable, no allowance has to be made for expansion, contraction or warping. This allows simple constructions to be used, especially where later veneering or painting will conceal them.

Butt joints are simple and quite strong when used with man-made boards to make box constructions. The joint can be strengthened by screwed or glued corner blocks, and exposed edges can be lipped, veneered, painted or stained as appropriate.

Corner rebate or lap joints are neater and do not need strengthening. Chipboard is not joined in this way, but plywood and blockboard can be lapped, taking care to cut along a joint in the laminations.

Mitre joints conceal the edges of the boards, and are especially useful when joining veneered material. Well cut mitres are quite strong when glued, but blocks are usually used as for butt joints.

Tongue and groove joints into a corner block or leg provide a strong construction which conceals the edges of the boards, allows shaping of the cabinet corners, and protects corners from chipping of veneers.

Dowelled joints are a strong and fairly simple method of joining these man-made boards and are especially suitable for veneered chipboard. Where a number of similar dowelled joints are to be drilled, make a metal drilling jig as shown and pin it in the correct position on each piece in turn, to guide the drill. Use a thick piece of metal to help keep the drill square. (*See* Dowel jigs.)

Slab construction – tee joints

Butt, through housing, stopped housing and dowelled joints can all be used for tee joints in man-made boards as they are in carcase construction.

Covering the edges of man-made boards

The edges of plywood, blockwood and chipboard can be covered in several ways depending on the quality of the job and the use to which it is to be put.

1. Paint. Carefully finished plywood edges can be painted, usually either black or a shade of brown similar to the veneer colour.

2. Veneer. Wood veneer can be applied to the edges of any man-made board. The simplest methods are using either pre-glued iron-on edging strips or strips cut from a sheet and glued with contact adhesive.

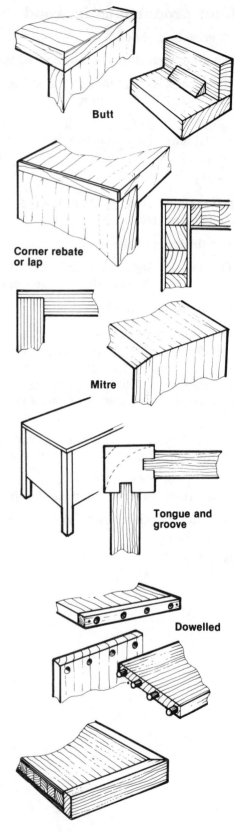

Butt

Corner rebate or lap

Mitre

Tongue and groove

Dowelled

3. Solid wood. Where the edges have to withstand knocks, strips of solid wood can be glued on. The corners are mitred. This method is the best way of edging boards which will be veneered later. The butt joint can be strengthened by using either a tongue and groove joint or a loose tongue.

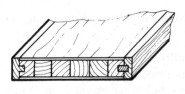

4. Plastic and metal edging strips. A wide variety of strips which either glue, screw or nail on are available. Alternatively, where a plastic laminate such as formica is used, matching strips can be cut from the same sheet.

Fixing table tops and underframes

Solid wood tops. Solid wood usually shrinks, mainly across the grain, in centrally heated buildings and expands in damp conditions. This movement is allowed for when fixing a solid wood top to an underframe.

Methods

1. *Wood buttons.* A set of buttons is made across the end of a board so that the grain is in the strongest direction.

Fit the projecting tongue into a shallow groove or mortise on the inside of the rail. Screw into the top.

The button top is sloped to make sure that the top is pulled tight down onto the rail (see right).

Allowance for movement at the end is made in the mortise, and at the side by a space between the rail and button shoulder.

2. *Metal plates.* Straight or right-angled 3 mm thick steel or brass plates are screwed to the rails with countersunk screws in round holes, and to the top with round head screws in slots (see below).

The diagrams show how the slots are arranged to allow for movement across the grain on a table corner, and a dual purpose bracket with slots for screwing at end, or at side of top.

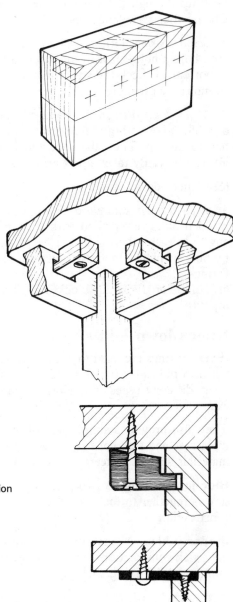

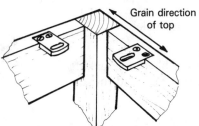

Grain direction of top

Man-made tops. Man-made boards are almost free from movement, and therefore fixing is much simpler.

Methods.

It is possible to screw through a flat top rail, but with a thick rail other methods are needed to avoid very long screws.

1. *Pocket screwing.* Cut a row of pockets inside the top rails with a gouge and drill down from the top into these pockets.

Drill up through the slot into the top and put in the screw. Choose the screw length carefully.

2. *Counterboring.* Drill a clearance hole through the rail and then bore a hole equal in diameter to the screw head. It is important to check the screw length and depth of counterbore carefully.

3. *Knock-down fittings.* To make a removeable top, one half of a bloc-joint fitting is screwed to the rail, and the other half to the top. The halves are joined by a screw so that the job can be easily taken apart and reassembled.

(*See* Knock-down joints.)

4. *Screwed blocks and glued blocks:* either, square-section wooden blocks are drilled with clearance holes at right angles to each other, and screwed to rails and top; or, a number of plastic modesty blocs are used (*see* Knock-down fittings);
or, square or triangular blocks are glued between rails and top.

Knockdown joints

'K.D.' fittings are used to make furniture which can be taken to pieces for moving and reassembled later. There are many different types and below we show only a few examples.

They also provide a simple way of making permanent joints in carcase and slab constructions, especially in difficult materials such as veneered chipboard.

Bloc-joint fitting. A two piece plastic K.D. joint which screws together to make a 90° angle joint in slab construction.

Modesty bloc. A small one-piece plastic block for making light slab constructions, for strengthening butt and mitred joints, and for fixing shelves, etc.

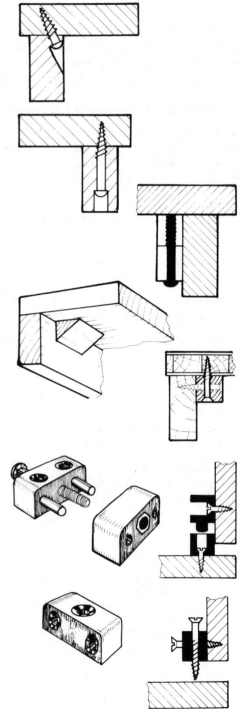

Scan fittings. These fittings are the most used way of making K.D. frame constructions. They can also be used for slab constructions. Each joint consists of a countersunk head machine screw with a socket for an *Allen key*, a brass collar to protect the wood where the screw head is tightened against it, and a cross-dowel into which the screw is tightened. Brass dowels can be used to prevent any rotation of the two pieces being joined.

Leg fastenings. This fitting is used where the joint has to be taken apart frequently and especially for joining legs. The hanger bolt remains in the leg, and the wing nut is unscrewed to take off the leg.

Joints in metal

Frame joints. When making metal frame constructions, such as stools or tables, it is sometimes necessary to make joints similar to woodwork joints. This is in order to increase the area of contact for brazing or hard soldering, to obtain a flush joint where two pieces cross, or to give a neat appearance, especially when joining tubes.

Butt joints are used when welding, but are often not strong enough for brazed joints because of the small area of contact.

Mitred joints are neat and especially useful for concealing the ends of square and round tubes.

Dowelled joints are a neat, easy way to make a stronger frame joint, for example when making a wrought iron gate. Spigots can be turned by holding the metal in a four jaw chuck or filed by hand. Alternatively, loose dowels can be used.

Halving joints are an alternative to dowelled joints. The cross-halving is the most used, because it is the best way to make a flush cross joint. The U-shapes are hard to cut out by hand.

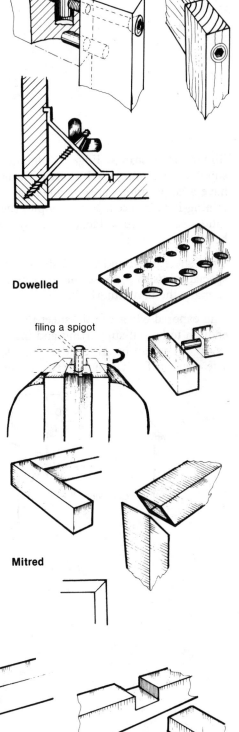

Dowelled

filing a spigot

Mitred

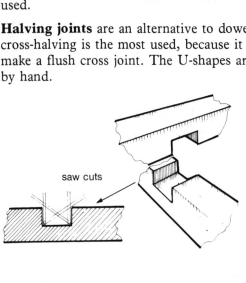

saw cuts

Halving

Dovetail joints are used to make very strong corner joints in flat pieces of metal.

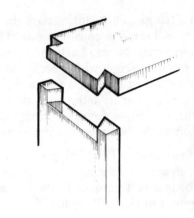

Sheet metal joints. Edge to edge butt joints are only suitable for joining thick sheet materials where the edges have a large contact area or where a strong method of joining is to be used. For example, they are used where mild steel is to be welded, or brass, silver and copper are to be silver soldered.

Thin sheet metal and coated sheet such as tinplate need special joints to increase the joint area for soft soldering, or to make the parts interlock.

The exposed edges of thin sheet metal are rarely strong enough to be self-supporting and may be dangerously sharp. They can be stiffened and made safe by forming a safe edge, or further reinforced by using a wired edge.

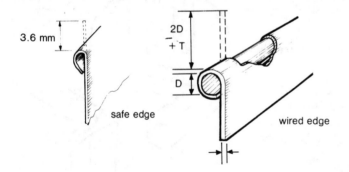

3.6 mm

safe edge

2D + T

D

wired edge

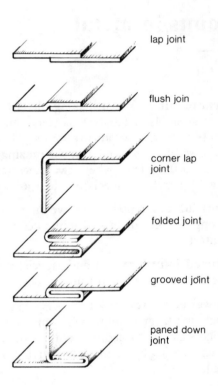

lap joint

flush join

corner lap joint

folded joint

grooved joint

paned down joint

15 Materials for craftwork (1) wood

Part 1　How a tree grows

Roots	These absorb water and mineral salts, and make crude sap.
Sapwood	This carries crude sap to the leaves.
Leaves	Plant food is manufactured in the leaves by the process of photosynthesis. In this process sugars are formed out of water (from the sap) and carbon dioxide (from the air) using energy absorbed by chlorophyll from sunlight.
Bast	This carries plant food down from the leaves to all parts of the tree.
Medullary rays	carry plant food from the bast into the cambium layer, sapwood, and heartwood, and store it.
Cambium layer	This contains cells capable of division to produce sapwood cells on the inside and bast cells on the outside, to make the tree grow.
Sapwood	is the living part of the tree. It consists of cellulose cells which have thin walls capable of absorbing moisture from the roots, and plant food to grow.
Heartwood	is the commercially most useful part of the tree. It consists of cells which have become clogged with gum and die. They are stronger, more durable, and more resistant to insect and fungal attack than sapwood, and provide the strength to support the tree. A young tree consists mainly of sapwood but as it grows it makes heartwood. Waste products are stored here.
Pith	is the centre of the trunk consisting of the original sapling, from which the tree grew, and is often soft.
Bark	is a protective covering to protect the tree from damage and extremes of temperature. It is made from the outer layers of bast as they die, and consists of a soft inner layer which expands as the tree grows and a hard outer layer.

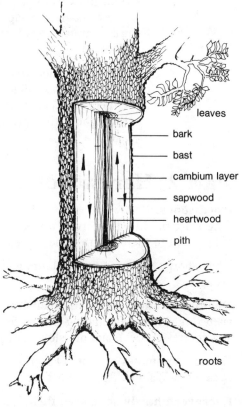

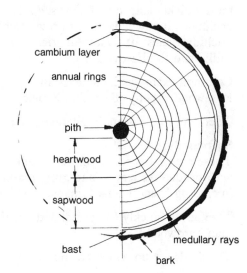

Annual rings   each represents one year's growth. In spring, the cambium layer makes wide thin-walled cells so that a large amount of sap can reach the leaves quickly. These cells are pale, soft and weak. In summer, the tree needs less sap, and so it makes narrow cells with thick walls which are dark, hard and strong. In winter, the tree rests and no sap flows. This cycle gives alternate pale and dark annual rings from which we can count the age of softwood trees.

Some hardwood trees (e.g. oak and ash) produce light and dark growth rings similar to, but less distinct than, those of softwood. Others (e.g. beech and mahogany) grow at an even rate throughout the spring and summer and so we cannot tell their age.

Part 2 Hardwoods and softwoods

Hardwoods.
These are produced by broad leaved trees (having leaves broad in width in proportion to their length) whose seeds are enclosed in fruit (e.g. apple, acorn).

They show a wide range of colours and grain patterns and are divided into two groups:

Deciduous hardwoods lose their leaves in winter. They grow in warmer *temperate* climates (including the British Isles, Europe, Japan, New Zealand, Chile and central U.S.A.), and are slow growing (100 years) and expensive.

Common examples include: Oak, Ash, Elm, Beech, Birch, Chestnut, Lime, Sycamore, Walnut, Apple and Pear.

Evergreen hardwoods keep their leaves all the year round, and therefore grow more quickly and to a greater size. They are usually softer and easier to work than deciduous hardwoods. They grow mainly in *tropical and sub-tropical* climates (including most of South America, central America, Indo-China, Africa, Burma, India, and the East and West Indies).

Common examples include: Mahogany, Teak, African Walnut, Afrormosia, Iroko, Rosewood, Ebony, Balsa and Sapele.

There are two European evergreen hardwoods, the Holly and the Laurel.

Softwoods.
These are produced by conifers (cone bearing trees). They are usually evergreen with needle-like leaves, and grow mainly in colder and cooler temperate climates (including Scandinavia, Canada, Northern Russia, and at high altitudes elsewhere).

They grow quickly (30 years) and are therefore cheaper, softer and easier to work than hardwoods.

The seeds are not enclosed, but are held in cones.

Common examples include: the many types of Pine, Spruce, Fir, Cedar, Larch and Giant Redwood.

Yew is a coniferous tree which does not produce cones. Larch is the only deciduous coniferous tree.

Note The names softwood and hardwood describe the leaves, seeds and structure of the trees, and not necessarily the timber produced. As a result, some hardwoods (notably Balsa) are light in weight and very soft to work, while some softwoods (e.g. Yew and Pitch Pine) are heavy and hard to work.

Commonly available forms of hardwood and softwood

Remember when ordering timber that the widths and thicknesses of all timbers are given as the rough sawn sizes. You can buy machine-planed timber either planed on both sides (P.B.S.) or planed all round (P.A.R.), but its size will still be described as the nominal (rough sawn) size, although it will actually be approximately 3 mm smaller in thickness and if P.A.R. in width too.

A *board* is a piece of wood less than 40 mm thick and 75 mm, or over, wide.

Common thicknesses are 12, 16, 19, 22 and 25 mm.
Common widths for softwood are from 75 mm to 225 mm.
Common widths for hardwood are from 150 mm to 330 mm.
Lengths normally start at 1.8 metres and go up to 6.3 metres.

A *plank* is a piece of wood over 40 mm thick.

Squares are square sections.

Common sizes for squares are 25 mm × 25 mm, 38 mm × 38 mm, and 50 mm × 50 mm.

Strips are rectangular sections narrower than 75 mm wide. Common sizes for strips are 25 mm × 38 mm and 25 mm × 50 mm.

Part 3 Conversion of timber

Conversion means the sawing of logs into usable sizes with the minimum of waste. There are many different methods to suit different timbers and purposes.

The two main ones are:

Plain sawing (also known as flat, through, and through and slash sawing). This is the simplest, cheapest and quickest method, but the boards warp and shrink badly because there are long annual rings in most boards. Only the centre board has short annual rings and will stay flat. (*See* Shrinkage.)

Plain sawing is used mainly for softwoods.

Quarter or radial sawing. True quarter sawing produces boards with short annual rings which are less liable to warp and shrink, are stronger, and show the figure of the wood. This is the attractive grain exposed by sawing along the medullary rays of some hardwoods.

True quarter sawing is more difficult, more expensive and slower than plain sawing, and wastes a lot of wood. Therefore, several near radial methods are used to reduce wastage and simplify sawing.

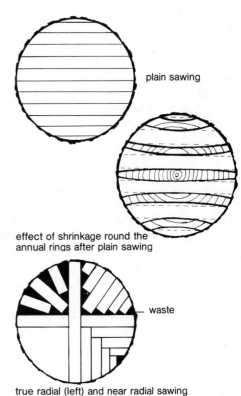

plain sawing

effect of shrinkage round the annual rings after plain sawing

waste

true radial (left) and near radial sawing

Properties and uses of a few common hardwoods

Name	Sources	Colour	Advantages
Beech	Europe including Britain.	White or pinkish brown, with flecks in grain from rays when quarter sawn.	Hard, tough, very strong and straight. The close grain polishes well and withstands wear and shocks.
Elm	Europe, including Britain.	Light reddish brown.	Tough, elastic, durable, fairly strong, fairly easy to work, medium weight, does not split easily. Good for use underwater.
Iroko	East and West Africa e.g. Nigeria, Ghana.	Initially yellow but darkens to dark brown.	Looks like Teak and has the properties of Teak, but is only half the price. Naturally one of the most durable timbers because it is oily. Needs no preservative outside.
African Mahoganies e.g. Sapele Utile	West Africa e.g. Nigeria, Ghana.	Pink to reddish brown.	Plentiful supply, available in wide and long boards, fairly easy to work, fairly strong, medium weight, durable. Finishes fairly well.
Meranti	Malaysia, Indonesia, Phillipines.	Dark red or yellow.	Red Meranti looks like Mahogany, but is cheaper. Fairly strong, fairly durable.
European Oak	Europe, including Britain, Russia, Poland.	Light to dark brown, with silver grain or ray figure when quarter sawn.	Very strong, very durable, hard, tough. Little shrinkage. Usually works fairly well with sharp tools. Finishes well.
Japanese Oak	Japan.	Yellowish brown.	Strong, durable, slightly lighter, milder and easier to work than European oak. Knot free. Cheaper than European oak.

Disadvantages	Uses
Not suitable for outdoor work because it is not durable when exposed to changes in moisture. Heavy, difficult to work, narrow planks and warps.	Most used hardwood in Britain. For furniture (especially chairs), floors, wooden tools, veneers, plywood, toys, turnery. Good for steam bending.
Tends to warp unless well seasoned. Cross-grained.	Garden furniture when treated with preservative, construction work, turnery, furniture.
Heavy, cross-grained.	Teak substitute. Furniture, interior and exterior joinery, cladding, floors, veneers, constructional work.
Some interlocking and variable grain, warps, hardness varies.	Shop fitting, furniture, cladding, floors, veneers, joinery plywood. Because the name includes a wide range of timbers, the properties and colours inevitably vary.
Does not polish as well as Mahogany. Fairly hard to work.	Interior joinery, furniture, construction work, Mahogany substitute. Red and yellow faced plywood. Can be used outside with suitable preservatives.
Heavy, expensive, open-grain. Contains tannic acid which corrodes iron and steel fittings and causes permanent blue stain on wood. Splits. Some Britsh Oak is harder to work. Sapwood needs preservative.	Boat building, garden furniture, gate posts, floors, construction work, veneers, high class furniture and fittings.
Slightly weaker and less durable than European Oak.	Interior woodwork and furniture. Good for steam bending.

Properties and uses of a few common hardwoods

Name	Sources	Colour	Advantages
Teak	Burma, India, Thailand.	Rich golden brown.	Hard, strong, one of naturally most durable timbers because it is oily. Highly resistant to moisture, fire, acids and alkalis. Very attractive straight grain. Works fairly easily. Does not corrode iron and steel.
Obeche	West Africa e.g. Cameroon, Nigeria, Ghana	Pale yellow	Straight grained variety works well, and stains and finishes well after filling the open grain.
Afrormosia	Africa generally.	Yellow to light brown with darker streaks. Tends to darken on exposure to light.	Works fairly well. Fairly durable.
Makoré	West Africa e.g. Ghana, Nigeria, Sierra Leone.	Light red with a striped figure.	Very durable. Stable when dry. Fairly easy to work. Stains and polishes well. Strong.
African Walnut	West Africa.	Bronze yellowish-brown with irregular dark lines.	Works fairly well. Attractive appearance. Available in large sizes.

Disadvantages	Uses
Difficult to glue because oils form a barrier that will not readily absorb adhesives. Gritty nature, blunts tools quickly. Very expensive.	High class furniture, veneers, laboratory benches, ships' decks.
Tends to be 'corky' when cutting joints. Not durable outside. Sometimes cross grained and difficult to work – avoid this type.	Hidden parts of furniture. Interior joinery, plywood core making and for veneering on. Work to be painted.
Stains in contact with iron in damp conditions. Grain is variable.	High class interior and exterior joinery. Floors, windows, sills, doors, gates, stairs, external cladding, furniture, constructional work.
Cross grain can make planing difficult.	High class interior and exterior joinery. Cladding, floors, veneers, plywood, furniture.
Cross grain can make planing and finishing difficult.	High class internal and external joinery, veneers, furniture. Sometimes used as a Teak substitute in furniture.

Properties and uses of a few common softwoods

Name	Sources	Colour	Advantages
Redwood (Scots Pine, Red Baltic Pine, Fir)	Northern Europe, Scandinavia, Russia, Scotland.	Cream to pale reddish-brown heartwood, cream sapwood.	One of cheapest and most readily available timbers. Straight grain. Fairly strong. Easy to work. Finishes well. Fairly durable.
Whitewood (Spruce)	Northern Europe, Canada, U.S.A.	Plain creamy white.	Fairly strong. Easy to work. Very resistant to splitting.
Douglas Fir (Columbian Pine)	Canada, U.S.A.	Attractive reddish-brown heartwood. Cream sapwood.	Available in long and wide boards. Knot free, straight grain, slightly resinous, therefore water resistant. Fairly strong, fairly durable, tough, fairly easy to work.
Western Red Cedar	Canada, U.S.A.	Dark reddish brown.	Contains natural preservative oils, therefore resists insect attack, weather and dry rot. Knot free, light weight, soft, straight grained. Fine, silky, attractive surface. Very durable, stately. Very easy to work.
Parana Pine	South America, especially Brazil.	Pale yellow with attractive red and brown streaks in heartwood.	Available in long and wide boards. Often knot free. Hard, straight grain. Fairly strong, works easily and well. Smooth finish. Fairly durable.

Disadvantages	Uses
Knotty. Sometimes has a blue stain from a harmless fungus.	Most used softwood in Britain. Suitable for all inside work and with suitable preservatives for outside work. Also for woodturning.
Small hard knots. Contains resin pockets. Not durable.	General inside work. Whitewood furniture.
Splits easily. Open grain with pronounced annual rings.	General outside construction work, masts, ladders, plywood.
More expensive than red and whitewood. Not very strong.	All kinds of joinery, especially outside. Widely used for cladding the outside of buildings, for roof shingles, for kitchens and bathrooms, and for panelling walls.
Lacks toughness. As expensive as some hardwoods. Tends to warp if not carefully seasoned and used.	Best quality internal softwood joinery, especially where attractive grain colour will show e.g. staircases, and built-in furniture.

Part 4 Seasoning

Seasoning is the removal of excess moisture from the wood by drying it after conversion.

Green timber is saturated with moisture (85% water).

Timber with less than 20% moisture content is immune from decay, especially dry rot, and therefore seasoning aims to reduce moisture content to below 18% for general use, and 12% for use in centrally heated and air conditioned buildings.

Correctly seasoned timber has:
1. Increased strength.
2. Increased stability.
3. Increased resistance to decay.

The two methods of seasoning are:

1. Air seasoning (the natural method). Boards are stacked in the open air with *sticks* (thin strips of wood) between them to allow air to circulate. The stack is raised clear of the ground on piers and has a roof to protect it from the weather.

The ends of the boards are painted, or have cleats (wood or metal strips) nailed across them to prevent the end grain drying more quickly than the rest of the board, as this causes splitting (checking).

Advantages. It is cheap and needs little skilled attention.

Disadvantages. It takes three to six years to dry. (Allow one year for every 25 mm thickness of wood.)

The moisture content can only be reduced to 15 to 18%.

2. Kiln seasoning (the artificial method). Boards are stacked on trolleys with sticks between them, and pushed into a kiln. The kiln is sealed and seasoning proceeds in three stages.

Stage 1. Steam is injected at low temperature to force free moisture out of the wood cells.

Stage 2. Steam is reduced and the temperature is increased to dry the wood.

Stage 3. Finally there is a flow of hot, almost dry, air.

Advantages. It takes only a few days or weeks and kills insect eggs in the wood (e.g. woodworm). It is possible to reduce moisture content to below 12%, making the wood suitable for use in centrally heated and air conditioned buildings.

Disadvantages. Kilns are expensive to build and to run.

It needs more attention and a lot of skill as incorrect drying will ruin the wood.

Identifying a quarter sawn board

Look at the growth rings on the end of the board.

plain sawn board

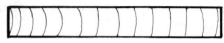

quarter sawn board

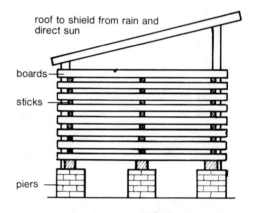

roof to shield from rain and direct sun

boards

sticks

piers

flat, dry, wood free site

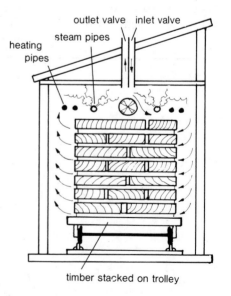

outlet valve   inlet valve

steam pipes

heating pipes

timber stacked on trolley

Testing moisture content

Wood is never completely dry in normal use and moisture content (m.c.) is the amount of water contained in the wood, as a percentage of its oven-dry weight. During seasoning, a sample is usually put in with the main stock and checked at intervals.

Method 1. Weighing.

(a) Weigh a sample of the wood to be tested (initial weight).
(b) Dry it in an oven until there is no further weight loss.
(c) Weigh the dry sample (dry weight).
(d) $\dfrac{\text{Initial weight} - \text{dry weight}}{\text{dry weight}} \times 100 = \% \text{ M.C.}$

Method 2. Electric moisture content meter.

Works on the principle that wet wood is a better conductor of electricity than dry wood. Two prongs are pressed into the wood, and the meter gives a direct reading of the moisture content by measuring the current which flows between them.

Part 5 Faults in timber

(A) Shrinkage

When seasoning removes water from timber, it shrinks considerably.

Most shrinkage takes place round the annual rings.

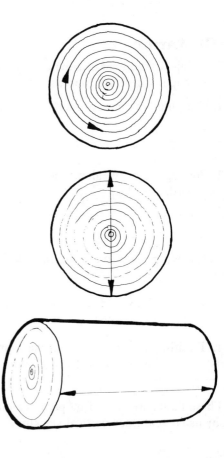

About half as much shrinkage takes place across the diameter as around the annual rings.

Very little shrinkage takes place along the length. (Can be ignored.)

If a log is allowed to dry before conversion it will split along the medullary rays as the annual rings shrink and try to shorten themselves.

When timber is seasoned after conversion, shrinkage affects the shape of the boards. As shrinkage shortens the annual rings, the most shrinkage occurs in those boards with the longest annual rings, and the shape of each board depends on which part of the log it comes from and on how it is sawn. (*See* Conversion.)

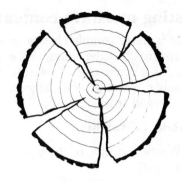

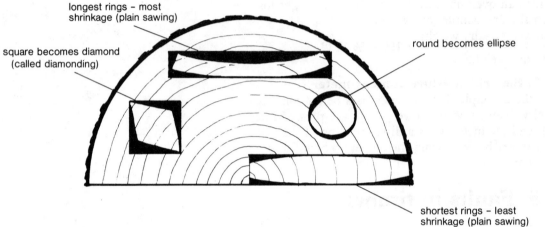

longest rings – most shrinkage (plain sawing)

square becomes diamond (called diamonding)

round becomes ellipse

shortest rings – least shrinkage (plain sawing)

(B) Warping

Warping is the general name for any distortion from the true shape. There are four ways in which wood warps.

1. Cupping – a curve across the grain.

2. Bowing – a curve along the grain on the wide surface of the board.

3. Springing – a curve along the edge of the board.

4. Twisting or *wind* – curved like a propeller (remember use of winding strips to test face-sides for twist).

These faults are caused by poor seasoning, uneven shrinkage and poor vertical stacking.

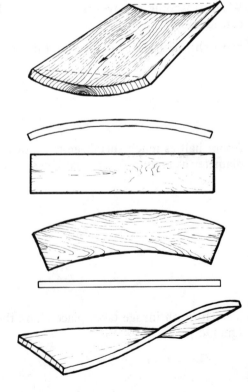

(C) Defects in timber

Defects are faults in the structure of the timber, which may reduce its strength, durability or usefulness.

Natural defects are caused by strong winds, lightning, fire, insect and fungal attack.

Artificial defects are caused by careless felling, conversion and seasoning.

1. Shakes. The separation of adjoining layers of wood usually caused by strong winds, poor felling, or shrinkage.

Cup shake. A partial separation of the annual rings.

Ring shake. A cup shake which has separated all the way round an annual ring.

Heart shake. A split along the medullary rays starting in the pith.

Star shake. Several heart shakes forming an approximate star shape.

Radial shakes or splits. Splits along the medullary rays starting on the outside, and caused by shrinkage around the annual rings after felling.

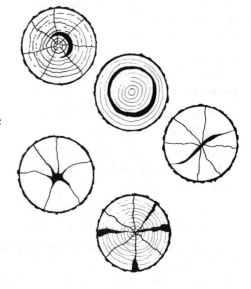

2. Knots are where branches grew from the tree. A large knot weakens the timber.

Live knots are where a living branch joined the tree. They are hard, tightly knit into the wood, light in colour and free from decay.

Dead knots are where a branch died or was cut off while the tree was growing. They are often dark in colour, soft, decayed, or loose.

3. Pitch pockets are saucer shaped hollows along the grain full of resin. The resin runs out when the pocket is opened. They are caused by damage to the growing tree.

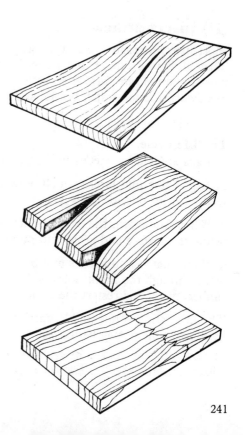

4. Checks are splits in the length of a board caused by bad seasoning.

5. Thunder shakes are hair-line cracks across the grain which are often impossible to see until the timber is converted. The board will usually break along the shake. This is especially seen in mahoganies.

6. Irregular grain is any variation of the grain from approximately parallel to the surface, which makes planing very difficult and weakens the wood.

Cross-grain is where the grain fibres are at varying angles to the surface, usually only in small areas of a board. Caused by cutting from logs where the grain is not straight, or around a knot in the wood.

Short or diagonal grain is where the fibres are not parallel to the surface although the board is cut from straight-grained timber. Caused by careless conversion.

Interlocking grain is where adjacent strips of grain fibre are angled in opposite directions so that whichever way you plane, some strips tear.

7. Waney edge. A board which shows part of the natural circumference of the tree.

8. Sapwood is the young, soft part of the tree, and is much more vulnerable to fungal and insect attack than heartwood.

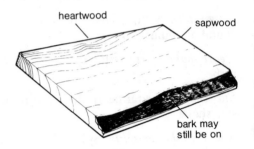

heartwood

sapwood

bark may still be on

It should, therefore, be removed during conversion before the timber is used for most purposes.

9. Case-hardening and honeycombing is when the timber is seasoned too quickly in a kiln, leaving the outer layers very hard, and causing the cell walls in the centre to collapse, resulting in short splits along the medullary rays.

(D) Insect attack

Most insect damage to wood in Britain is caused by beetles. They all have a similar four stage life cycle, and the three most important are furniture beetle (commonly called woodworm), death-watch beetle, and powder post beetle (lyctus).

The life cycle.

1. Eggs are laid by beetles in cracks in timber.

2. Eggs hatch into larvae which bore into the wood, and feed on it for one to fifty years.

3. When full grown the larvae hollow out tiny caverns just below the surface and grow into pupae.

4. Pupae hatch into beetles and bite their way out of the wood through the flight holes which we see in infested timber, mate, and restart the cycle.

The infestation is not visible until the flight holes appear by which time it may be too late.

Furniture beetle. This attacks hardwood, softwood and some plywoods, especially sapwood and old wood, and is responsible for 75% of known damage to timber in buildings.

It produces pellets of coarse, gritty powder, and honeycombs the inside of the timber with tunnels.

Death watch beetle. This attacks hardwoods, especially old oak structural timbers, and occasionally, softwood, usually where there is also damp and fungal attack. (*See* section E.) It is not normally found in houses or furniture and produces bun-like pellets of coarse dust which are easily seen.

Powder post beetle. This attacks only the sapwood of hardwoods. It reduces the inside of the timber to a very fine powder and produces flour-like bore dust.

Prevention.
1. Apply preservative to timber e.g. creosote or insecticides.

2. Keep furniture clean and wax polished to seal small cracks.

Treatment.
1. In a building, cut-out and burn infested timber wherever possible. This may not be possible when repairing furniture.

2. Apply a deep penetrating insecticide to kill larvae and give protection from renewed attack.

3. Fill old holes with stopper so that new holes can be spotted.

Treatment of serious infestation requires expert help.

(E) Fungal attack

All fungi which attack timber develop under similar conditions. They require:

1. Food. The cells of non-durable wood, especially sapwood.

2. Moisture. The moisture content of the wood must be at least 20%. (*See* Seasoning.)

3. Oxygen from the air.

4. Correct temperature. Unfortunately the temperature in Britain is never too hot or too cold for fungus.

5. Lack of air circulation.

Decay can be recognised by:
1. Softening and change of colour of the wood.

2. Loss of weight of wood.

3. A musty smell.

The main types of fungal attack are:

Wet rot (or white rot). A general name for a group of fungi which attack timber with 30% or more moisture content. It is the commonest form of rot, especially on outside woodwork. The wood becomes dark and spongy when wet, and brittle when dry.

Prevention. Treat with water repellant preservative.

Treatment. Cut out badly affected timber and dry the rest. Treat with fungicidal preservative.

Dry rot (or brown rot). This thrives in damp, unventilated conditions, on timber with 20% or more moisture content. It is called dry rot because it leaves the wood in a dry crumbly state. It is the most serious form of fungal attack and is very difficult to eradicate. It spreads either by sending out strands in different directions or by releasing millions of fine rust-red spores (like seeds) from the fruit bodies which grow on it. These can be carried by wind, animals or people to all parts of the building, while the strands can penetrate through walls to adjoining rooms.

Prevention. Keep woodwork dry and well ventilated and treat with preservative. Use naturally durable timbers.

Treatment. The cure must be prompt and thorough as even brickwork, concrete and steel girders will not prevent the spread of spores. Remove and burn all affected timber and debris up to at least 500 mm beyond the decay. Then sterilize all timber, walls, etc. in the area with a blow lamp and dry-rot fluid.

Correct causes of damp and bad ventilation, and prevent direct contact between new woodwork and brickwork.

Part 6 Veneers and man-made boards

Veneers

Veneers are thin sheets of wood. They can be made in several ways including:

Rotary cutting. After softening by steaming, the log is mounted between centres on a lathe, and slowly rotated against a knife to unroll a continuous sheet of veneer which is then chopped into sheets.

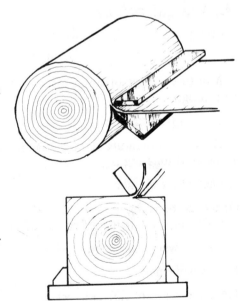

This method usually produces a plain veneer which is used to make the plies of plywood. It is the most used and cheapest method.

Slice cutting. After softening by steaming, the log is mounted on a machine bed which moves it against a knife to produce flat sheets.

This method usually produces interesting grain patterns for face veneers.

Man-made boards

Very wide boards of hard or softwood are rare, expensive and liable to warp.

Narrow boards joined edge to edge are time consuming to prepare and liable to warp.

Man-made boards are available in large sheets and are

stable. Plywood, blockboard, and laminboard have great strength in both directions because of the crossing of the grain in the layers.

Plywood is made from layers or plies of wood glued together so that the grain of each ply is at right angles to the next. There is always an odd number of plies so that the grain runs the same way on both outside pieces and hence stresses are balanced.

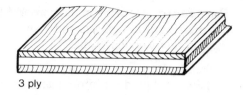

3 ply

Plywood can be faced with a veneer of decorative hardwood to improve its appearance, or with melamine to give a harder wearing surface.

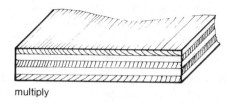

multiply

Plywood is graded for interior or exterior use depending on the water resistance of the glue used, and this is shown by code letters on each sheet.

W.B.P. – Weather and boil proof
B.R.   – Boil resistant
M.R.   – Moisture resistant
Int.   – Interior use only.

Plywood is also graded by the smoothness of the surface and number of defects in it. Plywood can be nailed near the edge without splitting. Thin plywood is flexible and can be formed into curved shapes.

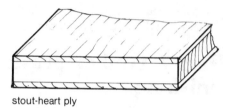

stout-heart ply

Usual sheet sizes are 2 440 × 1 220 mm and 1 525 × 1 525 mm.

Common thicknesses are 4, 6, 9 and 12 mm.

Blockboard and laminboard. Made by sandwiching strips of softwood between two plies. The strips are narrower in laminboard than in blockboard. They are usually made in interior grade only. The grain of the face plies runs at right angles to the core strips. The core strips are arranged with the heartside alternately on top and underneath (as when edge jointing boards) to avoid warping. Both block and laminboard can be faced with veneers of decorative hardwood.

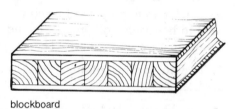

blockboard

It is usually cheaper to make blockboard than to make multiply over 12 mm thick.

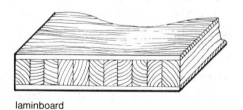

laminboard

Usual sheet size is 2 440 × 1 220 mm.
Common thickness is 18 mm.

Chipboard. Made by glueing wooden chips together under heat and pressure. Most chipboard is of *graded density* having smaller chips packed tightly together on the outside to give a smoother and stronger face. It is suitable only for interior use. Veneered and melamine-faced chipboard is widely used for worktops, shelves and furniture making.

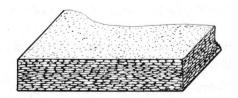

Usual sheet size is 2 240 × 1 220 mm.
Common thicknesses are 12 mm and 18 mm.

Hardboard. Made by mixing wood fibres with water and synthetic resin glue, hot-pressing it into sheets and leaving it to dry. It is not very strong and is usually fixed onto a wooden frame.

Standard grade is for interior use.
Tempered grade is impregnated with oil for exterior use and for bending to make curved shapes.
Can be melamine-faced or ready painted.
Pegboard is hardboard with holes in to hold display hooks.
Usual sheet size is 2 440 × 1 220 mm.
Common thickness is 3.2 mm.

Softboard (fibre-board). Made in the same way as hardboard, but less pressure is used. It is used for notice boards, and sound and heat insulation boards. Its low density makes it light, but weak.

Usual sheet size is 2 440 × 1 200 mm.
Common thicknesses are 9 mm and 12 mm.

Part 7 Timber preservation and wood finishing

Cleaning up and finishing wood

As much cleaning up and finishing as possible is done before assembly, but joints need to be levelled off and the outside of the job cleaned up and finished, after the cramps have been removed. The stages are:

1. The smoothing plane is used to remove marking-out lines and to clean the surface.

It must be sharp and set fine. For cross-grained wood move the cap-iron close to the cutting edge and move the frog to reduce the width of the mouth. Be careful not to plane off too much, especially from joints, and to keep the work square.

2. Scrapers are used to produce a very smooth surface on hardwoods only, especially on cross-grained timbers where a plane is not entirely effective.

They take off very fine shavings and there are two types:

(a) *Simple tool steel blade* (flat or curved) which is held between thumbs and fingers.

(b) *Cabinet scraper* (flat only) which has a blade held in a cast iron body similar to a spokeshave.

3. Abrasive papers are used to remove small faults from the surface. They scrape wood away by rubbing and should always be used wrapped tightly round a cork block to prevent damage to the wood. Take care not to round corners or rub hollows in flat surfaces.

There are three types:

(a) *Glasspaper* consists of pieces of ground glass, graded into sizes and glued onto backing paper. There are ten grades of cut. Sheet size 280 × 230 mm.

(b) *Garnet paper* consists of very hard stone, crushed, graded and glued onto backing paper. It is more expensive.

There are two types of garnet paper. The first is *open coated paper* with abrasive grains spaced out so that the paper does not clog when rubbing down paint or soft resinous woods, and when machine sanding. The second is *close coated paper* with grains packed together to give a regular surface suitable for rubbing hardwoods (all glasspaper has a closed coat).

(c) There are also special, tough, hardwearing grits used mainly for sanding machine discs, sheets and belts, and metal backed hand rubbers (e.g. aluminium oxide). These are graded by grit sizes.

4. Wire wool (steel wool) is used as a very fine abrasive, mainly in the final stages of polishing. Take care not to leave fine pieces of black wire stuck in the grain.

Grades of abrasive.

Grit size		Garnet paper	Glasspaper
220	Extra fine	6/0	Flour
180		5/0	00
150	Fine	4/0	0
120		3/0	1
100	Medium	2/0	$1\frac{1}{2}$
80		0	F2
60		$\frac{1}{2}$	M2
50	Coarse	1	S2
40		$1\frac{1}{2}$	$2\frac{1}{2}$
36		2	3

5. Finishing. After cleaning up, but before assembling, apply the chosen finish to as many parts of the job as possible. All inside surfaces should be finished before assembly because it is difficult to get a good finish in corners after glueing.

Mask areas which are to be glued with tape because glue will not stick on many finishes.

It is essential to check the surface of the wood very carefully before applying any finish because any faults will look worse afterwards.

Small dents may be removed by damping the surface with water or ironing over a damp cloth and allowing to dry.

Wood finishes

These are used to protect the surface of the wood from weather, insect attack, fungal attack, heat, liquids and dirt, and to improve the appearance of the timber.

The type chosen depends on the type of wood and the use to which it is to be put. The ones listed below are only a few of the many available.

French polish is made by dissolving Shellac in methylated spirit. It is available in a range of colours, mainly white (an amber shade) and browns. The wood may be stained first.

To use it apply the first coat with a brush to seal the grain. If necessary fill the grain with filler and leave to dry.

Lightly rub down and apply polish in long strokes along the grain with a cloth rubber and allow to dry.

Apply more polish with a circular motion of the rubber and finish with diluted polish.

Oil produces a good natural finish. It is especially suitable for naturally oily timbers (e.g. Teak and Iroko).

It is suitable for inside and outside use, but requires regular recoating. Some examples include teak oil and linseed oil.

Olive oil is used for woodware which will come into contact with food.

To use oil, rub in well with a cloth and wipe off the surplus. Allow one week between coats.

Wax polish produces a dull gloss finish and shows the natural grain of the wood. It was originally made by shredding beeswax and dissolving it in turpentine.

To use it seal the grain with white french polish. Then lightly rub down with fine glasspaper when dry, rub wax into the grain and allow to dry again. Finally, polish with a brush and/or soft cloth.

Plastic finishes (e.g. clear polyurethane varnish, etc.) produce a good gloss, eggshell or matt surface and show the natural colour of the wood.

They are widely used for furniture because they are heat proof, immune to most liquids and very durable. Some are also suitable for outside use.

To use, apply with brush, spray or cloth and rub down lightly between coats. They can be diluted with white spirit (turps subs.) to help them soak into the grain and obtain a natural finish.

Varnish is a solution of resins in oil or spirit. It produces a hard, durable, waterproof, glossy, transparent finish, and is used on internal and external joinery, but not usually on furniture.

It is used as for plastic finishes but using a brush only.

Filler, a paste used to fill the grain to make the surface smooth. The colour must be matched to the wood and applied after staining if needed. Then clean off the surplus by rubbing across the grain and leave to dry.

Stain. Wood is stained to imitate other woods or to enhance its appearance.

Matching colours is difficult so always test stains on scrapwood.

Do not stain after filling because filler stains darker than wood.

Paint is suitable for internal and external use. There are many types so select for the job and read the instructions.

To use it, key the surface by glasspapering at 45° with coarse glasspaper (S2). Treat knots with knotting or french polish to prevent resin staining the finish, or causing peeling.
Apply one coat of primer and fill nail holes and cracks with putty or filler. Then apply one or two coats of undercoat followed by one or two coats of gloss, eggshell or matt finish. Rub down lightly between coats.

Wood preservation

Some timbers are naturally immune from decay (*see* Some common hardwoods and softwoods), and all wood finishes protect the wood to some extent, but exterior woodwork and structural timbers may require more thorough treatment than painting or varnishing.

Wood preservation means treating wood with solutions which make it poisonous to fungus, insects and marine borers, as well as protecting it from the weather.

Common types of preservatives

1. *Tar oils*, for example *creosote* which is the best known preservative. It soaks into the grain and gives a matt brown finish. It is cheap, permanent, safe to handle and does not affect metals.

2. *Water soluble chemicals* (e.g. Zinc Chloride) are for use where timber will be used in dry conditions.

3. *Preservatives contained in non-water soluble solvents* penetrate deeply into the timbers and then evaporate leaving the preservatives in the wood cells. They are usually proprietary preservatives which are more expensive than creosote, but penetrate better when brushed or sprayed on.

How to use preservatives

1. Brushing or spraying on is a simple way of treating timber already made up, but gives only surface protection because the preservative does not penetrate far into the timber.

2. Soaking the timber in tanks of hot and/or cold preservatives gives better penetration than brushing and spraying and needs only simple equipment.

3. Forcing the preservative into the timber under pressure gives the greatest penetration, but requires expensive equipment.

Cleaning brushes. French polish – methylated spirits.
Cellulose paint and varnish – cellulose thinners.
Polyurethane varnish and paint – white spirit or cellulose thinners.
Oil based paint and varnish – white spirit (turps subs.).
Emulsion paint and some modern oil-based paints – soap and water.
Creosote – paraffin.

There are a number of brush cleaners and paint removers on the market which will soften hard brushes used for all but cellulose finishes.

16 Materials for craftwork (2) metal

The production of iron

Iron ore, usually in the form of iron oxide in rocks is mined or quarried and taken to a steelworks. There it is graded and crushed to reduce it to a maximum size of 100 mm cubes. Small particles are mixed with coke and heated to form a clinker of similar size called *sinter*.

Once lit, a blast furnace runs continuously until the heat resistant bricks of the refractory lining start to burn away, usually after about two years. The raw materials, coke, limestone, iron-ore and sinter, are continuously poured in through the double bell charging system which prevents hot gases from escaping during charging.

Heated air is blasted into the bottom of the furnace from the blast or bustle pipe, through the tuyères, to make the coke burn fiercely.

The iron in the ore melts and collects in the well at the bottom of the furnace. The limestone acts as a flux to make impurities float on the surface of the molten iron in the form of a liquid slag, which can be tapped off. The iron and slag are tapped off at regular intervals.

The hot waste gases go through a gas cleaning plant before either being reused to heat the blast to 800°C, or being burnt off.

The iron produced is 90 to 95% pure, and it is used in one of three ways.

1. In a modern integrated steel works it is conveyed in its molten state straight to the steel making furnaces.

2. It is fed into a pig casting machine which makes it into small iron bars (pig-iron) for future remelting, for example, in an electric arc furnace.

3. It is refined into cast iron which is a strong but brittle metal especially suitable for making intricate castings such as engine cylinder blocks and cylinder heads simply, easily and economically.

The production of steel

The raw materials for steel making are iron from the blast furnaces, scrap iron and steel. The amount of each used depends on the type of steel being made and the process used. Because there are many different types of steel, for example, mild steel, tool steels, stainless steel and steel alloys, there are many variations in the techniques used. All steelmaking however, involves removing impurities and

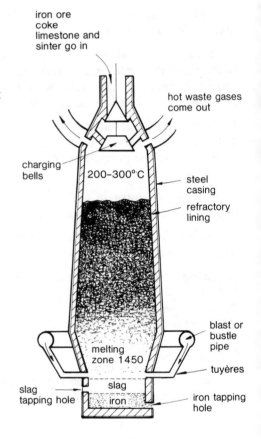

iron ore
coke
limestone and
sinter go in

hot waste gases come out

charging bells

200–300°C

steel casing

refractory lining

melting zone 1450

blast or bustle pipe

tuyères

slag tapping hole

slag

iron

iron tapping hole

excess carbon from the iron, and adding small amounts of other elements.

The basic oxygen furnace. This is the most important method for making large tonnages of widely used steels and one furnace can make 350 tonnes or more in 40 minutes.

The furnace is tilted and charged first with 30% scrap and then with 70% molton iron. With the furnace upright, a watercooled oxygen lance is lowered to just above the surface of the metal, and oxygen is blown into the melt at very high speed. It combines with carbon and other unwanted elements to remove them from the charge. During the blow, lime is added as a flux so that the oxidized impurities form a slag on the surface ready for tapping off later.

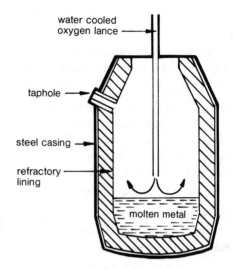

After the blow, the steel which has been made is tapped out through the taphole into a ladle. The converter is then tipped upside down to empty out the slag.

The electric arc furnace. This method is used to make both large tonnages of widely used steels and, because of the precise control it gives over the composition of the steel, special high quality steels. A large furnace can make 150 tonnes of steel in four hours.

The furnace is charged only with cold scrap. To charge the furnace, the carbon electrodes are withdrawn and the swivel roof is swung open so that the cold metal can be dropped in. The roof is swung closed and the electrodes are lowered. When the electric circuit is completed between the electrodes and the metal, a powerful arc is struck which produces a temperature of about 3 500°C to melt the metal.

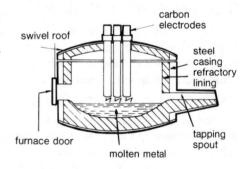

Lime, fluorspar and iron oxide are added to combine with the impurities in the metal and form a slag. Additions are made to get the required type of steel. The slag is poured off through the furnace door by tilting the furnace which is then tilted the other way to tap off the steel.

Converting the molten steel

After tapping from the furnace, the molten steel is first cast in one of three ways.

(a) It can be cast into ingots by pouring it into moulds to solidify. The size of each ingot depends on the use to which it will be put. Red hot ingots can then be rolled between heavy rollers to make slabs, blooms, billets and heavy sections such as girders, or forged by pressing or hammering into shape.

Slabs are usually 75 to 254 mm thick and up to two metres wide. They are used to make plates, sheets, strips, pipes and tinplate.

251

Blooms are usually 150 to 300 mm square, while *billets* are usually 50 to 125 mm square. They are used to make structural shapes, bars, rods and wire.

All these shapes are in 7 to 10 metre lengths.

(b) It can be cast into slabs and blooms by the continuous casting process where molten steel is channelled down through a water-cooled tube until it has solidified on the outside. It is then passed through water sprays and rollers until completely solidified, and it is finally cut to length.

The advantage of this method is that the steel travels straight from the furnaces, through the continuous casting plant to the rolling mill. The casting of ingots, the reheating of the ingots, and the rolling of ingots into slabs, blooms and billets ready for further processing are all eliminated, and the inevitable wastage of some steel at each extra stage avoided.

(c) It can be poured into sand moulds to make steel castings.

Black steel and bright steel. Metal which has been rolled to shape while hot is known as black bar because it has a coating of black oxide all over it. The best example of this is the black mild steel used for forgework.

To convert this to a bright finish (as for example, on bright drawn mild steel), and to make the sizes more accurate, the black steel is first pickled in dilute sulphuric acid to remove the oxide, washed, dried and oiled, and then rerolled cold.

The bright steel is finally drawn through a series of gradually reducing dies to make accurately shaped rods, flats and wire.

The production of aluminium

Aluminium ore, known as bauxite, is mined or quarried, crushed and dried before being refined into alumina (aluminium oxide). This is done by dissolving the bauxite in a hot caustic soda solution, filtering out impurities and collecting the aluminium oxide which remains in precipitation tanks.

The filtered oxide is washed and heated to 1000°C to give alumina. This is ready for the second stage of refining where it is dissolved in a flux of molten cryolite in a steel furnace. This furnace has a refractory lining and an inner lining of carbon which forms a cathode. Blocks of carbon are suspended in the melt to form anodes, and a large current is passed between the anodes and the cathode to heat the furnace to about 1000°C. As the alumina melts, molten aluminium of 99 to 99.8% purity collects in the bottom of the furnace. The oxygen from the aluminium oxide combines with carbon from the anodes to form carbon dioxide which escapes as a gas.

The aluminium is tapped off and cast into ingots ready for further processing.

The production of copper

Copper ore, often containing a very low percentage of copper, is mined or quarried and then crushed and ground into a fine powder. Large quantities of waste can then be removed by the flotation process, where grains of copper float on the surface of the liquid while the rock particles sink.

The resulting copper concentrate is smelted in a reverberatory furnace, where lime is added as a flux to form most of the impurities into a slag, which is then tapped off.

The *matte* of copper and iron sulphides remaining after smelting is taken to a converter where compressed air is blown through it. This oxidizes the iron to make a slag, and blows off the sulphur as a gas. The copper which is now 99% pure, is cast into cakes known as *blister* copper.

To obtain pure copper blister, copper is used as the anodes in electrolytic cells where the copper is gradually dissolved and redeposited on cathodes made from pure copper sheet.

When the cathodes have grown into blocks of copper, they are melted and cast into copper ingots ready for conversion into wire, plates, sheets, strips, tubes, rods, castings and powders.

Definitions of properties of materials

Various words are used to describe the properties of materials and for this purpose they have exact meanings. In general conversation the same terms are often used inaccurately, and it is important that when we are discussing materials we should understand exactly what they mean, and use them accurately.

The most commonly used terms are defined below and are used in the following chapters.

Hardness is the resistance of the material to cutting and surface indentation.

Toughness is the amount of energy the material can absorb without breaking and measures its ability to withstand shocks. It is the opposite to brittleness.

Tensile strength is the maximum force the material can stand in tension (pulling apart), compression (crushing), torque (twisting) and shear (sideways pressure), without breaking.

Malleability is the amount of shaping which can be done by hammering, rolling or pressing without the material breaking.

Ductility is the length to which the material can be stretched without breaking.

Elasticity is the length to which the material can be stretched and still return to its original length when released. The elastic limit is the point beyond which it remains stretched.

Heat and electrical conductivity is a measure of how well the material will conduct heat or electricity.

Ferrous and non-ferrous metals. All metals belong to one of these two groups.

Ferrous metals are those which are made mainly of iron with small amounts of other metals or other elements added, to give the required properties. Almost all ferrous metals can be picked up with a magnet.

Non-ferrous metals are those which do not contain iron, for example, aluminium, copper, lead, zinc and tin.

Pure metals and alloys. All metals are also either pure metals or alloys.

A *pure metal* consists of a single element, which means that it is a substance having only one type of atom in it. The common pure metals are aluminium, copper, iron, lead, zinc, tin, silver and gold.

An *alloy* is a mixture of two or more pure metals, or one or more pure metals mixed with other elements.

Alloys are made in order to create materials which have combinations of properties not all available in the pure metals, and to fulfil needs for which no pure metal is suitable. For example, while pure aluminium is soft and ductile, the addition of small amounts of other elements can produce aluminium alloys which are stronger than mild steel, have improved hardness, and are corrosion resistant while still retaining the lightness of aluminium.

The identification of ferrous metals

Metal	Test		
	Drop on anvil	Nick and hammer in vice	Grind
Mild steel	Medium pitched ring	Bends before breaking. Shows uniform grey lustre on fracture.	A long thick stream of pale yellow sparks which explode and fork.
Carbon steel	High ringing note	Bends a little and then breaks. Silvery white, fine, crystalline structure.	Orange sparks burst from a thick stream of lines.
High speed steel	Medium metallic ring	Resists blow and then breaks cleanly. Very fine, crystalline structure.	Dull red sparks barely visible close to the wheel.
Grey cast iron	Dull note	Snaps easily. Coarse, dark fracture.	Dull orange stream of sparks close to the wheel.
White cast iron	Very dull note	Breaks cleanly. Finer, white fracture.	Dull red stream of sparks close to the wheel.

The heat treatment of metals

Heat treatment is a way of making metals more suitable for processing or for the jobs which they have to do. For example, a piece of high carbon steel being used to make a cold chisel must be annealed (softened), so that it can be shaped, and then hardened and tempered so that it can cut other metals.

There are three stages in heat treatment.

1. Heat the metal to the correct temperature.

2. Keep it at that temperature for the required length of time (soaking).

3. Cool it in the correct way to give the desired properties.

Annealing makes the metal as soft as possible to relieve internal stresses, and to make it easier to shape.

Mild steel is heated to bright red heat, soaked for a short time, and left to cool slowly.

Tool steel is heated to bright red heat, soaked for a short time, and left to cool *very slowly* in hot ashes. The more slowly the metal cools, the softer it will be.

Copper is heated to cherry red heat and quenched in water.

Gilding metal is heated to salmon pink heat and quenched in water.

Brass is heated to dull red heat and left to cool.

Aluminium is covered with soap, heated gently until the soap turns black and left to cool.

Normalising returns work hardened steel to its normal condition after forging or previous heat treatment.

Steel is heated to red hot and left to cool.

Hardening increases the hardness and tensile strength of tool steel in order to make cutting tools, springs, hard, wear-resistant bearing surfaces, etc. Hardening can only be carried out on carbon and alloy steels. The higher the carbon content of the steel, the harder it will be.

Steel is heated to cherry red heat, soaked for a short time and quenched vertically in oil, brine or tepid water. Quenching horizontally or in cold water can cause cracking. Hardened metal is brittle and unusable.

Tempering removes the extreme hardness and brittleness from hardened steel, and makes it tougher so that it can be used. Increasing the tempering temperature reduces hardness, but increases toughness, and the final compromise between hardness and toughness depends on the purpose for which the steel is to be used.

The hardened steel is cleaned so that the tempering colours can be seen, heated to the required tempering colour and immediately quenched in water.

Tempering colours. As the metal is heated it changes colour, and below are given examples of different degrees of tempering.

Colour	Approx. temperature	Uses
Light straw	230°C Hardest	Planer blades, lathe tools, scribers, scrapers, dividers, emery wheel dressers.
Dark straw	245°C	Drills, taps, dies, reamers, punches.
Orange/brown	260°C	Lathe centres, shears, hammer heads, plane irons.
Light purple	270°C	Knives, scissors, woodwork chisels.
Dark purple	280°C	Saws, cold chisels, rivet sets, axes, table knives.
Blue	300°C Toughest	Springs, screwdrivers, chuck keys, vice jaws, spanners, needles.

Case hardening is a method of putting a hard surface coating onto steels which do not contain enough carbon for hardening and tempering. Carbon is burnt into the surface of the metal so that it can be hardened to give a wear resistant shell and a tough break resistant core.

Mild steel is heated evenly to dull red heat, and dipped or rolled in carbon powder which melts and sticks to the surface. Repeated heating and dipping burns the carbon into the metal and thickens the carburized shell. When the required thickness of shell has been built up, surplus powder is cleaned off with a wire brush and the metal is heated to bright red heat and quenched in water to harden it.

Properties and uses of common non-ferrous metals

Name	Melting point	Composition	Properties	Uses
Aluminium	650°C	Pure metal.	Greyish-white, light, soft, malleable, ductile and highly conductive to heat and electricity. Corrosion resistant (a thin inert film of oxide forms and protects the metal from further attack). Can be welded and soldered by special processes.	Aircraft, boats, railway coaches, engine cylinder heads, blocks, pistons and crankcases, window frames, saucepans, aluminium foil for packaging and insulation, electrical conductors and cables, castings.
Aluminium alloys e.g. Duralumin	650°C	Aluminium + 4% copper and 1% manganese.	Ductile, malleable, light, work-hardens, and machines well.	Aircraft and vehicle parts.
L.M.4 casting alloy		Aluminium + 3% copper + 5% silicon.	Good fluidity in pouring, good machineability, improved hardness, toughness and corrosion resistance.	General purpose casting alloy.
L.M.6 casting alloy		12% silicon.	High fluidity.	Complex castings.
Copper	1 100°C	Pure metal.	Red, malleable, ductile, tough. High heat/ electrical conductor. Corrosion resistant. Hot or cold working is possible. Cold working increases hardness and strength and requires frequent annealing. Easily hard and soft soldered.	Wire, especially electrical cables and conductors. Water and central heating pipes. Soldering iron bits and welding nozzles. Copper foil for car radiators, printed circuits and gaskets. Roofing, castings.
Copper alloys				
Brass	980°C	65% copper + 35% zinc (approximately).	Yellow, very corrosion resistant though it tarnishes easily. Harder than copper. Casts well, easily machined and easily hard and soft soldered. Good heat/electrical conductor.	Castings, forgings, ornaments, valves, propellers.

Properties and uses of common non-ferrous metals

Name	Melting point	Composition	Properties	Uses
Copper alloys **Bronze**	980°C	90 to 95% copper + 5 to 10% tin. Sometimes other elements e.g. phosphorous for phosphor-bronze.	Reddish-yellow, harder and tougher than brass, hard-wearing, corrosion resistant and easily machined.	Bearings, springs, instrument parts, gears. Air, water and steam valves and fittings. Pumps, castings for statues.
Gilding metal		85% copper + 15% zinc.	Golden colour, corrosion resistant and easily hard and soft soldered. Enamels well. Annealed and worked cold.	Beaten metalwork, jewellery, architectural metalwork.
Lead	330°C	Pure metal.	Bright and shiny when new, but rapidly oxidizes to a dull-grey. The heaviest common metal. Soft, malleable, corrosion resistant and immune to many chemicals. Very easy to work. Readily joined by 'burning'.	Coverings for power and telephone cables. Protection against X-rays and radiation. A main constituent in many soft solders, paints, printing type, bearing metals. Roof-coverings and flashings.
Tin	230°C	Pure metal.	White, soft, corrosion resistant in damp conditions.	Tinplate, making bronze, soft solders, printing type metal.
Tinplate		Thin sheet steel coated with pure tin.	Mild steel core is strong and ductile. Tin coating bends with the steel without separating and protects it from corrosion. Resistant to and non-toxic for use with a wide variety of foods.	Tin cans etc. Light sheet metalwork.
Zinc	420°C	Pure metal.	Bluish-white, ductile, a layer of oxide protects it from further corrosion. Easily worked.	Making brass. Zinc chloride soft soldering flux and wood preservative. Coating for steel galvanized corrugated iron roofing, tanks, buckets, etc. Rust-proof paints, intricate die castings.

Properties and uses of common ferrous metals

Name	Melting point	Composition	Properties	Uses
Cast iron	1 000 to 1 200°C	Remelted pig iron with small additions depending on use, and scrap steel.	A wide range of alloys with varying properties. Hard, brittle, cheap, strong, rigid in compression and self-lubricating.	Used for heavy crushing machinery.
			White cast iron is very hard, brittle and almost unmachineable.	
			Grey cast iron is readily machineable, easily cast into intricate shapes, and corrosion resistant in damp conditions.	The most used type. Used for car cylinder blocks and heads. Vices, machine tool parts, car brake drums and discs.
			Malleable cast iron is white cast iron annealed to make it softer, more ductile, more machineable and to increase tensile strength.	Horticultural machinery and agricultural implements. Machine handles and gear wheels. Intricate shapes which must withstand rough work such as plumbing fittings.
Steels	1 400°C	Alloys of iron and carbon.	Properties, working, qualities and uses vary considerably with the different types of steel.	
Low carbon steels		Less than 0.15% carbon.	Soft, ductile, tough and malleable.	Wire, rivets, thin sheets, cold pressings, drawn tubes.
Mild steels		0.15 to 0.30% carbon.	High tensile strength, ductile, tough, fairly malleable, softer than medium and high carbon steels. Because of low carbon content it cannot be hardened and tempered. Must be case-hardened.	General purpose steel, girders, angle iron, plates, sheet, tubes, drop forgings, nuts and bolts etc.
Medium carbon steels		0.30 to 0.70% carbon.	Stronger and harder than mild steel, but less ductile, tough and malleable.	Garden tools, shafts, axles, springs, wire ropes.

Properties and uses of common ferrous metals

Name	Melting point	Composition	Properties	Uses
High carbon steels		0.70 to 1.40% carbon.	Hardest of the carbon steels, but less ductile, tough and malleable. Hardness and toughness are improved by heat treatment.	Hammers, wood, metal and plastic cutting tools, such as chisels, drills, files, lathe tools, taps and dies. *Silver steel* is a high carbon steel.
Alloy steels		Any steel to which other elements have been added.	Properties depend on elements added.	
Stainless steel		18% chromium and 8% nickel added.	Corrosion resistance.	Sink units, kitchen ware, tanks, pipes, aircraft.
High speed steel		Medium carbon steel, tungsten, chromium and vanadium.	Retains hardness at high temperatures. Brittle. Can be hardened and tempered.	Cutting tools for lathes, etc.
High tensile steel		Low carbon steel, nickel and chromium.	Exceptional strength and toughness.	Gears, shafts, engine parts.
Manganese steel		High carbon steel and manganese.	Extreme toughness.	Chains, hooks etc.

Commonly available forms

Metals can be bought in a wide range of shapes and sizes, and you should always try to design jobs which use these standard sections. It is advisable to check what materials are in stock before starting, or to look in a stockholder's catalogue to find out what is available. The following sketches show the common shapes and some of the most used sections.

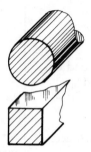

Round rod 5, 6, 8, 10, 12, 16, 20, 25, 32, 40, 50 mm diameter.

Squares 5, 6, 8, 10, 12, 16, 20, 25 mm square.

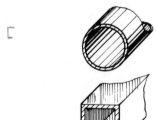

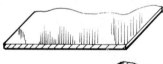

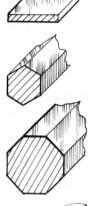

Flats	12 × 1.5 mm	20 × 1.5 mm	25 × 1.5 mm
	12 × 3 mm	20 × 3 mm	25 × 3 mm
	32 × 3 mm	40 × 3 mm	50 × 3 mm
	12 × 6 mm	20 × 6 mm	25 × 6 mm
	32 × 6 mm	40 × 6 mm	50 × 6 mm

Hexagons 6, 8, 10, 12, 16, 20, 22, 25 mm across flats.

Octagons 6, 8, 10, 12, 16, 20, 22, 25 mm across flats.

Sheets 0.60, 0.80, 1.00, 1.2, 1.6, 2.0, 2.5, 3 mm thick.

Round tubes 5, 6, 8, 10, 12, 16, 20, 25, 32, 40 mm outside diameter.

Square tubes 12, 20, 25 mm square.

Rectangular tubes 50 × 30 mm.

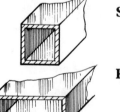

Angles 12 × 12 mm, 18 × 18 mm, 25 × 25 mm.

Cleaning-up and finishing metal

Finishing bright steel.

Stage 1. After shaping with coarse file and smooth file, complete filing by drawfiling. Always work in the same direction along the metal and make sure that each stage removes all marks left by the previous one. Keep your files clean to avoid pinning.

Stage 2. Finish by using different grades of emery cloth, first coarse, then fine, and finally after all marks have been removed add a little oil to the fine cloth for final finishing. Always wrap emery cloth round a flat file to avoid rounding corners and work in the same direction as the drawfiling marks.

Stage 3. To protect the metal from rust, smear it with Vaseline or light grease.

Oil finishing black steel.

Stage 1. Remove all loose scale from forging, grease, etc.

Stage 2. Either dip the metal in machine oil and burn it into the metal, or heat the metal to dull red heat and quench it in oil. Old sump oil containing carbon can be used to give a blacker finish and reduce costs.

Stage 3. Wipe off surplus oil and polish with black boot polish.

Painting metal.

Stage 1. Thoroughly clean and degrease the metal. Paraffin or special degreasers will clean badly affected parts while hot water with soda or detergent will remove light oil and dirt.

Stage 2. Find a dust free place to work, and make arrangements for supporting the work while painting and drying before starting.

Stage 3. For maximum protection apply primer, undercoat and topcoat. For inside work one or two coats of topcoat alone are adequate. Do not allow the paint to collect in corners or run. Paint awkward parts first, and then larger, flat, more noticeable areas. Two thin coats are always better than one thick one. Keep brushes clean and paint tin lids sealed.

Cleaning copper and brass.

Stage 1. Dip into an acid pickle consisting of one part sulphuric acid to ten parts water. Always use brass tongs as steel will contaminate the pickle.

Stage 2. Clean the metal with pumice powder and a damp cloth, and then remove any blemishes with wetted water of Ayr stone.

Stage 3. Finally polish on a polishing machine with a linen mop and tripoli buffing compound and/or by hand using metal polish.

Lacquering.

Stage 1. Thoroughly clean, polish and degrease the metal.

Stage 2. Apply the lacquer or varnish with a best quality soft paint brush to preserve the finish.

Coating with plastics

There are several widely used ways of coating metal with plastics. This is usually done to protect the metal from corrosion, to provide electrical insulation, or to improve its appearance.

Common examples include vegetable racks, refrigerator shelves and baskets, dish drainers, supermarket trolleys and baskets, metal furniture, steering wheels, and tool handles.

The method most suitable for school is to dip the pre-heated metal into a tank of fluidised thermoplastic powder such as polythene, P.V.C., nylon or cellulose acetate butyrate. Polythene is the most used coating powder because it is reasonably cheap, pleasant to handle, tough and durable.

Fluidization is where air is blown through a powder to make it behave like a liquid, so that when an object is dipped into it all parts are evenly coated.

The fluidizing tank has a porous base so that air can be blown at low pressure through the powder above, until the powder bubbles.

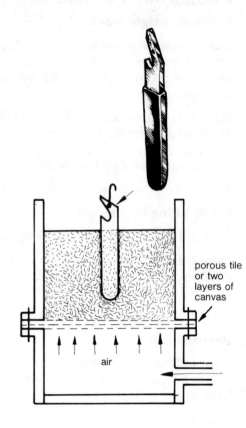

porous tile or two layers of canvas

air

Method.

1. Clean and thoroughly degrease the job. Arrange a suitable method of suspending it during heating and dipping.

2. Heat the job to 180°C in an oven. A thin wire construction will need to be hotter than a thick piece of metal.

3. Dip the job in the fluidized plastics powder for a few seconds.

4. Return it to the oven to fuse the coating into a smooth glassy finish. Overheating will discolour or burn the coating.

5. Hang it up to cool without touching it. Trim any rough edges with a sharp knife.

17 Materials for craftwork (3) plastics

The manufacture of plastics

Unlike wood and metal, plastics are man-made materials. They are often thought of as one material called plastic but this is wrong, and they are really a group of materials with widely varying properties. Suitable plastics can be found to take the place of the traditional materials, such as wood and metal, for many purposes.

Plastics are distinguished from other chemical compounds by the large size of their molecules. While most substances have molecules made up of less than 300 atoms, plastics molecules contain thousands of atoms. They are therefore known as *macromolecules*.

Sources of plastics

A few plastics are made by modifying natural substances which already have large molecules (*see* Fig. 1) but most of those used today are man-made, and are therefore known as synthetic plastics.

Fig. 1. Sources of natural plastics

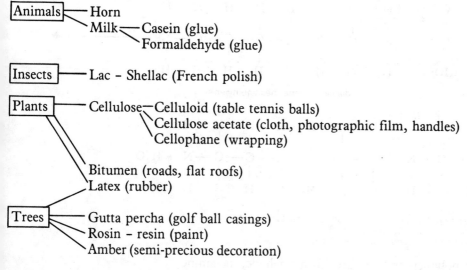

The main source of synthetic plastics is crude oil, but coal and natural gas are also used. During the refining of crude oil, liquids of various densities, such as petrol, paraffin and lubricating oils, and highly volatile petroleum gases, are produced. These gases form the basis of the plastics industry. Although complex and expensive equipment is needed to manufacture plastics, the basic process is simple.

The gases are broken down into *monomers* which are chemical substances consisting of a single molecule, and thousands of these are then linked together in a process called *polymerization* to form new compounds called *polymers*. Most polymers are made by combining the element carbon with one or more of the elements oxygen, hydrogen, chlorine, fluorine and nitrogen.

There are two main methods of polymerization

1. Addition polymerization is where polymers result from the chemical linking of thousands of identical small molecules (*see* Fig. 2).

Fig. 2. Polyethene (commonly called polythene)

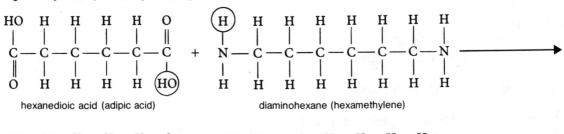

ethene (ethylene) monomer   polyethene polymer

Other common addition polymers include polypropene (polypropylene), polyethenyl ethanoate (polyvinyl acetate), polyphenylethene (polystyrene), polymethyl 2-methylpropenoate (acrylic).

2. Condensation polymerization is where two different monomers which react with each other are linked together to give a larger molecule with the splitting off of a small molecule, usually water. After the reaction the resulting larger molecule still contains two reactive groups, and therefore the reaction goes on and on, making a larger and larger molecule (*see* Fig. 3).

Fig. 3. Polyamide (commonly called nylon 6.6)

hexanedioic acid (adipic acid)   diaminohexane (hexamethylene)

Condensation product of 1 molecule of each reactant
(ringed atoms give water). This is repeated
thousands of times to form a polymer chain.

Other common addition polymers include urea formaldehyde, melamine formaldehyde, phenol formaldehyde.

Ways of changing plastics

The properties of plastics materials can be changed in three ways.

1. *We can lengthen or shorten the chains making up the polymers.*

For example, fifteen ethene monomers combine to make a paraffin wax, while several thousand combine to make polyethene (*see* Fig. 2).

2. *We can change the basic monomer.*
For example, if we replace one of the hydrogen atoms in the ethene monomer (*see*

Fig. 2) with a chloride atom we have a vinyl chloride monomer. These can then be linked to make a polyvinyl chloride (P.V.C.) polymer.

Fig. 4. P.V.C.

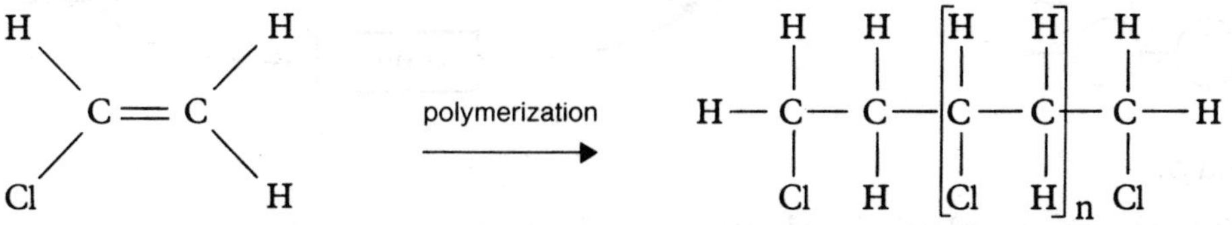

3. *We can combine two or more monomers* to make a new material. This is called *copolymerization* and the new material is a *copolymer*.

For example, a small amount of vinyl acetate monomer mixed with vinyl chloride monomer makes PVAC (vinyl chloride/vinyl acetate copolymer), which is easier to process than P.V.C. for such jobs as pressing gramophone records and vacuum forming, because it combines the toughness of P.V.C. with greater heat stability during shaping.

Fig. 5. P.V.A.C.

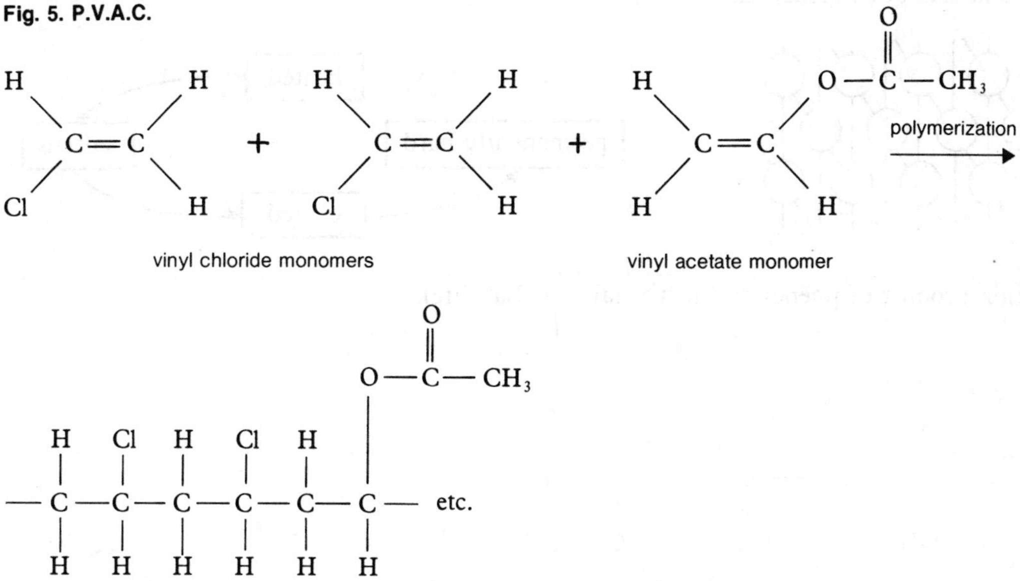

vinyl chloride monomers   vinyl acetate monomer

Thermoplastics and thermosetting plastics

There are two basic types of polymer chain formation and each behaves differently when heated. This difference allows us to separate plastics into two main groups.

1. Thermoplastics

These plastics are made up of lines of molecules with very few cross linkages. This allows them to soften when heated so that they can be bent into different shapes, and to become stiff and solid again when cooled (*see* Fig. 6). This process can be repeated many times.

Fig. 6.

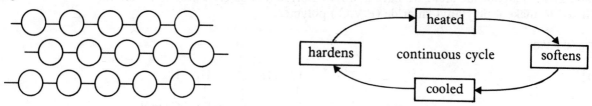

See also Figs. 2, 3, 4 and 5.

Plastic memory. Each time a thermoplastic is reheated, it will try to return to its original flat state, unless it has been damaged by over-heating or over-stretching. This property is known as plastic memory.

Three quarters of the plastics used are thermoplastics.

2. Thermosetting plastics

These plastics are made up of lines of molecules which are heavily cross-linked. This results in a rigid molecular structure (*see* Fig. 7). Although they soften when heated the first time, and can therefore be shaped, they then become permanently stiff and solid, and cannot be reshaped.

Fig. 7.

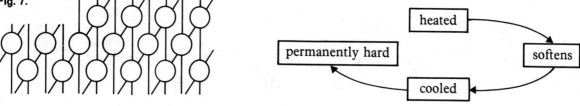

e.g. Condensation product of phenol and methanal (e.g. Bakelite).

Bakelite

This is repeated thousands of times in both directions.

Properties, uses and commonly available forms of plastics

Before the raw materials can be converted into finished products, other substances may have to be added to give the required properties.

These may include:

Plasticizers to soften the final product and make it less brittle.
Dyes and pigments to give the required colour.
Heat stabilizers to give resistance to heat during manufacture or in use.
Inert fillers to improve the properties by increasing flexibility, hardness, or toughness for example, or to save money by increasing the bulk of the material.
Catalysts to control the speed of a chemical reaction.
Fire – retarding additives.
Foaming agents to make plastic foams.

Raw materials manufacturers produce plastics in many convenient forms for use by other industries. These include powders, granules, pastes and liquids, and semi-finished products such as sheets, slabs, rods, tubes and films.

Many of these forms are either not available in small quantities, or are not suitable for working by the methods available in school or at home. We have, therefore, included in the properties and uses chart, only those which are readily available for school and home use.

The identification of plastics

Although it is very difficult to identify all the many different plastics, especially where two or more have been used together, or when additives have been used to alter their properties, it is useful to be able to recognise the most used ones.

The following chart shows some simple tests which will help in this, and the results of them for some common plastics.

In general, most thermoplastics will cut cleanly, become flexible at 200°C or less, and melt to a viscous liquid if heating continues, while thermosets will produce powdery chips when cut, and bubble and decompose before softening.

The identification of common plastics

Common name	Technical name	Cut with sharp knife	Hit with hammer	Bend at room temperature	Put in water	Scratch with finger nail
1 Polythene	Polyethene	Easy and smooth	Very strong	L.D.-flexible H.D.-fairly stiff	Floats	Yes
2 Polyvinyl chloride (P.V.C.)	Polychloro-ethane	Easy and smooth	Fairly strong	Plasticized – flexible Rigid – stiff	Sinks	Plasticized – yes Rigid – no
3 Polystyrene	Polyphenyl-ethene	Fairly hard	Weak	Stiff	Sinks	No
4 Expanded polystyrene	Expanded polyphenyl-ethene	Crumbles	Crumbles	Breaks	Very buoyant	Yes
5 Acrylic or PMMA or polymethyl-methacrylate	Polymethyl (11)methyl-propenoate	Splinters	Brittle	Breaks	Sinks	No
6 Polypropylene	Polypropene	Easy and fairly smooth	Very strong	Stiff	Floats	No
7 Nylon	Polyamide	Fairly easy and smooth	Very strong	Stiff	Sinks	Yes
8 Cellulose acetate	A modified natural material	Easy and smooth	Strong	May be flexible	Sinks	No
9 Urea formalde-hyde	Urea methanal	Chips	Brittle	Very stiff	Sinks	No
10 Melamine formalde-hyde	Melamine methanal					
11 Phenol formalde-hyde	Phenol methanal					
12 Polyester resin	Unsaturated polyester resin	Difficult and chips	Brittle	Very stiff	Sinks	No

Effect of burning

	Softens	Ignites	Colour of flame	Smoke	Nature of flame	Continues to burn on its own	Smell
1	Yes	Easily	Blue with yellow tip	Little	Burning droplets go out when hit floor	Yes	Candle wax
2	Yes	With difficulty	Yellow	White, heavy soot formation	May drip	No	Hydro-chloric acid
3	Yes	Easily	Orange/ yellow	Black with sooty smuts	Burning droplets	Yes	Sweet
4	No	Easily	Orange/ yellow	Black with sooty smuts	Drips continue to burn	Yes	Sweet
5	Yes	Easily	Yellow with blue base and clear edges	None	Drips continue to burn. Bubbles before burning. Spitty flame (crackles)	Yes	Strong, sweet, fruity smell
6	Yes at a higher temper-ature than polythene	Easily	Yellow with clear blue base	Little	Burning droplets go out when hit floor	Yes	Candle wax. Different from polythene
7	No	Difficult	Blue with yellow tip	Little	Melts to a free flowing liquid which drips carrying a flame.	Yes	Like burning hair.
8	Yes	Easily	Dark yellow	Little	Material crackles and shrivels.	Depends on type	Like vinegar
9–11	No	Difficult	Pale yellow with light blue green edges	Little	Plastic swells, cracks, turns white at edges. Glows red after flame is put out.	No	Pungent burning smell
12	No	Easily	Orange/ yellow	Lots of black smoke with smuts	Very smoky	Depends on type	Fruity

Properties and uses of a few common thermoplastics

Common name	Chemical name	Properties
Low density polythene	Low density polyethylene	Wide range of colours. Tough. Good chemical resistance. Good electrical insulator. Flexible, soft. Fades unless light stabilized. Attracts dust unless anti-static. Service temperature 60°C, provided there is no mechanical stress.
High density polythene	High density polyethylene	Wide range of colours. Fairly stiff and hard. Stiffness and softening point both increase with density. Can be sterilized. Good chemical resistance. High impact and shock resistance (special grades). Fades unless light stabilized. Service temperature 80°C, provided there is no mechanical stress.
Rigid P.V.C. (polyvinyl chloride)	Rigid polychloroethane	Wide range of colours. Stiff, hard. Tough at room temperature. Can be used outdoors if suitably stabilized. Light weight. Very good acid and alkali resistance. Particularly good for fabricating.
Plasticized P.V.C. (Polyvinyl chloride)	Plasticized polychloroethane	Wide range of colours. Soft, flexible. Good electrical insulator.
Polystyrene	Polyphenylethene	Stiff, hard. Wide range of colours. Can be made impact resistant.
Expanded polystyrene	Expanded polyphenylethane	Very buoyant. Light weight. Absorbs shocks. Very good sound and heat insulator. Crumbles easily. Burns readily unless flame-proofed.

'ses	Common forms
queezee bottles and toys. Plastic acks and sheets. Packaging film. elecommunications cable nsulation. T.V. aerial lead nsulation.	Powders. Granules. Films. Sheets. Wide range of colours.
Milk crates. Bottles, barrels, tanks, ipes. Chemical pumps. Machine arts (e.g. gear wheels). Housewares e.g. buckets, bowls).	Powders. Granules. Films. Sheets. Wide range of colours.
ipes, guttering and fittings. Bottles nd containers. Gramophone ecords. Chocolate box liners. Curtain rails. Roofing sheets. Shoe oles. Brush bristles.	Powders. Pastes. Liquids. Sheets. Wide range of colours.
eathercloth, suitcases, tabletop overings. Sealing compounds, Underseal. Dip coatings. Hosepipes. lectrical wiring insulation. Wall overings (vinyl wallpaper). Floor overings (vinyl tiles etc.).	Powders. Pastes. Liquids. Sheets. Wide range of colours.
ood containers. Disposable cups, utlery, plates. Model Kits. efrigerator linings. Film. Kitchen are. Toys, radio cabinets.	Powders. Granules. Sheets. Wide range of colours.
ound insulation. Heat insulation. ackaging.	Sheets Slabs } Usually white. Beads

Properties and uses of a few common thermoplastics

Common name	Chemical name	Properties
Acrylic or Polymethyl methacrylate (PMMA)	Polymethyl(11) methylpropenoate	Stiff, hard, glass-clear. Very durable outdoors. Easily machined, cemented and polished. Good electrical insulator. Safe with food. Ten times more impact resistant than glass. Splinters easily. Scratches easily.
Polypropylene	Polypropene	Very light, floats. Very good chemical resistance. Good fatigue resistance (e.g. integral hinges). Hard. Can be sterilized. Impact resistant even at low temperatures. Service temperature of 100°C. Rigid. Good mechanical and electrical properties.
Nylon	Polyamide	Hard, tough, rigid, creep resistant. Good bearing surface. Self-lubricating. Resistant to oil, fuels, and chemicals. Good fatigue resistance. High melting point. Very resiliant. Wear and friction resistant.
Cellulose acetate	(A modified natural material)	Tough. Can be made flexible. Hard, stiff. Resiliant. Light weight.
Polyester resin	Unsaturated polyester resin	Good electrical insulator, good heat resistance. Stiff, hard, brittle alone but strong and resiliant when laminated. Resistant to ultra-violet light for outside use. Strongly exothermic, this can lead to cracking. Contracts on curing.

Uses	Common forms
Light units and illuminated signs. Watch and clock glasses. Record player lids. Simple lenses. Aircraft canopies and windows. Car rear light units. Skylights. Furniture. Baths. *Perspex* sheet. Cladding for buildings	Rods } Usually clear. Tubes } Sheets are clear, translucent and opaque. In a wide range of colours.
Crates. Chair shells and seats. Waste and chemical pipes and fittings. Packaging film. String, rope, sacks, cloth, carpets, strapping tape. Car and domestic appliance parts, e.g. air-cleaners, battery cases. Medical equipment (e.g. syringes), containers with integral hinges.	Powders. Granules. Sheets. Rods. Colour naturally pale pink/white, but can be pigmented.
Gear wheels, bearings, automotive, agricultural, general communications and telecommunications equipment parts. Power tool casings. Curtain rail fittings, packaging, film, clothing, combs.	Powder. Granules. Chips. Rod. Tube. Sheet. Extruded sections. Usually white or cream. Other colours including black obtainable.
Photographic film. Tool handles. Transparent, flexible box lids. Pen cases. Toothbrush handles. Car steering wheels.	Powder. Sheet-clear and in a range of colours. Film. Rod – yellow/amber shade. Extruded sections – usually fluted.
G.R.P. boats, car bodies. Chair shells, ducting, garden furniture, etc. Translucent panels for building. Encapsulating and embedding castings.	Liquids. Pastes.

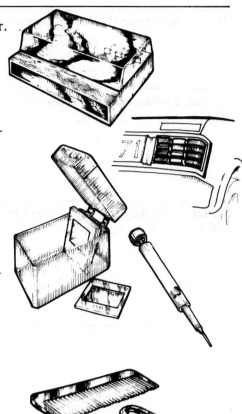

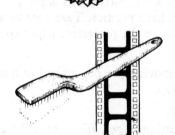

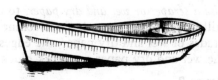

Properties and uses of a few common thermosetting plastics

Common name	Chemical name	Properties
Urea formaldehyde (U.F.)	Urea methanal	Stiff, hard, strong, brittle. Heat resistant. Wide range of colours.
Melamine formaldehyde (M.F.)	Melamine methanal	Stiff, hard, strong. Heat resistant. Wide range of colours. Resistant to weak chemicals. Stain resistant.
Phenol formaldehyde (P.F.)	Phenol methanal	Stiff, hard, strong, brittle. Heat resistant. Makes high strength fabric or paper reinforced engineering laminates. Limited colours because it darkens under light.

Part 5 Cleaning-up and finishing plastics

The following instructions apply particularly to acrylic, but will be found suitable for most hard plastics. Take care to avoid scratching the surface of plastics at all times. Leave the protective paper covering on, where supplied, for as long as possible.

After removing the paper the last traces of adhesive can be washed off with warm, soapy water.

Stage 1.
After cutting, *plane, file or sand* the edges to remove saw marks. If using a disc or belt sander on thermoplastics, use a coarse abrasive and light pressure to avoid overheating. If filing, finish by draw filing.

Stage 2.
Use a scraper or wet and dry paper, to obtain a completely smooth edge. Scraping will leave the edges ready for machine polishing. By using progressively finer grades of wet and dry paper, the edges can be made ready for hand finishing. Use the wet and dry paper on a cork block to keep the edges square.

Stage 3.
To avoid overheating when *machine polishing* thermoplastics, keep the work moving lightly against a soft mop coated with a mild abrasive.

Uses	Common forms
Light coloured electrical fittings and domestic appliance parts such as cooker knobs. Adhesives (especially for wood laminating).	Powder. Granules. Colours: white, cream.
Tableware such as *Melaware*. Decorative laminates. Electrical insulation. Synthetic resin paints.	Powder. Granules. Laminate sheets, e.g. formica. Colour–clear unless pigmented.
Dark coloured electrical fittings and parts for domestic appliances, such as electric kettle, iron and saucepan handles. Bottle tops, door handles. Paper and fabric reinforced laminates.	Powder. Granules. Reinforced sheet and rod e.g. *Tufnol*. Colours include black, brown, red and green.

When *hand polishing* use progressively finer grades of abrasive polish. Rubbing down compounds, as used for rubbing down car paintwork, valve grinding pastes or special polishes, can be used.

For example, on Perspex we would use Perspex No. 1 (abrasive polish), Perspex No. 2 (fine polish), Perspex No. 3 (anti-static polish).

Domestic metal polish is a fine finishing abrasive.

Deep surface scratches can be removed from most plastics by using progressively finer grades of wet and dry paper, valve grinding paste, or rubbing down compound. Shallow scratches can be removed by using special polishes or domestic metal polish.

Heating thermoplastics will cause marks which have been removed to reappear (plastic memory). Therefore, final polishing should be left until all heating is finished.

Wet and dry paper (silicone carbide paper) is graded by grit sizes.

Common grades are: 60 – 120 grit coarse.
200 – 320 grit medium.
400 – 600 grit fine.

Technology questions

Tools

1. Name specifically the cutting tools you would use to carry out *four* of the following operations. In *two* cases show how the design of the principal tool is suited to its particular job.

(a) Sawing an elliptical hole (major axis 125, minor axis 75) in the middle of a 200 × 150 × 18 thick multi-ply yoke for thermoforming sheet plastics.

(b) Cutting to a uniform depth a stopped housing joint in a 250 wide side of a solid wooden book case.

(c) Making the ø8 holes in the end of a 35 × 20 chair rail to join by dowels the front and back legs.

(d) Milling a stopped 4 wide keyway in an axle, using a vertical milling machine.

(e) Making the joints in a rectangular gilding metal box with mitred corners.

(f) Cutting a piece of 50 thick expanded polystyrene into a predetermined curve.

(L)

2. Fig. 1 shows the cutting ends of three tools used to make cylindrical holes. Account for the differences in shape. By reference to each tool, explain why its particular shape makes it suited to its specific use.

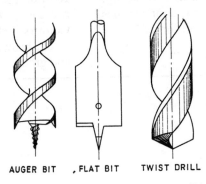

AUGER BIT　, FLAT BIT　TWIST DRILL

Fig. 1

(L)

3. Explain the difference between the two tools in each of the following pairs and state a use for each tool:

(a) set-square and try-square,
(b) twist bit and twist drill,
(c) brace and wheelbrace (or hand drill),
(d) firmer gouge and scribing gouge.

(O&C)

4. (a) Make a clear sketch of a forstner bit. When would you use it?

(b) By means of sketches, either cross-sectional or exploded views, show how the jaws of a brace grip a bit.

(O&C)

5. (a) Show with sketches the difference between a cutting gauge, a marking gauge and a mortice gauge, and state a use for each of these tools.

(b) How would you test a try square to ensure that it shows an accurate 90° angle? (A protractor or set square is not to be used.)

(O&C)

6. Name the tools/drills which you could use to produce the following round holes:

Type of hole	Tool/drill
Up to 50 mm diameter flat bottomed hole in wood	
50 mm diameter hole in tinplate	
25 mm diameter hole in brickwork	
6·5 mm diameter hole in mild steel	
6·5 mm diameter hole in acrylic sheet	

(WJEB)

7. For what purposes are the following tools used: router, plough plane and rebate plane? Your answer should include notes and sketches of *the work accomplished* by these tools.

(O&C)

8. Explain why the tools listed below are efficient for the work they have to undertake. Diagrams should form an important part of your answer.

(*a*) Straight tin snips,
(*b*) engineers' pliers,
(*c*) bossing mallet,
(*d*) hacksaw.

(O&C)

9. List the sequence of events in 'dry-cramping' a flat-frame, prior to gluing-up. List *three* main checks for accuracy and state methods of correction.

(O&C)

10. Choose two of the following and in each case draw a sketch, label three main parts, and explain the method of use:

a) a sash cramp; *b*) a strip heater; *c*) a toolmakers clamp.

11. Choose *two* of the following and state what they are used for. In each case draw a sketch and label *three* parts.

(*a*) A try-square; (*b*) A hacksaw; (*c*) An injection moulding machine.

12. (*a*) The tools listed below have already been ground to the correct angle. Describe how you would sharpen each of these.
   (i)   A 25 mm firmer chisel.
   (ii) A jack plane blade.
   (iii) A turning gouge.
(*b*) Draw the end of a centre bit and use your drawing to explain how this should be sharpened.
(*c*) Give *one* reason why oil is necessary when sharpening tools on an "oilstone"?
(*d*) Make a drawing of an oilstone slip or slipstone and give *one* example of its use.

(YREB)

Processes

13. The simple carrying handle shown in fig. 2 is to be used for lightweight duties. It may be made in a school workshop of aluminium alloy HE9WP, or beech veneers or polypropylene.

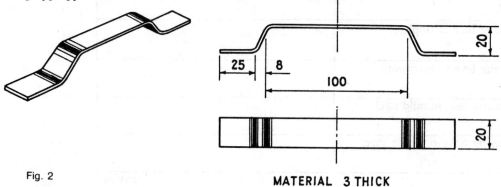

Fig. 2

MATERIAL 3 THICK

Choose one material and in detail describe a simple tool or mould to enable 100 of the handles to be made. Give full details for their manufacture, indicating materials, construction, functional dimensions and finish. Credit will be given for simplicity of design, ease of manufacture, ease of operation and the economic use of materials.

(L)

14. Fig. 3 shows two wooden handles. Handle A is to be fitted into a veneered laminboard drawer front of 20 total thickness, and handle B into a veneered hardboard sliding door of 7 total thickness.

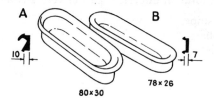

Fig. 3

Describe in detail, as in an instruction leaflet, how you would fit and fix *both* of these handles, detailing the tools to be used. The overall length and width of the handles is given. Both handles have semi-circular ends. Use the following table.

Op. no.	Description	Sketch	Tools required
1.			

(L)

15. Fig. 4 shows a view, part sectioned, of a free running cast iron pulley in a mild steel support. Make separate *bold* annotated diagrams to show how a bearing shaft may be retained by means of four of the following:

(a) split cotter pins,
(b) internal circlips,
(c) external circlips,
(d) a socket headed set screw,
(e) a headed and part threaded shaft and appropriate nut(s).

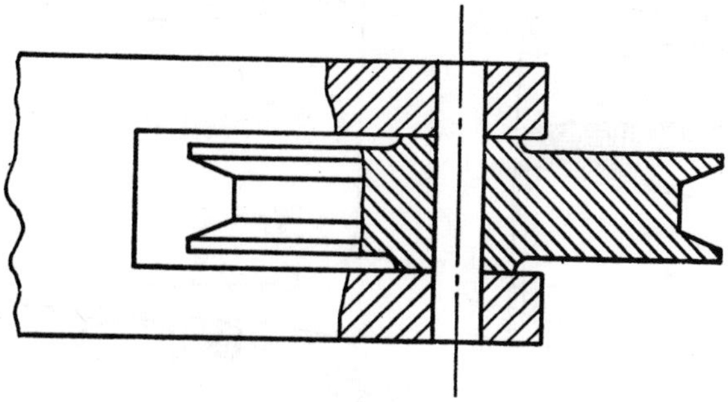

Fig. 4

(L)

16. Fig. 5 shows a forged screwdriver bit used in a carpenter's bit brace when working with long, large gauge screws.

(i) State the material from which the bit should be made, and list its important properties.
(ii) With the aid of *bold* annotated sketches, describe in detail the stage by stage operations by which the bit would be made in your school workshop.

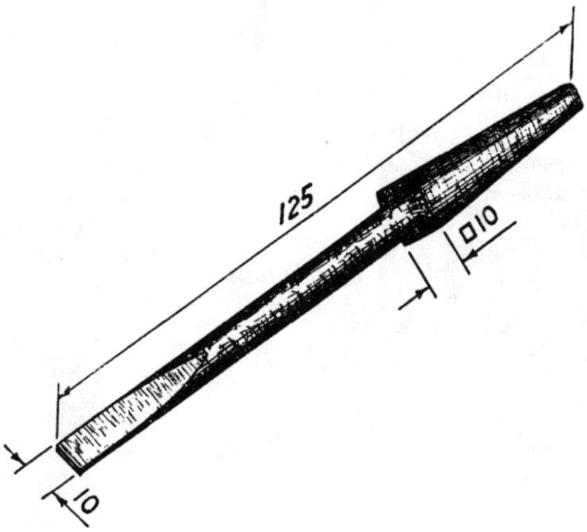

Fig. 5

(L)

17. Fig. 6 (over) represents a sheet from a sketch book showing five different bases for a table lamp. The lamp shade is clear polyester resin reinforced with glass filament. Describe in detail the stages you would follow to make *one* of the bases, naming the tools and equipment you would use. Start by naming the material. Set out your answer using the column headings given below. The fitting of the adapter is to be included in your description.

Process	Detailed description of method	Tools/equipment	Sketches of the process and/or set-up
1.			

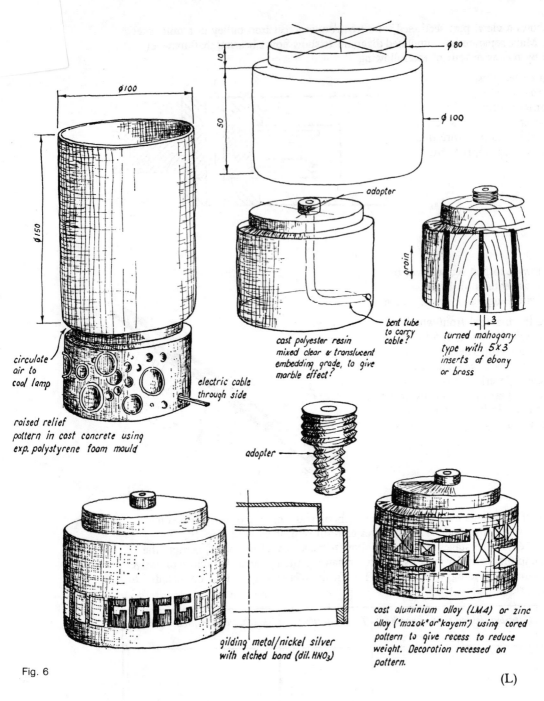

circulate
air to
cool lamp

electric cable
through side

raised relief
pattern in cast concrete using
exp. polystyrene foam mould

adopter

cast polyester resin
mixed clear & translucent
embedding grade, to give
marble effect?

bent tube
to carry
cable?

turned mahogany
type with 5×3
inserts of ebony
or brass

grain

3

adopter

gilding metal/nickel silver
with etched band (dil. HNO₃)

cast aluminium alloy (LM4) or zinc
alloy ('mazak" or "kayem") using cored
pattern to give recess to reduce
weight. Decoration recessed on
pattern.

Fig. 6

(L)

18. Small trays as shown in fig. 7 are to be made
from 3 thick acrylic sheet by the plug and yoke
method of thermoforming.

(i) With the aid of *bold* annotated sketches
describe in detail:

(*a*) the form of the plug and yoke to be
used,

(*b*) the stage by stage sequence of
operations needed to produce a tray.

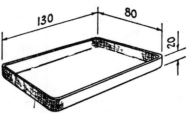

Fig. 7

(ii) Name two other methods by which the trays could have been made in your school workshop using plastics materials. For each method state the advantages or disadvantages compared with the plug and yoke method.

(L)

19. Set out a well illustrated instruction sheet for *one* of the following processes:

(i) making a loose tongue joint between the edges of two solid wood boards 18 thick 150 wide × 500 long,

(ii) making a butt seam in a cylindrical vessel ø75 × 100 long × 0.90 gilding metal, using a high melting point silver solder.

(iii) making a hot air welded flat butt joint between two pieces of PVC sheet 3 thick. In addition make an annotated sectional elevation of the welding tool to show how it works.

(L)

20. A small riven slate-topped table is shown in fig. 8. It is to be made of solid wood. The joint at *A* is to be a lap dovetail, and the joint at *B* is to be a haunched mortice and tenon.

(i) With the aid of *bold* annotated sketches, describe in detailed procedural order the marking out of *either* joint *A or* joint *B*.

(ii) Sketch an alternative form of construction for *either* joint *A*, if lipped and veneered laminboard were to be used, *or* joint *B*, if the upright were to be of 20 × 20 × 0.90 wall thickness BDMS tube and the bottom rail of solid wood.

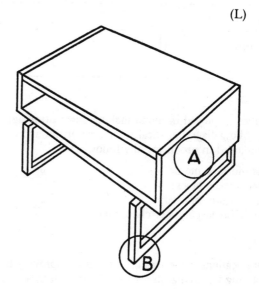

Fig. 8

(L)

21. Fig. 9 shows an elevation, half sectioned, of a small bowl to be made of gilding metal. The body is to be raised from flat sheet. With the aid of a series of bold annotated diagrams, describe in detail the stages you would take to *raise and planish* the bowl. State all the tools and equipment you would use.

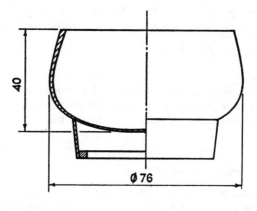

Fig. 9

(L)

22. List the adhesives you would employ to join the following:

Applications	Adhesives
A clear gemstone to its metal setting	
The wooden laminate forming the laminated member of a bridge	
Two pieces of wood which are subsequently to be parted	
Cloth to wood	
Plastic laminate to plywood	

(WJEC)

23. The techniques employed in mouldmaking and casting apply, in many cases, to a range of materials. Show diagrammatically the similarities and differences between the processes employed in producing the following:

(a) a vacuum-formed mould;
(b) a concrete screen block;
(c) a cast aluminium bracket;
(d) a glass-reinforced polyester chair shell.

(WJEC)

24. In certain applications, adhesives are not only improving but in some instances are actually replacing traditional joints in various materials. List *two* examples where this occurs and discuss the significance of the statement.

(WJEC)

25. The traditional type of toolbox has a lid which opens upwards. What type of lock would you fit to this box? Describe, with the aid of sketches, how you would fit such a lock.

(O&C)

26. (a) Name *three* different types of glue used in woodworking.
(b) Describe, in detail, how you would glue up a flat frame construction. What tests would you make to ensure that the frame is true?

(O&C)

27. Describe with freehand drawings:

(a) two different ways of edge jointing boards for a table top;
(b) how you would fix such a table top to the underframe and allow for shrinkage. Indicate the grain direction of the table top in your answer.

(O&C)

28. (a) If you wished to buy some woodscrews, what information would the storekeeper need in order to supply you with the correct item?
   (b) By means of a cross-sectional diagram, show clearly how you would prepare two pieces of hardwood to receive a countersunk wood screw which holds them together.

(O&C)

29. How would you fit a pair of brass butt hinges to a small box? State *two* causes for the lid not closing properly and explain how you would rectify these faults.

(O&C)

30. Illustrate and describe the uses of the following in the casting of metals: (a) pattern; (b) mould; (c) core; (d) cope and drag.

(O&C)

31. The correct setting of a lathe tool is vital for successful turning. Consider the design of a lathe toolpost and explain how the tool may be securely fixed and adjusted. Clear, annotated drawings must form an important part of your answer.

(O&C)

32. Explain the stages in the making of a tray, using resin and glass fibre. How could the tray be made more visually interesting?

(O&C)

33. Describe how it is possible to produce a vacuum formed mould from which a pendant can be made, using casting resin. Illustrations must form an important part of your answer.

(O&C)

34. (a) Describe in detail with the aid of sketches how you would make a set of four egg cups based on the form shown in fig. 10. Your answer should include all the details of the materials used, and how the egg cups would be finished.
   (b) Comment critically on the design of the egg cups.

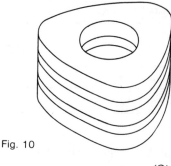

Fig. 10

(O)

35. Fig. 11 shows three views of a model boat hull. The hull, which should be hollow to accommodate a motor, could be made from a number of materials. Explain step-by-step, using sketches where possible, how the hull could be made in one material. Give reasons for your choice of material.

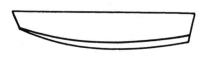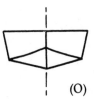

Fig. 11

(O)

36. Assume that you have been asked to design and make a goblet; a basic outline is shown in fig. 12.

    (a) Show by means of an annotated sketch how the form illustrated could be developed or would need to be modified when a specific material is used.

    (b) Explain in detail with the aid of sketches how the goblet you have designed would be made.

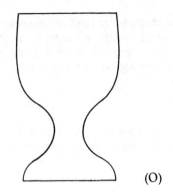

Fig. 12   (O)

37. Fig. 13 shows two elevations of a nut-cracker (hidden detail is not shown).

    (a) Suggest how part No. 1 might be made.

    (b) Explain in detail how the thread on part No. 2 is produced.

    (c) Show how part No. 3 could be made to swivel on part No. 2.

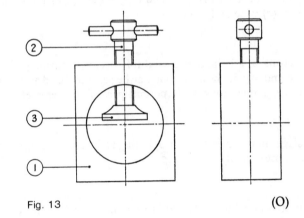

Fig. 13   (O)

38. Give *one* example of a product normally manufactured in plastic by *each* of the following processes:

Process	Product
Vacuum forming	
Injection moulding	
Extrusion	
Compression moulding	
Laying-up (G.R.P.)	

(WJEC)

39. Illustrate suitable knock-down joints for the following situations:

    (a) Legs of 18 mm square stainless steel tube (wall thickness 1·5 mm) joined at right angles to teak rails for a small table (section of rail 50 mm × 16 mm).

    (b) Ends of plastic laminated blockboard panels joined at right angles for the top joint of a bookcase. The blockboard is lipped on all edges with 18 mm × 18 mm beech.

Your answers should be expressed graphically with appropriate labels on exploded drawings.

(WJEC)

40. Name the joints or techniques which could be employed in the following wood constructions:

Locations	Joints or techniques
Jointing the bottom to the side in a chest of drawers made of solid timber	
Manufacturing of a curved base rail of a rocking chair by glueing strips of wood	
Linking a number of narrow boards edge to edge for cladding a ceiling	
Jointing a square table leg to a rectangular rail level with the top of the leg	
Jointing a drawer back to a drawer side in solid timber	

(WJEC)

41. Name the following techniques/processes in metalworking:

Techniques/processes	Name
Softening of metal by heating	
Shaping a bowl from a disc of copper using a hammer and stake	
Squaring the end of metal rod in lathe	
Heating non-ferrous metal in acid to remove oxides	
Producing a thread inside a hole using the lathe	

(WJEC)

42. Consider the design of a lathe and explain the purpose of the tailstock. State clearly how it may be used in connection with taper turning.

(O&C)

43. Describe an article that you have recently designed and made which has relied mainly on forging or silversmithing techniques. Describe in detail the making of one important part of this design and state why you think the construction and shaping of this piece is particularly suitable for the article as a whole. Large, well-labelled freehand drawings must form an important part of your answer.

(O&C)

44. When drilling acrylic sheet, what special drills, drilling speeds or other precautions would help to prevent the material from splintering at its edges? If the hole were 12mm diameter or more, how could such a hole have its edges highly polished?

(O&C)

45. Sketch 2 different types of mechanical stay for use on the fall front of a small cabinet, and state the circumstances under which you would choose one or the other. Indicate particular factors to be considered when fitting each pattern of stay.

(O&C)

46. 'Temporary' and 'permanent' are two words frequently used in connection with joining metals. Name *two* methods of temporary and *two* of permanent joining. Describe in detail how one of the permanent methods you have named would be carried out in the workshop.

(O&C)

47. When cutting internal and external threads by hand, which should be cut first and why?

Explain in detail the cutting of an internal thread by hand.

Describe how a lathe tailstock is frequently used to start cutting an external thread.

(O&C)

48. Name *two* different bonding materials which would prove successful when two or more pieces of acrylic need to be bonded together. List the steps necessary to produce a simple acrylic pendant and include the final polishing process.

(O&C)

49. Make clear illustrations of *two* methods by which a glass panel might be fitted to a display-cabinet lid or door. Full provision should be made for the replacement of the glass, if broken.

(O&C)

50. Describe the stages in two of the following:

(a) filing a piece of acrylic sheet to a rectangle after it has been sawn, and cleaning-up and polishing the edges;
(b) planishing, cleaning-up and finishing a small copper bowl;
(c) fitting a plywood bottom to a softwood box, and cleaning-up and finishing the outside of the box.

51. Use notes and diagrams to describe in the correct order two of the following:

(a) the stages in rivetting together two 6 mm thick pieces of bright drawn mild steel using a 3 mm diameter countersunk steel rivet, including preparing the hole and calculating the length of rivet;
(b) the stages in laying-up a fibre glass reinforced plastics tray on a previously made former;
(c) the stages in screwing a 12 mm thick piece of hardwood to a 30 mm thick piece of hardwood using a No. 8 countersunk steel woodscrew.

52. Use notes and sketches to explain two of the following:

(a) vacuum forming a tray to hold drawing instruments, (include notes on how the vacuum forming machine works, and the design of the mould);
(b) the difference between a frame construction and a carcase construction, (include sketches of one example of each showing the joints used);
(c) the stages in hardening and tempering a tool steel screwdriver blade.

53. Using sketches wherever possible, describe the stages in *two* of the following processes:

    (*a*) soldering the seam of a copper cylinder, indicating how the metal is held together during this operation;

    (*b*) cutting out and the complete shaping of a 200 mm diameter hole in a piece of acrylic 300 mm × 300 mm × 3 mm thick;

    (*c*) marking out a common mortice and tenon joint, listing all the tools needed.

54. Use notes and sketches to describe *two* of the following:-

    (*a*) drilling and tapping a blind hole in metal;

    (*b*) bending a piece of acrylic 100 mm × 50 mm × 3 mm thick into the shape shown in fig. 14;

    (*c*) how a plywood panel could be fitted into a door frame.

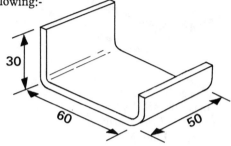

Fig. 14

55. Use notes and sketches to explain *two* of the following processes:

    (*a*) press-moulding a plastic dish, giving details of the mould and the moulding and finishing operations;

    (*b*) knurling an aluminium screwdriver handle on a centre lathe;

    (*c*) fixing two pieces of wood together using a countersunk headed screw, naming all the tools used in their correct order.

56. Fig. 15 shows one end of a bookrack that will stand on a table. Use clear drawings and notes to show

    (*a*) the type of joint which you would use to join the shelf to the end,

    (*b*) how you would mark out and cut this joint,

    (*c*) any modifications that you would suggest to the bookrack end to improve its functional design,

    (*d*) how you would assemble and glue together the finished rack.

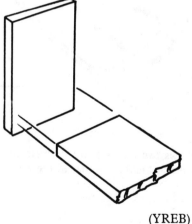

Fig. 15

(YREB)

57. *Either* (*a*) Explain stage by stage how you would mark out and make the sliding stay shown in fig. 16 from a length of bright mild steel, 25 mm × 4 mm. Include in your answer the name of any tools that you would use.

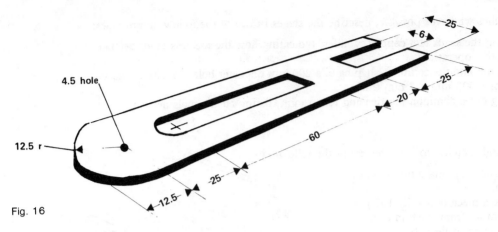

4.5 hole

12.5 r

60

25

20

25

6

25

25

12.5

Fig. 16

Or (*b*) Explain stage by stage how you would make the salad server shown in fig. 17 from strips of ash veneer, 300 mm × 45 mm × 1·5 mm. Your answer must include the making of any necessary moulds or formers. Include in your answer the name of any tools that you would use.

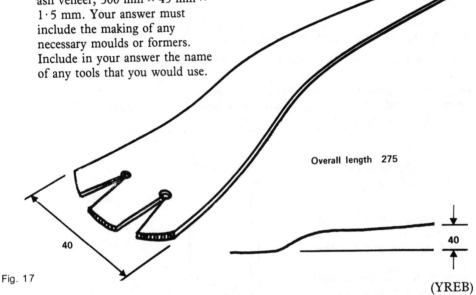

Overall length 275

40

40

Fig. 17

(YREB)

58. (*a*) Fig. 18 shows two pieces of tube which form part of a go-kart frame. They are to be fitted and brazed together at the angle shown.

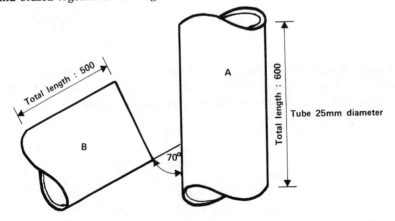

Total length : 500

Total length : 600

A

B

70°

Tube 25mm diameter

Fig. 18

Explain in detail how you would

    (i) mark out the joint at the end of tube B (your answer must include a drawing showing the two pieces of tube fitted together in their finished position),
    (ii) cut the joint,
    (iii) prepare the pieces for brazing,
    (iv) hold the pieces in position for brazing and test the joint angle,
    (v) braze the joint.

(b) Using drawings and brief notes, show how you would join two similar pieces of tube together at the angle shown in fig. 19 without using heating or adhesive.

Fig. 19

(YREB)

59. Fig. 20 shows a small, round dish to be made in copper. Using notes and drawings, describe how you would make this dish, starting with a 110 mm square piece of metal for the dish and a piece of metal 50 mm × 150 mm for the base.

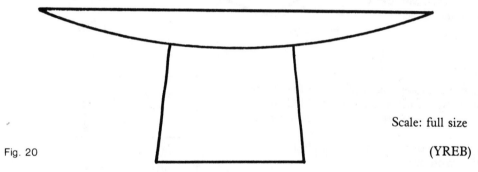

Scale: full size

Fig. 20   (YREB)

60. Fig. 21 shows part of a mild steel brazing hearth stand that fixes on to a bench. Explain in detail how you would

(a) cut the thread on screw A,
(b) cut the thread on component B,
(c) produce the 45° bevel on the end of screw A,
(d) modify the end of screw A so as to reduce the possibility of damage to the underside of the bench,
(e) mark out, drill and fix the crosspin C.

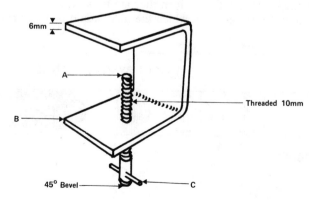

6mm

A

Threaded 10mm

B

45° Bevel

C

Fig. 21   (YREB)

61. Fig. 22 shows one of a large number of round, plastic endstops for tubular steel chair legs to be made by injection moulding.

   (a) Describe in detail how you would make the mould.

   (b) What material would you use for the mould?

   (c) What plastic would you use for making the endstop? Give *one* reason for your choice.

   (d) Describe the sequence of operations for making the endstop, starting with the raw plastic until the endstop is complete.

Dimensions:-

Bore   19mm ø

Height   20mm

Wall thickness 3mm

Fig. 22

(YREB)

62. (a) You are to make the glass-reinforced plastic skateboard deck shown in fig. 23.

     (i) Name *two* important features of the mould.

     (ii) What type and weight of glass-reinforcement would you use?

     (iii) What type of resin would you use?

   (b) Describe in detail

     (i) the moulding of the skateboard deck, which is to be of a red colour,

     (ii) the finishing stages,

     (iii) *two* safety precautions necessary when working with glass-reinforced plastic.

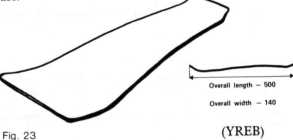

Overall length – 500

Overall width – 140

Fig. 23

(YREB)

Materials

63. Fig. 24 (a) shows the proportions of a simple line motif on a link. The motif is used to decorate each link of a bracelet or a belt by some form of surface treatment or overlay.

The links may be made of wood, or metal or plastics or a combination of materials.

   (a) State: (i) the purpose for which the links are to be used,

            (ii) the size of the links,

            (iii) the material(s) from which they are to be made.

   (b) Describe fully the processes by which the links would be made and finished.

Fig. 24(a)

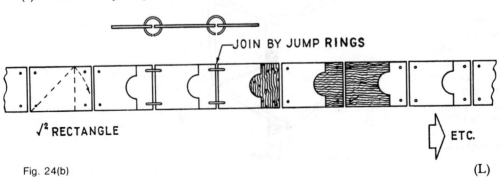

JOIN BY JUMP RINGS

√² RECTANGLE

ETC.

Fig. 24(b)

(L)

64. By effecting certain changes, the initial strength of some materials can be improved. Amongst the changes possible are:

(a) a modification of the material itself,
(b) an alteration to an established form of construction,
(c) an alteration to the basic form in which the materials are manufactured.
  (i) State one specific method of strengthening each of the following materials: wood, metal and plastics.
  (ii) For *two* of the three examples describe in detail the processes whereby strengthening is achieved.

(L)

65. Explain briefly the *difference* between each of the following pairs of processes:

(i) the extruding and drawing of metal,
(ii) the hammer and caul methods of veneering wood,
(iii) the rotational moulding and blow moulding of plastics.

For each of the six processes state *one* property which must be inherent in the material if the process is to be successful.

Select a pair of processes from (i), (ii) or (iii) above and
(a) with the aid of diagrams describe both processes,
(b) give an example of a specific article made by each process described in (a) above.

(L)

66. (i) Chess set pieces made of aluminium tube are to be anodised and dyed. Half the set is to be maroon and half black.
  (a) Draw and label a circuit diagram for the anodising process.
  (b) Describe in detail, naming the materials used, the procedure for anodising and dying the black pieces. Assume that the metal has just been shaped.

(ii) A milk bottle carrier, made of brazed ø5 BDMS round bar is to be plastics coated.
  (a) Draw and label a fluidizing tank for doing the job.
  (b) Describe in detail, naming the materials used, the procedure for plastics coating the carrier.

(iii) Redraw the table given below, to occupy a whole page, and complete it for the articles listed.

Article	Name and characteristics of an ideal timber	Appropriate protective coating and/or finish with reasons for choice.
Garden fence Garden seat Kitchen cabinet Tray frame of solid wood with veneered plywood base Sailing dinghy Cooking spoon/spatula Salad bowl		

(L)

67. Seasoned timber is usually described as 'kiln-dried' or 'air-dried'.

Write an account of these two methods of seasoning. Approximately what moisture content would you expect to find in the seasoned timber?

(O&C)

68. Write notes on the following: (a) the case hardening of mild steel; (b) the hardening and tempering of tool steel, mentioning the colours and temperature range involved; (c) the essential difference between iron and steel.

(O&C)

69. What do you understand by the term *thermoplastic material*?

Explain and illustrate how acrylics may be used to produce a simple yet effective piece of sculpture. Your answer should include references to the bending and polishing of the material.

(O&C)

70. Explain, with sketches if necessary, what is meant by:

(a) Cup shake. (c) Cambium layer.
(b) Warping. (d) Waney edge.

What is 'figured' oak? How is the log cut in order to obtain such 'figure'?

(O&C)

71. List *five* insulating materials and in *each* case give examples of their use.

	Materials	Examples of use
(i)		
(ii)		
(iii)		
(iv)		
(v)		

(WJEC)

72. List suitable materials you would employ for the following examples and the surface finish you would use in *each* case.

Example	Materials	Surface finish
Cheeseboard		
Garden shed		
Laboratory worktop		
Window frame		
Card table top		

(WJEC)

73. Manufactured boards frequently present unsightly edges when used in furniture. If the face surface is to be veneered, describe the sequence of masking such edges in order to improve appearances and durability.

(O&C)

74. Write notes on the working properties of the following materials and give *one* example of the use of each metal:

(*a*) copper,   (*c*) mild steel,

(*b*) aluminium,   (*d*) cast iron.

(O&C)

75. Timber moves as a reaction to changes in humidity. In which direction of the grain does such movement occur? Draw *two* examples of woodwork constructions which compensate for such movement.

(O&C)

General

76. Answer the following *very briefly*, starting each sub-section on a new line.

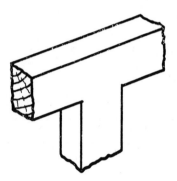

Fig. 25

(*a*) Sketch in 'exploded' form two joints suitable for the construction shown in fig. 25. Name the joints.

(*b*) What factors should be specified when ordering wood screws?

(*c*) State two methods by which acrylic sheets may be shaped with the aid of heat.

(*d*) Name the tool used for producing external threads.

(*e*) Why is it an advantage to have silver solder of different melting points?

(*f*) State a possible cause of a saw binding in a cut.

(*g*) Give an example where annealing would be necessary.

(*h*) G.R.P. is an abbreviation of Glass Reinforced Plastics. Give the name of the plastic.

(*i*) What is knurling?

(*j*) Name two types of (i) hardwood, (ii) softwood, (iii) thermoplastics.

(*k*) Make a sketch of an Allen key.

(*l*) By means of a sectioned freehand sketch show how a pop rivet is used to secure together two pieces of sheet metal.

(O) (Part question)

77. Answer the following *very briefly*, starting each sub-section on a new line and doing all the drawings on the writing paper.

(*a*) Sketch and name two corner joints suitable for a wooden box.

(*b*) Show, by means of a series of simple sketches, the correct procedure for joining two pieces of wood together by means of a countersunk screw.

(*c*) Sketch and name two types of hinge.

(*d*) Name the wood finish best suited to the following:
(i) a teak coffee table;
(ii) mahogany woodwork on a boat;
(iii) interwoven fencing.

(e) Name three types of manufactured board and give an example of the use of each.

(f) Name two methods of casting metal and give an example of a metal commonly used for each process.

(g) Give a common household example of vacuum-forming.

(h) What is meant by the term *extrusion*?

(i) When drilling the end of a length of round bar on the lathe, what tool is used before the drill, and why?

(j) Sketch turning tools suited to metal.

(k) State three different ways in which metal components may be joined permanently.

(l) What is meant by the term *work hardening*.

(m) Name two methods of joining plastics.

(O) (Part question)

78. Fig. 26 shows a simple cylindrical container for pencils, paint brushes, etc. It could be made from a wide variety of materials.

Explain in detail how it might be made in a material of your choice.

Fig. 26

(O)

79. Discuss the safety factors which should generally be observed when working with woods, or metals, or plastics, or combinations of these materials. It may help if you consider safety factors under three main headings:

(a) materials;

(b) tools, machines and general equipment;

(c) factors affecting the person.

(O&C)

Index

= **wood**

 = **metal**

 = **plastics**